GOOGLE
SITES
MADE EASY

Websites Designed the Easy Way

By James Bernstein

I0491839

Bernstein, James
Google Sites Made Easy
Part of the Digital Design Made Easy series

For more information on reproducing sections of this book or sales of this book,
go to **www.madeeasybookseries.com**

Contents

Introduction

Since the internet has been around since 1983 (depending on who you ask), you would think that there are many websites available for you to visit and you would most definitely be right. Websites come and go with new sites popping up daily and if you are a business owner and don't have your own website then you are not running your business up to its full potential.

Nowadays, the internet is the first place people go when they are looking to buy a new product or get some type of service. In fact, the internet is where most people go when looking for just about anything. So if you have something you want to share with the world, creating a website for it is the best way to get your products, services or ideas out there.

Google Sites is Google's website creation tool, and you don't need any HTML coding experience to use it and its fairly easy to get a basic website up and running in a short amount of time. And if you want to put a little extra effort into your work, you can actually create a very professional site for your business or personal use. And best of all, it's free to use and publish your site on the internet for all to see!

If you have used software such as Google Slides, Microsoft PowerPoint or Microsoft Publisher then you should have no problem getting up and running with Sites since it has the same look and feel as these other programs where you simply drag and drop text and images where you would like them to go. Of course there is a little more to it than that but after you spend some time with Sites you should get the hang of it fairly quickly.

The goal of this book is to get you up and running with Google Sites and show you how to make great looking websites for your business or personal use. I will also go over other advanced features such as how to publish your website online and even how to use your own custom domain name. So on that note, let's get our ideas online!

Chapter 1 – Introduction to Google Sites

If you are reading this book then you are interested in creating a website for yourself or maybe for someone else. If you have spent any amount of time online "surfing" the internet then you know there are a wide variety of websites out there with many different styles and degrees of professionalism. So you will need to decide on how deep you want to go into your site design and then choose the tool that is right for you.

Who Should Use Google Sites?

Google Sites is not the best tool for everyone to use because there is much more powerful software available to create websites such as Adobe Dreamweaver and WordPress. But if you don't have the computer skills necessary to use these programs you will need to find something more user friendly. There has been a trend recently to make software or apps that don't require as much technical skill to use and this is where Google Sites comes into play.

If you have let's say intermediate computer skills then Sites should be fairly easy to learn without too much of a learning curve… or too much of a headache! And if you normally use any word processing or presentation software then that will help you get a handle on Sites.

Sites comes with several templates that you can also use to help get your ideas in place, so you don't have to be a design expert to make a great looking website. Once you apply one of these templates you can then adjust it to your liking by changing things such as typestyles and graphics to make it your own.

So if you have some ideas in your head and some average computer skills then you should be able to create a decent looking website that you can then make live to share with the world. And if you need help with your ideas, you can always share your site with others so they can contribute to its design and content as well.

Creating a Google Account

In order to use Sites, you will need to have a Google account to log in with. If you have a Gmail account then you already have a Google account, and you can use that account for Sites. Most people use the free Google accounts even though there are subscription based accounts that give you additional features but for the home or small business user, the free account works just fine.

If you are planning on just using a free account to login and don't have one then it's very easy to sign up for one. To begin, simply open your web browser and navigate to **https://accounts.google.com/** and you will be prompted to enter your account details such as name, desired email address and a password to go along with your new account.

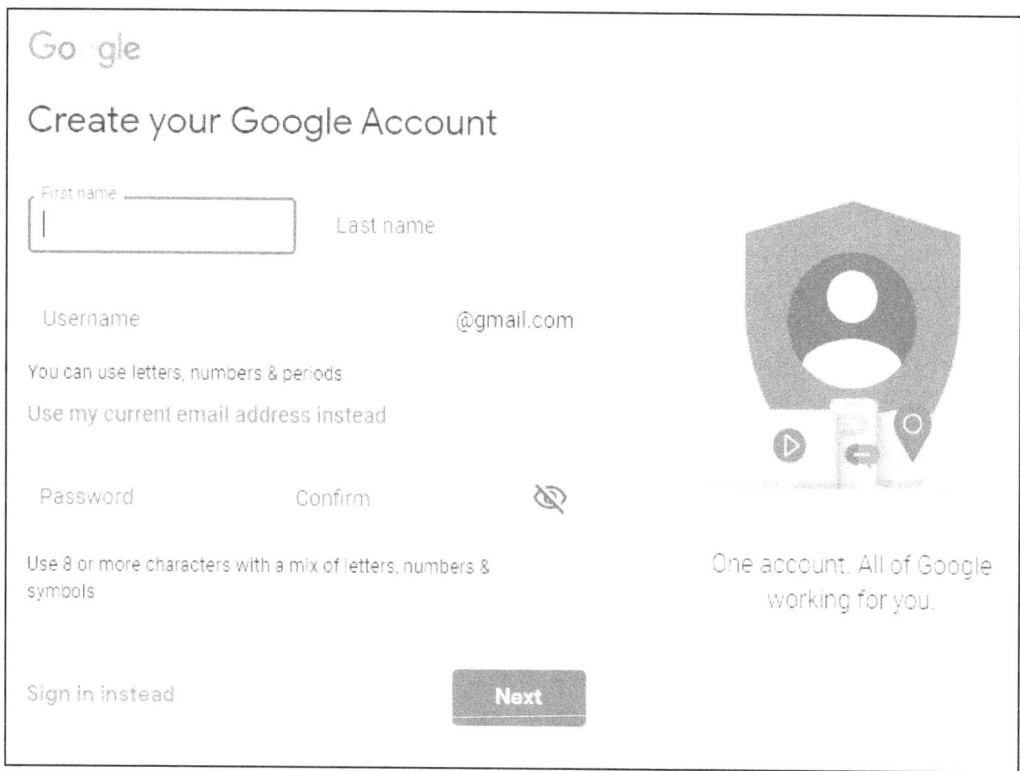

Figure 1.1

Simply enter your first and last name and choose a username, which will also be used for your Gmail email account ending in *@gmail.com*. If the username has already been taken, then you will be prompted to enter a new one. Notice that there is an option that says *Use my current email address instead*. This can be used if you do not want a Gmail email address, but still want to create a Google account with your current email address.

Then you will need to come up with a password that has 8 or more characters and uses letters, numbers, and symbols (such as **!** or **#** for example) and click on *Next*.

After that, you will need to enter your phone number so Google can verify it is really you. It will send you a six digit number via text message that you will have to enter in the next step. Doing this will also tie your phone number to your Google account, which comes in handy for things like password recovery if you forget your password. If you don't have a smartphone you can have Google call you with the code instead of texting it.

Next, you enter a recovery email address (which can also be used for password recovery), as well as your birth date information. The birth date information is used because some Google services have age requirements. The gender information it asks for is optional and is not shown to other Google users. You can also edit your Google account later if you wish to change or add anything.

If you *don't* want your number to be used at all, simply click on *Skip,* and you will be brought to the *Privacy and Terms* agreement, which you can read if you like. To continue, you will need to click on the *I agree* button. Finally, after clicking on *I agree,* your account will be created, and you will be logged in automatically. If you are on the Google home page, then you will see your first initial up in the right hand corner. You can go into your settings and edit your profile and add a picture if you like.

Sites Interface
Once you have your Google account created you can then go to the Sites website to get started on your website. To do this, open your favorite web browser and navigate to **sites.google.com**. If you don't have a web browser preference you might want to use Google Chrome for the best results, but any browser should work just fine since Google likes you to use their apps for everything. If you are not logged into your Google account then you can do so from here.

If you are interested in learning about some of the more popular and commonly used Google Apps then check out my book titled **Google Apps Made Easy**.
https://www.amazon.com/dp/1798114992

If you are new to Sites then you will not see anything too exciting when you first log in. Figure 1.2 shows that I have the option to start a new site or to open one of the existing templates that are available for me to use. Since I don't have any existing websites created with this particular Google account, nothing shows under *Recent sites*.

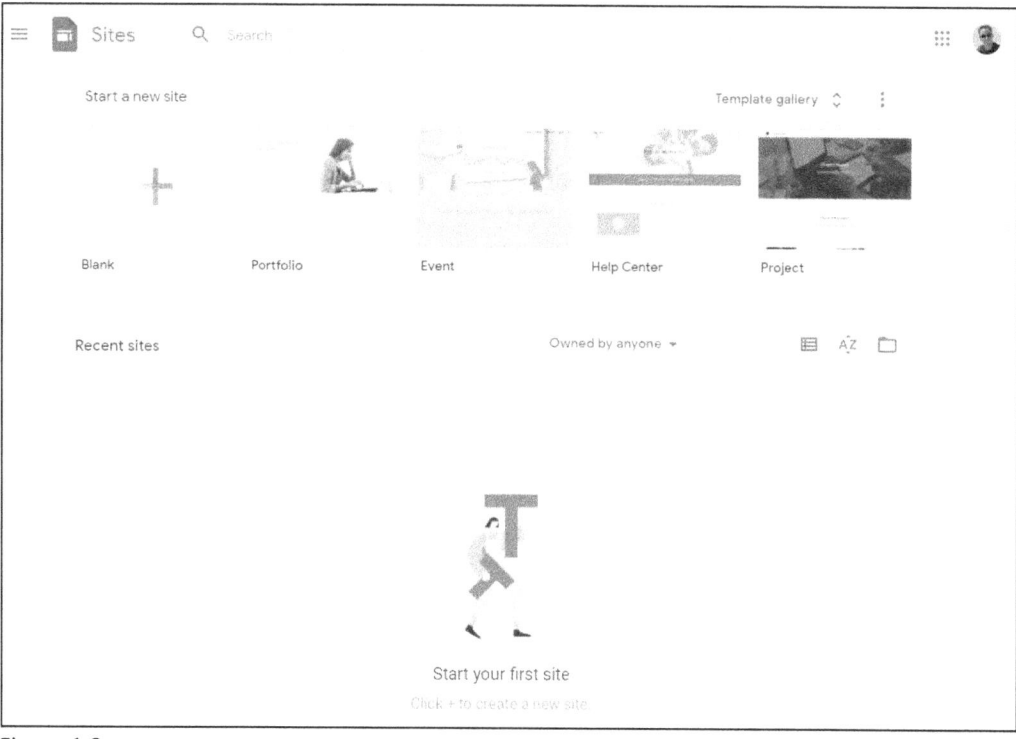

Figure 1.2

If I did have websites with this account I would be able to sort them alphabetically or change the view from a list view to a grid view. I could also open a site that I have stored in my Google Drive or on my local computer by clicking on the File Picker (folder icon).

The section that says *Owned by anyone* is where you can set what files you see to include sites that have also been shared by you. You can also change it to be *Owned by me* or *Not owned by me* depending on which sites you wish to see in your listing of files.

If I were to click on one of the arrows next to where it says *Template gallery* I would then be shown all of the available templates that I can use organized by type. I will be showing you how to use a template in the next chapter even though I prefer to start from scratch with a blank site.

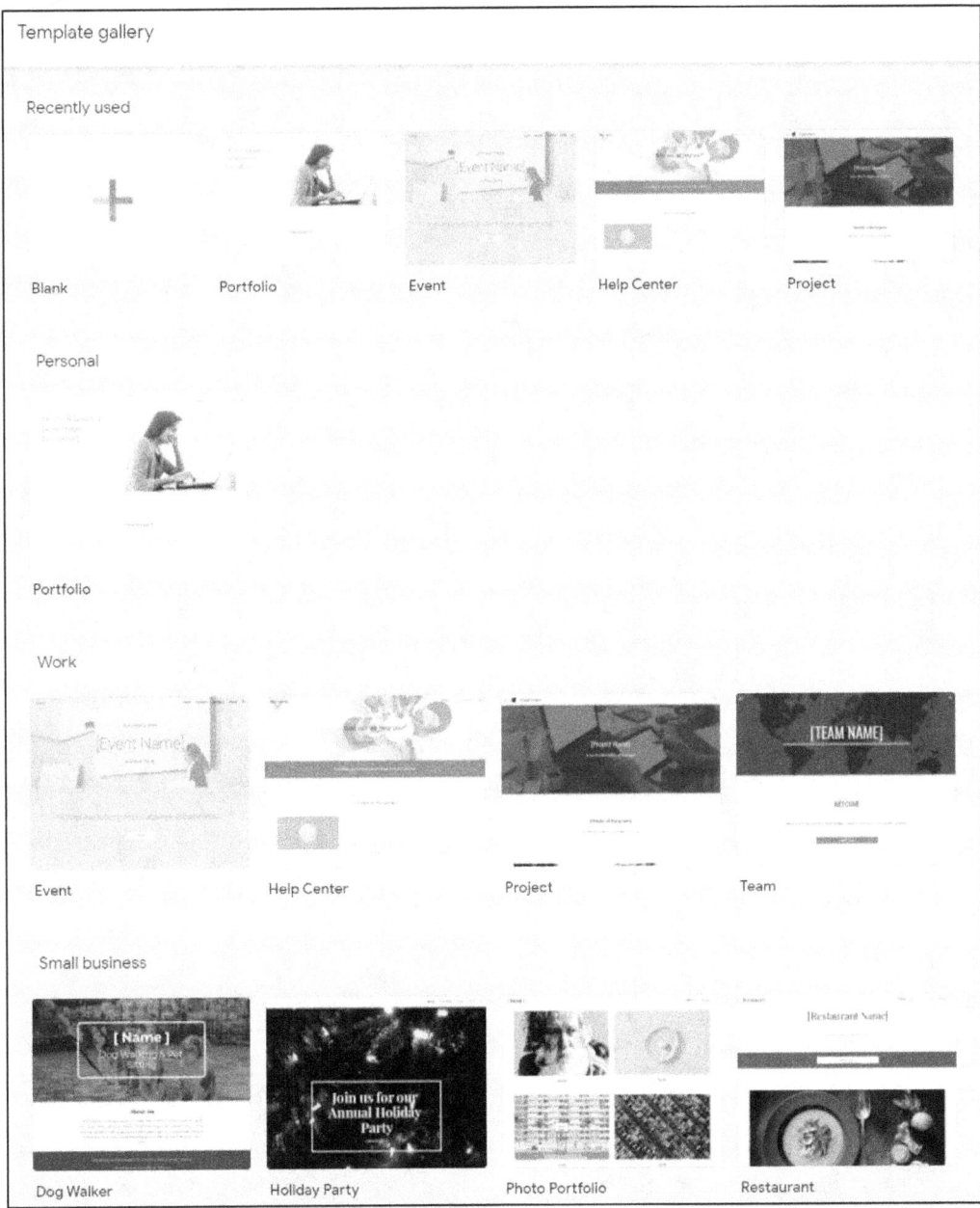

Figure 1.3

Clicking on the three vertical lines (or the hamburger as it's commonly called) at the top left of the Sheets interface will give you some choices such as opening up a different Google App such as Docs or Sheets, some basic settings and also give you access to your Google Drive. Chapter 5 is all about Google Drive and if you are going to be using Sites or any other Google Apps, then you might want to have an idea of how it works.

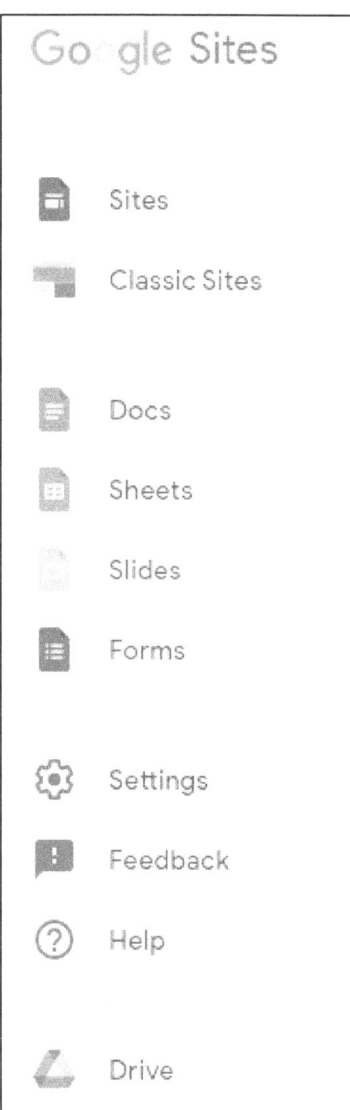

Figure 1.4

You might have noticed the icon for Classic Sites in figure 1.4. This may or may not be there by the time you read this book. Here is the timeline for the Classic Sites end of life.
- May 2021: New website creation will no longer be available.
- October 2021: Editing existing Classic sites will be disabled.
- December 2021: Classic sites will no longer be available.

If you click on the *Help* icon under the Sites menu then you will be taken to a fairly useful help website where you can find answers to commonly asked questions and also search for help on your topic of choice.

Chapter 2 - Editing Basic Website Components

Once you have an idea of how you want your website to be laid out you can then start adding items such as sections, background, text and images to your design to see how these items all come together. And if something isn't looking the way you imagined it would be, all you need to do is change it so it does!

Using Templates
Like I mentioned earlier, I prefer to start with a blank site rather than use any of the built in templates but that doesn't mean you will necessarily feel the same way. So to begin this chapter I will show you how to use a template to get your design started and then switch over to a new blank website to show you how it's done from scratch.

To use one of the included templates, simply click on the one you like to get started. I will use the template that is named *Project*. As you can see in figure 2.1, Sites loaded the template and it includes a banner image, text area and also some sections that include their own sample images.

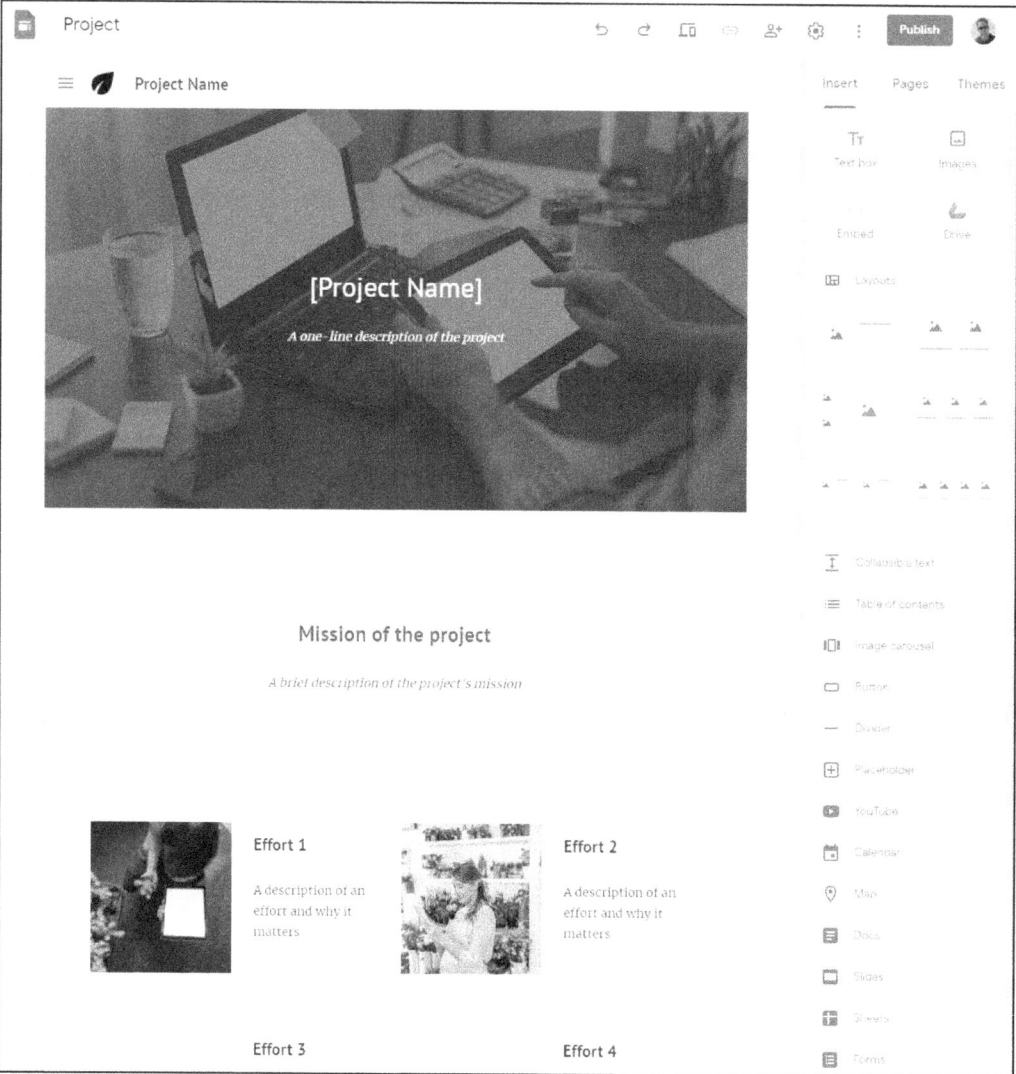

Figure 2.1

If I click on the *Pages* section at the upper right of the screen I will see that this template also includes three additional pages (History, Team and FAQ) that you can edit to suit your needs. If you don't like a particular page from a template, then you can simply delete it by clicking the three vertical dots next to that page and choosing *Delete*.

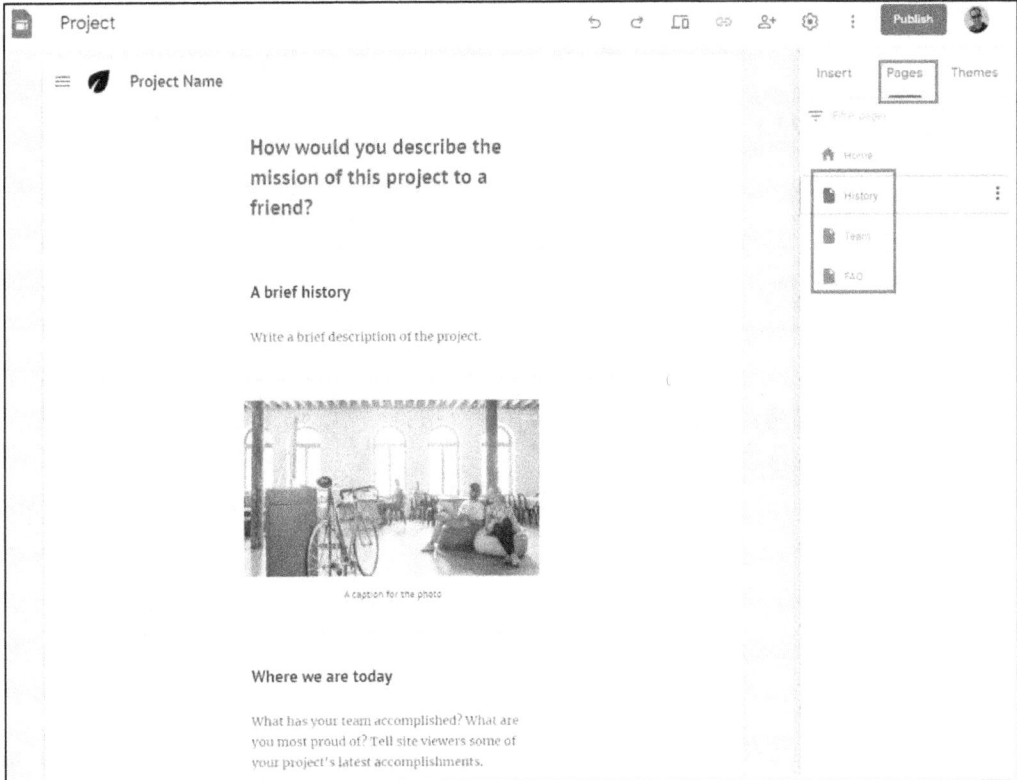

Figure 2.2

So as you can see, the Sites templates are a good way to get started on your website if you do not have any of your own ideas that you particularly like. As I go through creating a website from scratch, you will see how the procedures I use for this will also apply to editing a template.

Creating a Website From Scratch

Now that I have my template website on hold it will show up under my sites (under Recent sites in this case) if I need to go back to it. Just like most of the other Google Apps, your work gets saved as you do it, so you don't need to remember to click on a save button as you do with other software.

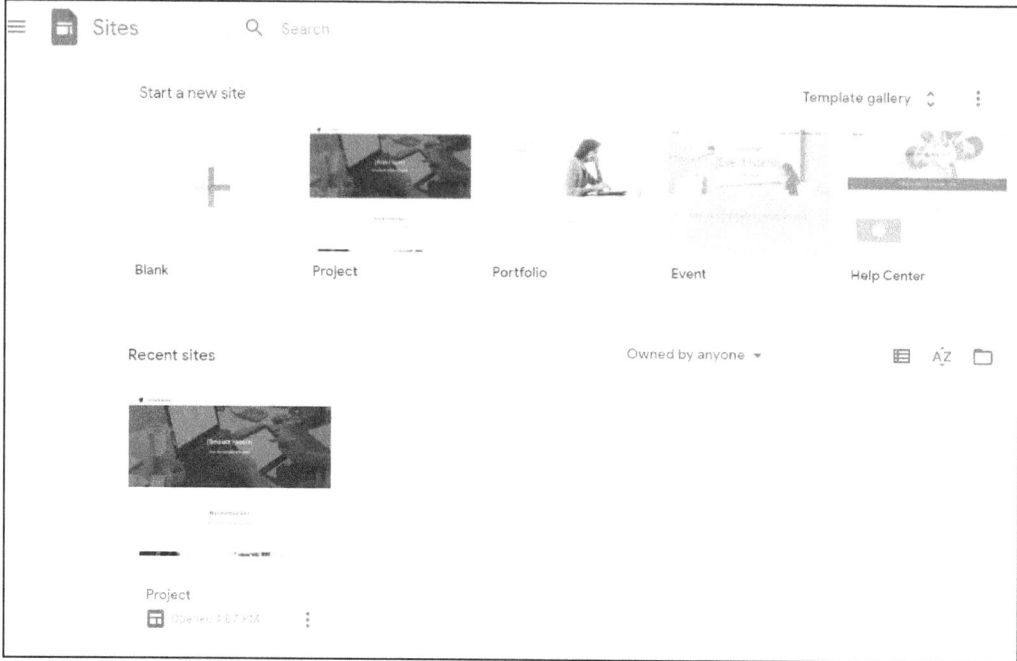

Figure 2.3

To create a website from scratch I will click on the *Blank* + button and it will bring up a new blank site as shown in figure 2.4. This will be my home page and starting point for my website. This will also be the landing page that people will see when they go to your website using its URL (Uniform Resource Location) or address as it's more commonly called.

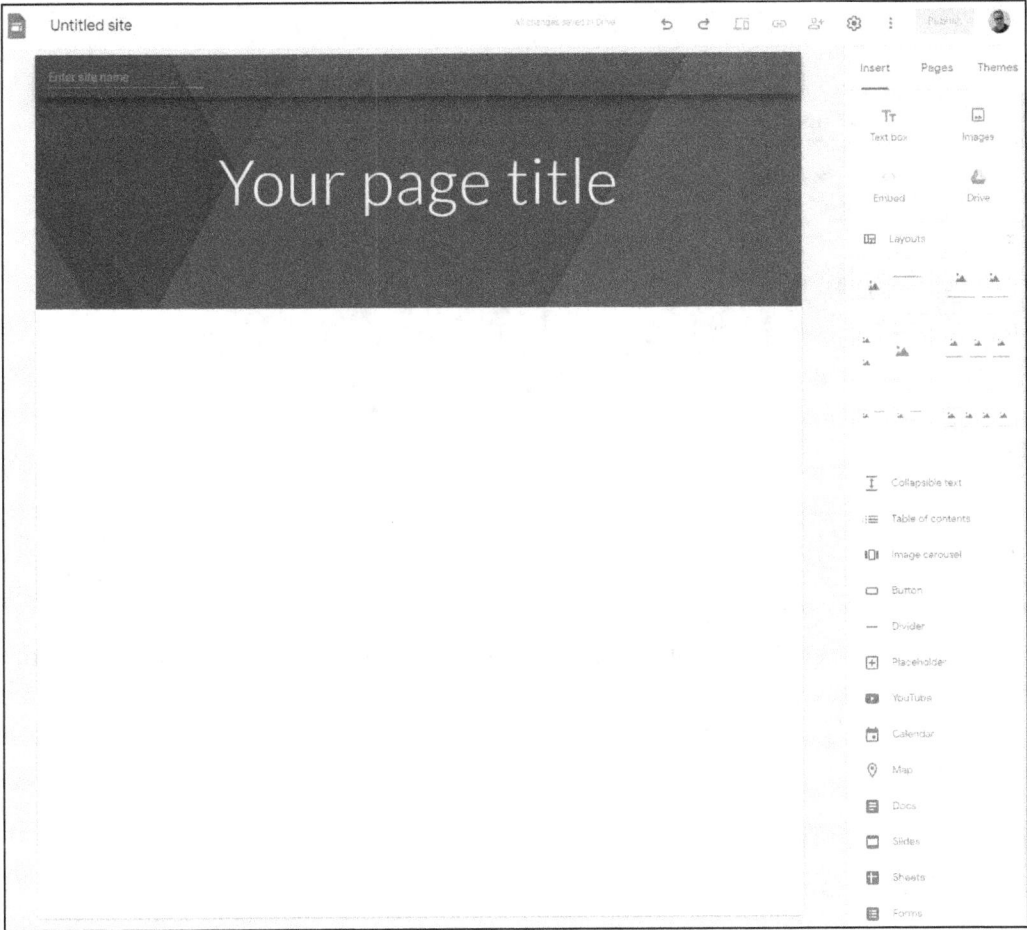

Figure 2.4

Changing Your Site Name, Logo and Homepage Image

I will begin by changing the name of the site from Untitled site to something more fitting. In this book I will be creating the website for my Computers Made Easy computer book series and then have it live for you to view for yourself as you read this book. So in that case, I will change the name to *Computers Made Easy*. When you name the file the first time it will take that name and make it the site name as seen in figure 2.5. You can change the site name without changing the file name after that if needed.

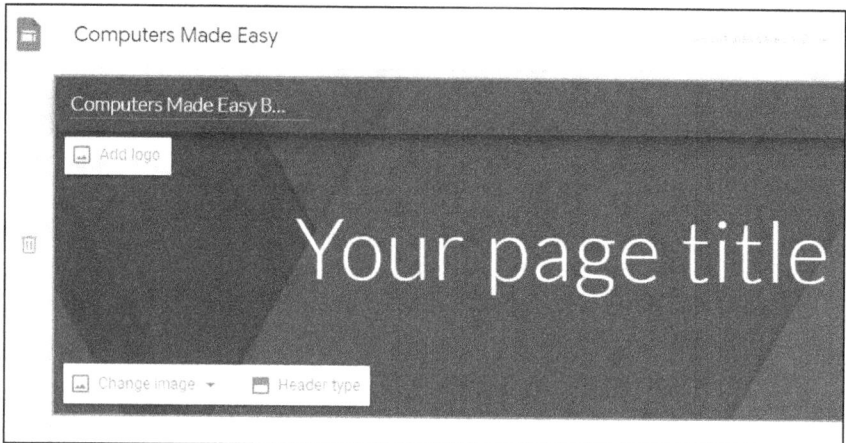

Figure 2.5

When I hover my mouse near the website name I get an option to add a logo if I have one for my website. This logo can be your company name or any design that you have that represents your product or service. When I click on the *Add logo* button it takes me to the Sites settings and then the *Brand images* section. From here I can select a logo image file from my Google Drive or upload one from my computer. I will upload my logo from my computer since that is where I have it saved.

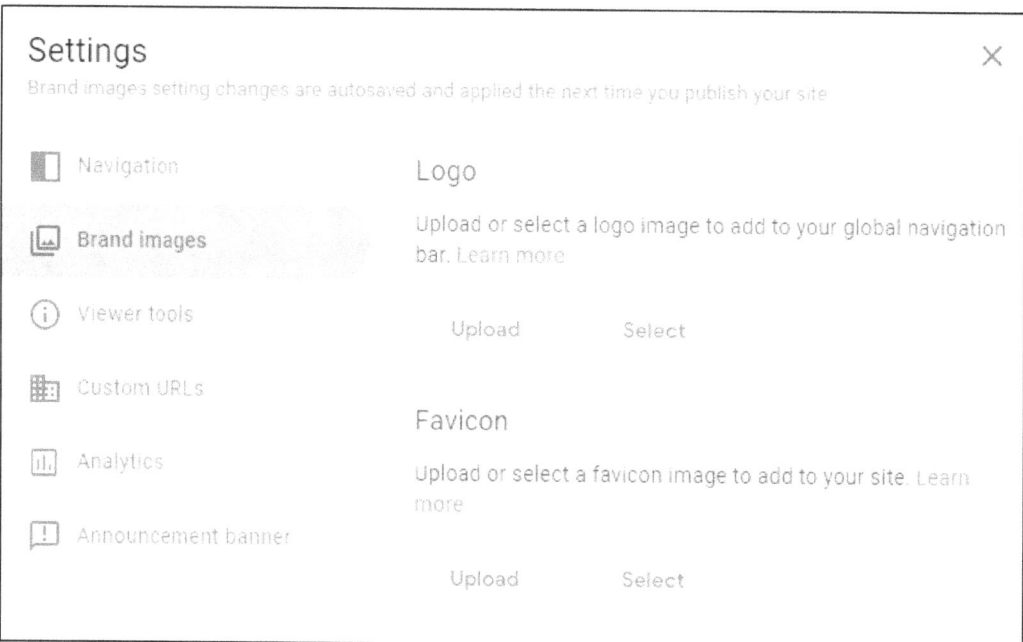

Figure 2.6

When you upload your logo you have the option to add some alt text to that image and this is what is displayed when someone hovers their mouse over an image. It can be used to add a description for that image if desired and you have probably seen this on other websites.

Sites will also give you an option to use a color or colors based on the colors used in your image. My image is orange and black, so Sites gives me the option to use orange as a theme for my website if I choose to take their advice. You can always try this and then change it to something else later if you don't like the way it looks.

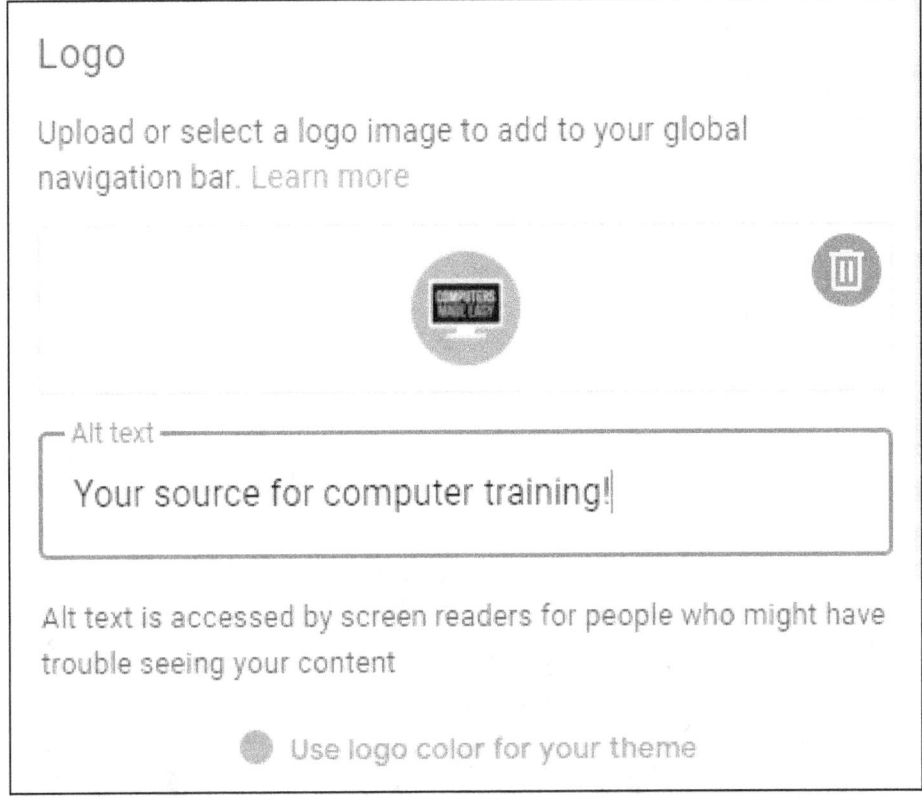

Figure 2.7

While I am in the Brand images section I will also use the same image for my *Favicon* icon. The favicon is what you see in your web browser on the tab for that site as seen in figure 2.8. For my OnlineComputerTips.com website, I use a favicon that says OCT which shows in the browser when someone goes to my website.

Figure 2.8

When you add your favicon to your site page it might not show up in your browser but that doesn't mean it's not working. Since you most likely saved your site with the default favicon then that's what it will be using. If you clear your browser cache then it should show up after that.

Now my site logo shows at the top left side of the page and will show on any other pages I create as well.

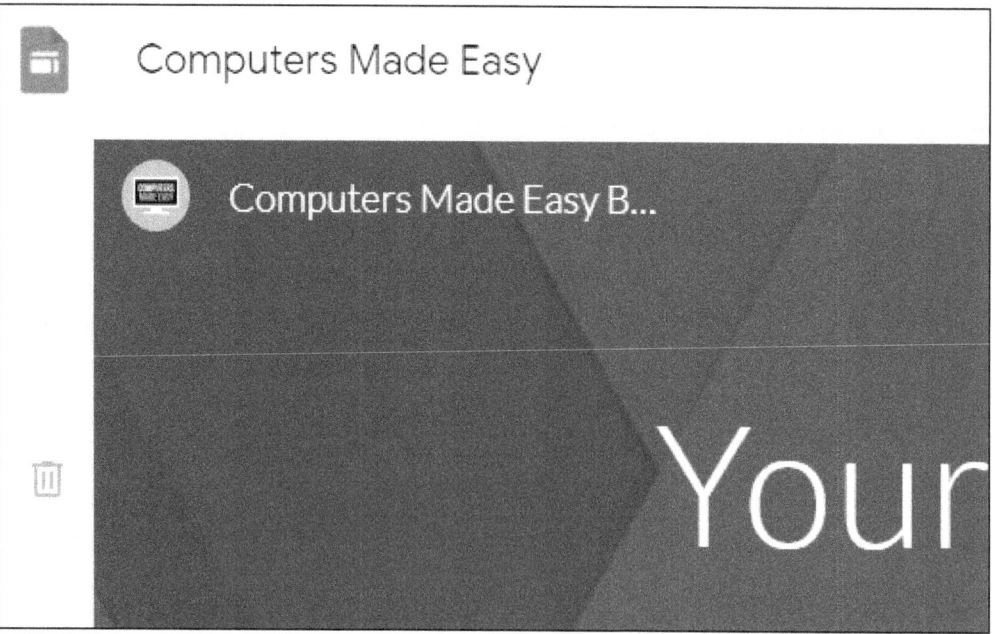

Figure 2.9

Next, I will change the main page image and text at the top of the page to something that makes a little more sense. If you click on the Change image button that appears when you hover over your image you can then choose where your new image will come from.

- **Gallery** – Here you have the option to use one of the built in images offered by Google
- **By URL** – If you have the address of an image you want to use online then you can paste in a link to that image
- **Search** – The search option lets you search for images that are free to use for your site
- **Your Albums** – If you have any photos stored within your Google account you can select one from here
- **Google Drive** – If you have any photos stored in your Google Drive then you can select one from Drive itself

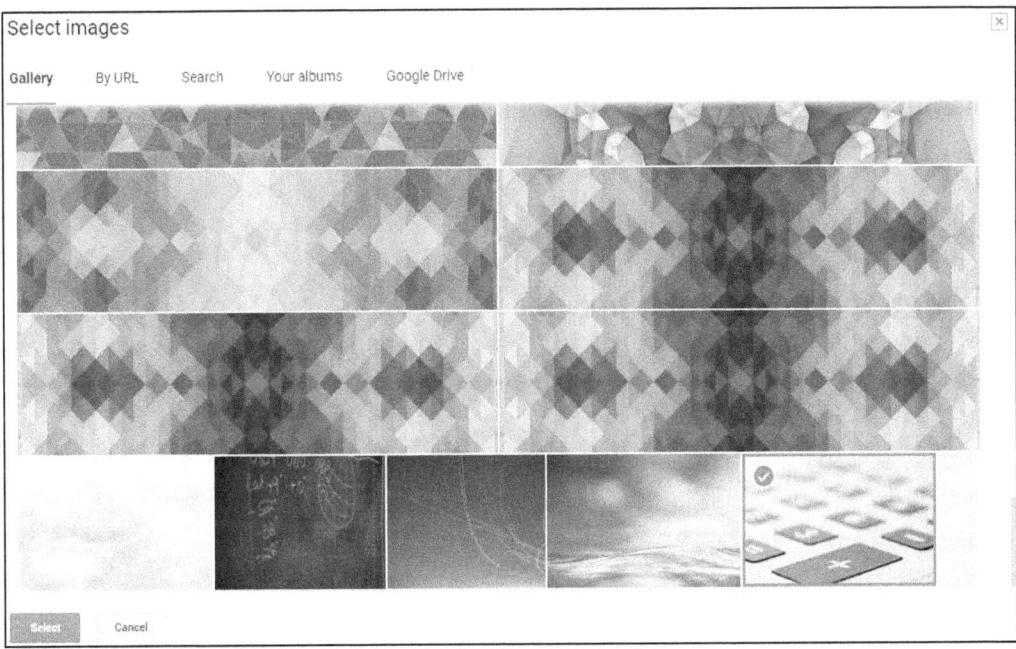

Figure 2.10

For demonstration purposes, I went with a keyboard image from the gallery and then changed my font to something a little bolder. I will find something a little more appropriate later or maybe even use an animated image instead. More on that later!

Figure 2.11

Adding Sections and Using Layouts with Text and Images

Now that I have my basic home page banner image and title, it's time to add some sections to the page so I can add some information pertaining to the website's content. The best part about using Sites for your website is that it is so easy to change things around if you decide you want to go for a different look or change any of the content on your pages.

Sections are used to divide up your page into, well sections. These sections can have text or images and you can resize and move these sections as needed. You can even copy them to make it easy to add the same information or images to another page.

The best way to make a new section is to double click on the area where you would like to add the new section to bring up the wheel menu that has a variety of choices as to the type of section you can create.

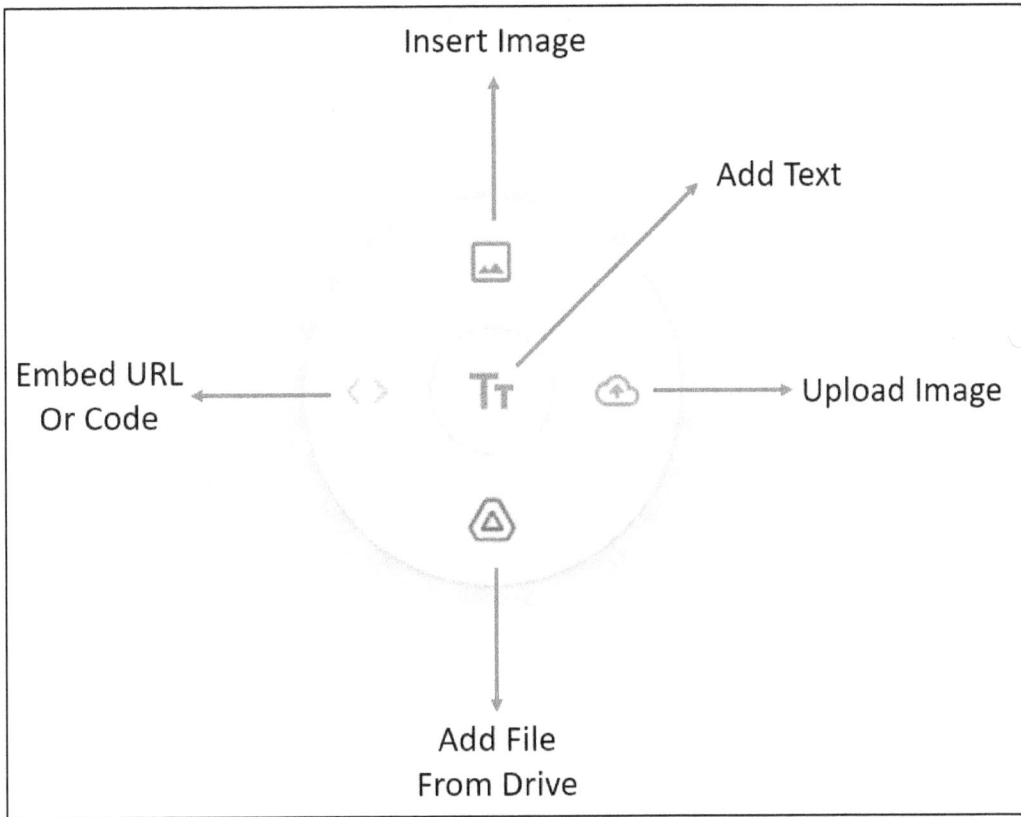

Figure 2.12

To begin with, I will click the text option to add some text to my homepage. By default, it will place the section at the top of the page, and I can then add my text and format it to make it fit the page.

Figure 2.13

When you are working in a section you will have some choices that appear to the left of that section as seen in figure 2.13. You can use these icons to change the section background, duplicate the section or delete the section. I will now add more text to my section and do a little formatting to make it fit the look that I am going for.

Once I add my section\text formatting, I can then resize the text block by clicking on it, so it makes a blue box around the text. From there I can shrink or resize the text box as needed. There will also be a pencil icon that appears for editing or a trash icon for deleting the text (or other objects).

Figure 2.14

Next, I will use one of the layout options to see how it fits with the layout of my site. The layouts are located under the *Insert* section on the right side of the window and all you need to do to apply one of them is to click on it.

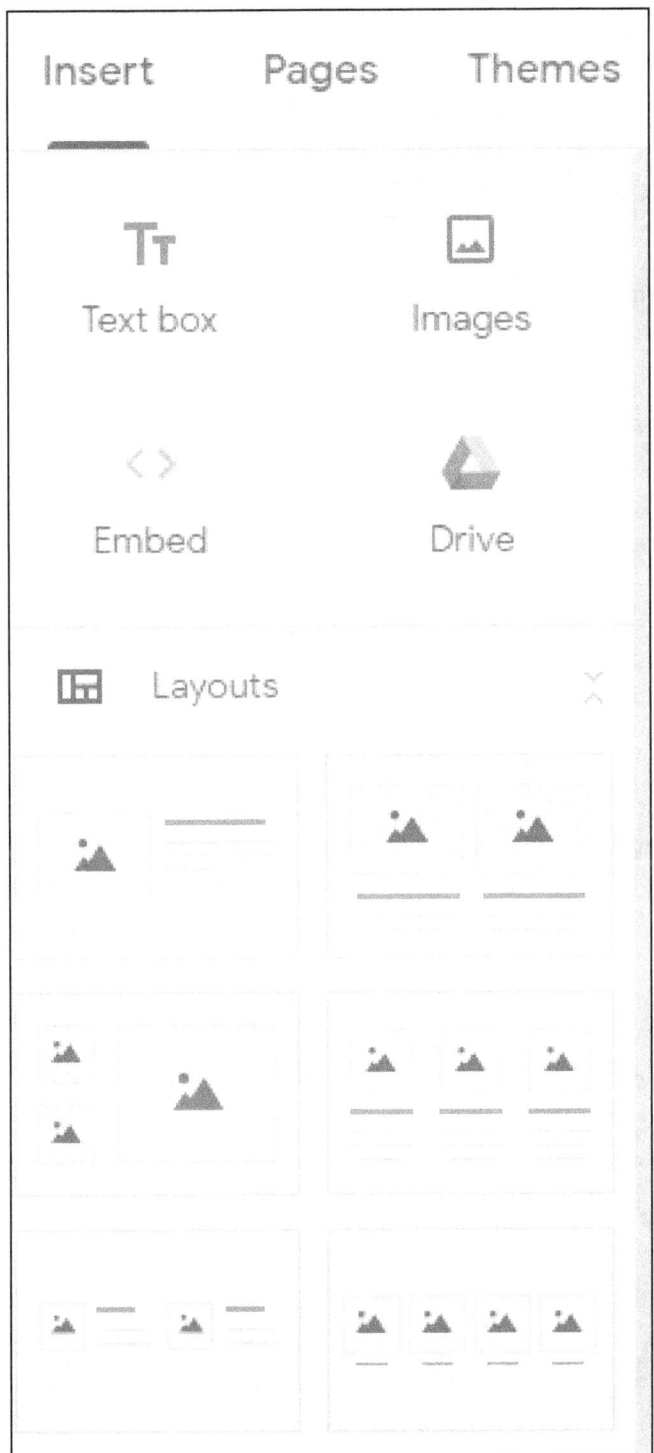

Figure 2.15

I will use the first layout that has one section with space for an image as well as some text.

Figure 2.16

Then I will use this space to add an image of the cover of the latest book in my series as well as a description. I will click on the + sign to upload the book cover picture and then simply edit the existing text that comes with the layout. I will also apply a light grey section background (Emphasis 1) from the *Section Background* palette that appears to the left of the section as I am working on it. The results are shown in figure 2.19.

You can upload your webpage images the same way you did for your banner image on the homepage. You have the option to upload an image from your computer, select one provided by Google or insert one you have stored on your Google Drive. If you take a look back at figure 2.15 you will notice that you have an option to insert images from the side navigation options as well.

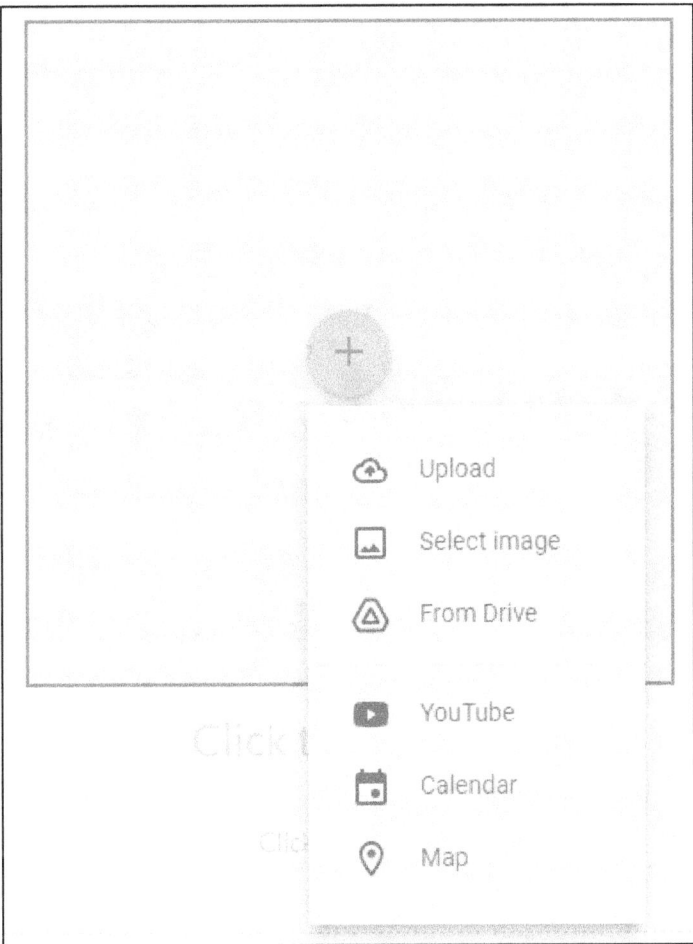

Figure 2.17

If you use an image from your Google Drive then you will need to set the permissions for that image so that other people can view it. To do so, go to that file in your Google Drive, right click it and choose the *Share* option and at the bottom where it says *Get link*, click where it says *Change to anyone with the link*.

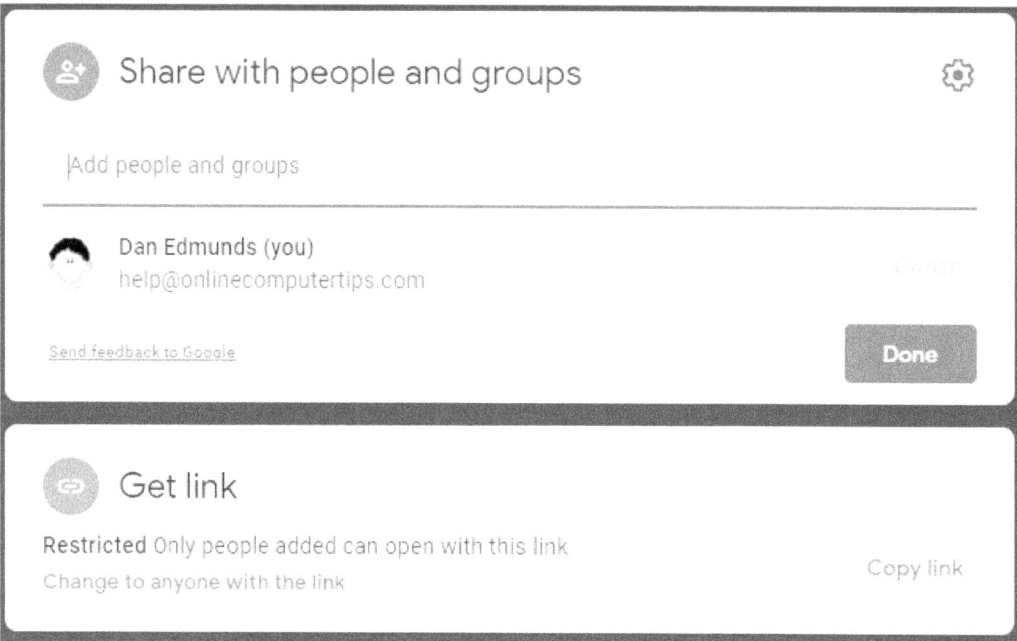

Figure 2.18

Computers Made Easy Book Series

Welcome to the Computers Made Easy Book Series website

Here you will find information about the Made Easy books that cover a variety of computer\technology topics such as Windows, networking, Microsoft Office, Google Apps, computer hardware, smartphones and much more. Each book was written with the user in mind and structured so that readers with any skill level would be able to follow along. Feel free to browse the various book subjects to learn more about what each book has to offer!

GOOGLE DOCS MADE EASY
Online Collaboration For Everyone

JAMES BERNSTEIN

Latest Release

With the growing trend of working and attending classes from home, there has been an increased need for the ability to share your work online with other people on your team or from your classes.

Emailing documents back and forth can get messy and when you have multiple copies of your work in a bunch of different emails, then things tend to get missed or even lost.

Everyone knows about Google and how they are one of the leaders when it comes to online technology and applications so one would assume they would have a solution for anything you need to accomplish over the Internet. Google Docs has been around for years but is gaining even more popularity since you can create your documents and share them with others without having to install any additional software on your computer or leave your house. And best of all, it's totally free to use and all you need is a free Google account to get started.

The goal of this book is to get you up and running with Google Docs and cover all the things you need to know to get you started creating professional looking documents and collaborating with your coworkers and classmates. It sticks with the basics yet covers all aspects of the application to help you accomplish your goals without needing to be a computer genius.

Figure 2.19

Finally, for the home page I will add some navigation links to the bottom of the page for items such as contact information and other resources. To do this I will double click again to get the wheel menu and add click on the text option. If your new section ends up in a different place from where you intended it to go simply click on the section until you get a four sided pointer and then drag the section to where you would like it to be on the page.

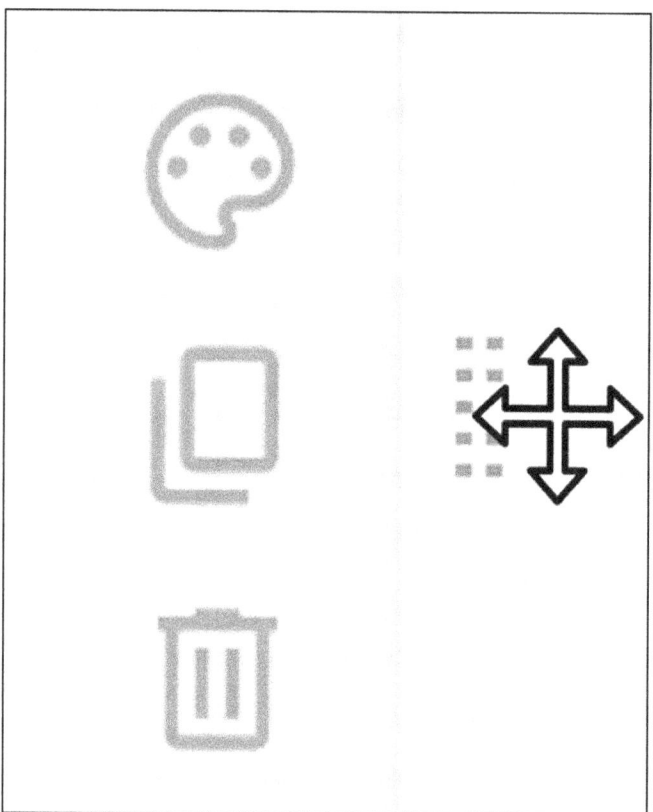

Figure 2.20

To add the sections at the bottom of the page I will create a new section and then add individual text boxes in that section rather than trying to use spaces or tabs to separate each bit of text to make sure it looks correct when viewing the site live later on. I can create the first text box that says **Contact** and then copy and paste it two more times for the **Computer Help Website** and **Order Your Copy Now** text areas and then just drag them where I want them. Then I will add the same section formatting that I have at the top of the page and change the font, so things have a uniform look to them. I will add some links to these text items later when I go over adding hyperlinks.

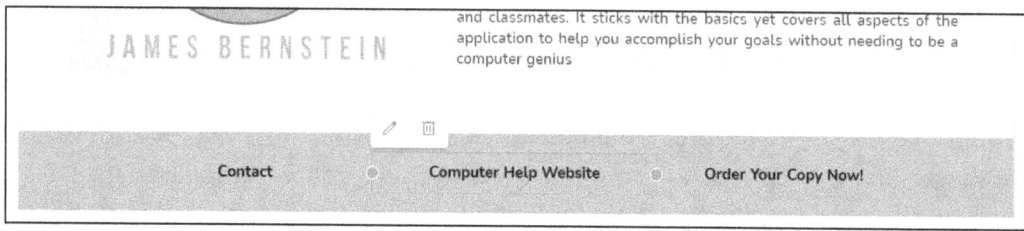

Figure 2.21

Adding Additional Pages to Your Site

Now that I have my basic homepage setup, it's time to add some additional pages for the books in my series. I will base these pages on book categories such as Windows, Microsoft Productivity, networking and so on.

To add a new page all I need to do is go to the *Pages* section at the upper right side of the window and then click on the + icon to add a new page.

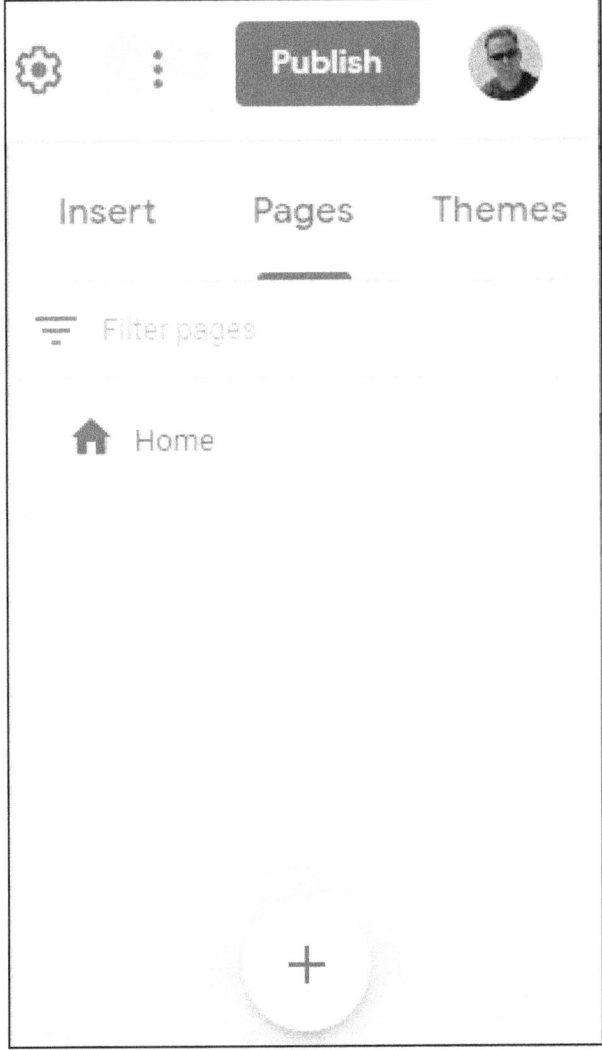

Figure 2.22

Then I will need to type in the name for the page and click on *Done*. If you click on *Advanced* you will have an option to add a custom path to your page. If I just leave mine as is then the new page URL will contain windows-books based on the name I typed in the box. If I wanted to make the page shorter to maybe just be **windows** or longer to be **windows-based-training** then I can add either one to the *Custom path* section.

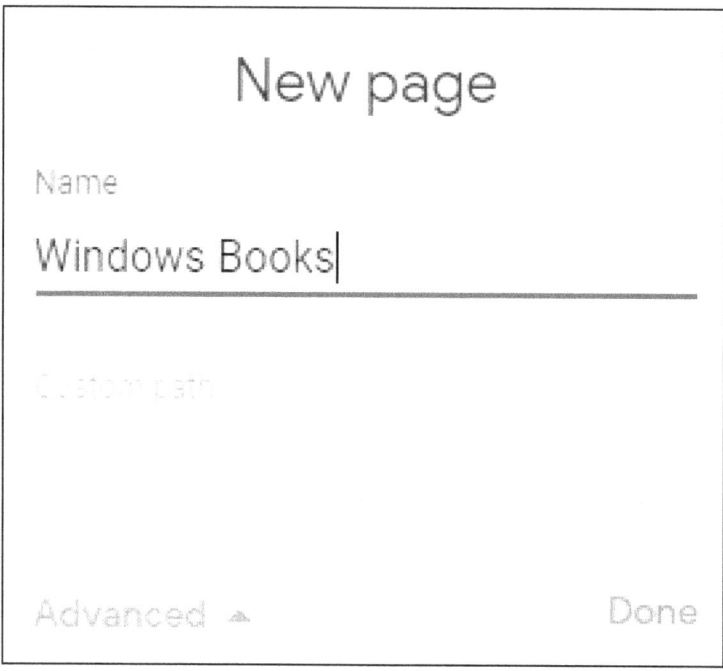

Figure 2.23

Now that I have added my new page it shows up under my Home page in the Pages section. Sites used the same banner background image that was used on the home page and also used the original default text.

Figure 2.24

I will now add the pages for my other book categories. As you can see in figure 2.25 that your list of pages can grow very quickly so keep that in mind when creating your website.

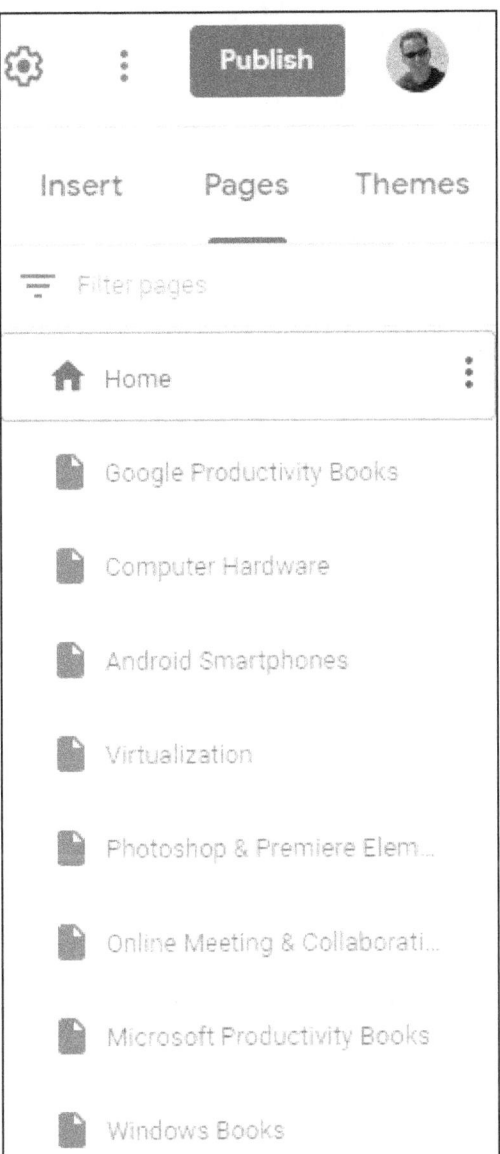

Figure 2.25

When creating your website you will most likely not need to have every page accessible from the homepage but rather be a subpage of an existing page. For example, you might have a website about dogs and have a link for the breeds page on the homepage and then have subpages on things like training or feeding be a subpage for each specific breed and these subpages will only be accessible from the breed pages and not the home page.

To make a page a subpage of an existing page, all you need to do is drag that page onto another page to make it a subpage. If I drag my Windows Books page on top of my Microsoft Productivity page it then becomes a subpage and won't show up on the homepage. You will get a better idea of how this works when I get to the next section on site navigation.

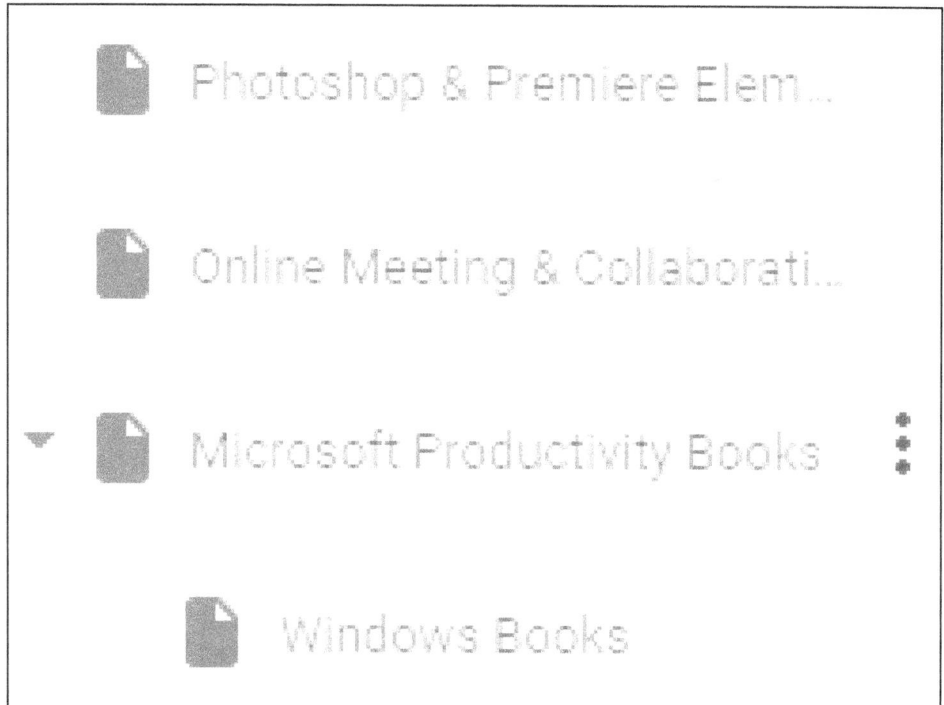

Figure 2.26

You might have noticed the three vertical dots next to each page from the Pages section. Clicking on these dots will bring up some additional configuration options that you can apply to your pages.

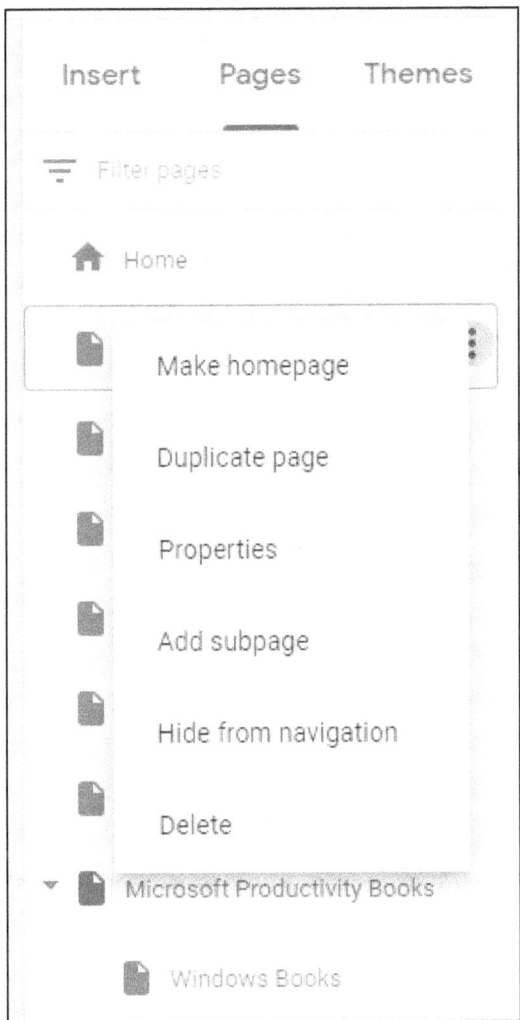

Figure 2.27

The choices you will see will vary based on what type of page you are clicking on such as the homepage or a subpage.

- **Make homepage** – If create another page and then decide that you would like to make it the main page for your site then you can set it as the homepage. This will make your current homepage a secondary page for your site and won't delete it.

- **Duplicate page** – Here you can make an exact copy of an existing page and simply give it a new name during the copy process.

- **Properties** – If you would like to change the name of a page or set a custom path, you can do so from here.

- **Add subpage** – This allows you to create a new subpage from scratch rather than making an existing page a subpage by dragging it to the current page.

- **Hide from navigation** – If you don't want a page to be shown in your site navigation at the top of the page then you can hide it from here. You can tell when a page is hidden because its icon will have a line through it.

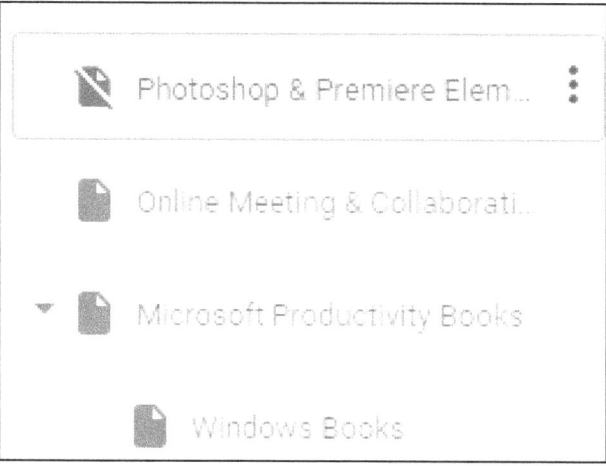

Figure 2.28

- **Delete** – This will remove a page from your website. If you change your mind then you can use the Undo option to get it back.

Site Navigation Settings & Previewing Your Website

Now that I have added some new pages, they will show up in the navigation area of my site on the home page. Then when I click on *More* it will show the pages that don't fit across the top. Notice under *Microsoft Productivity* that there is another arrow indicating that there is a subpage underneath this page. Figure 3.30 shows a zoomed in view so you can see it a little better.

Figure 2.29

Figure 2.30

You might have noticed that it looks a little busy at the top of the page with all of these book categories. You can change the site navigation from showing on the top to showing on the side by clicking the *Settings* gear icon at the top right of the page and then going to the *Navigation* section.

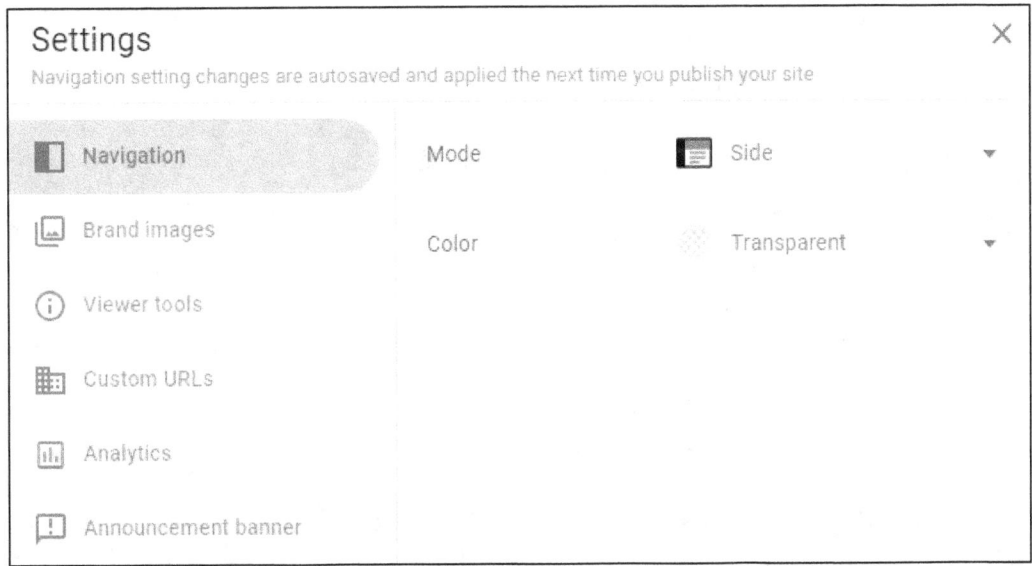

Figure 2.31

Now that I have made this change, I will get a three line menu (hamburger) icon at the top right of my page (figure 2.32) and when I click on it, I will get a navigation menu that appears with all of my other site pages (figure 2.33). As you can see in figure 2.33, I have an additional arrow that I can click on next to Microsoft Productivity Books to show its subpage.

Figure 2.32

Figure 2.33

When I preview my site in my browser it shows up without the hamburger icon and actually has the navigation pane on the left side of the page. If my browser was not maximized (full screen) then I would see the hamburger icon once again.

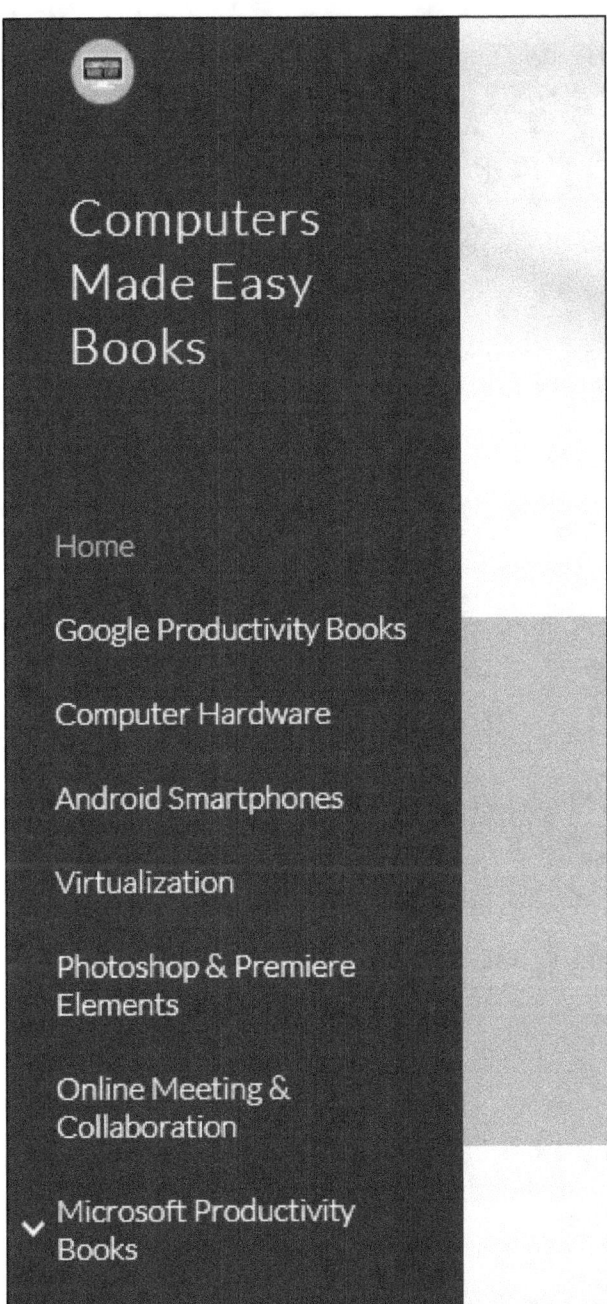

Figure 2.34

I mentioned that I was able to preview my site and what I meant by that is that you can see how your website will look "live" at any time by clicking on the *Preview* button in the toolbar while in Sites. From here you can see how your page will look on a computer, tablet or smartphone by clicking the appropriate button. Then you can click on the X to exit the preview or also the back button in your browser.

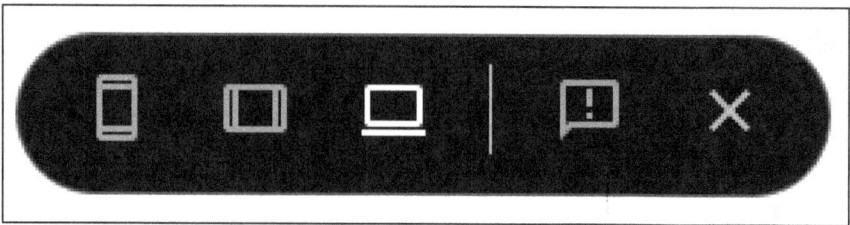

Figure 2.35

One thing that you will notice when previewing your site is that the layout in regards to sizing and positioning will not look the same as it does in editing mode. You need to keep in mind that this will also vary between devices and screen resolutions used with different computers so try and make things look the best they can for your preview mode since that's what people will be seeing.

And while I'm on the topic of the toolbar, figure 2.36 shows what each icon will do when you click on it.

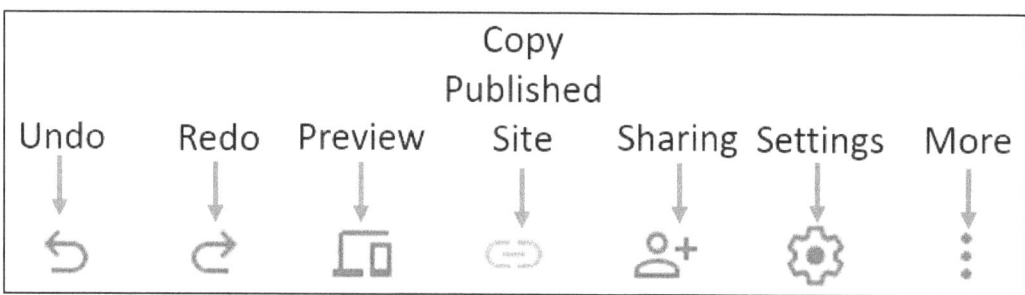

Figure 2.36

I will be getting into more of these options as I go along in this book but for now I will add some basic content to my other pages and then we can continue with some more advanced site settings and features.

Chapter 3 – Adding Advanced Website Components

Now that I have gone over how to add the basic components to your website it's time to get into some of the more advanced features and show you how to spruce things up a bit and make your site look more professional.

One thing to keep in mind when using Sites is that you are limited to what the application can do so if there is some feature that you really need that can't be done with Sites you will either need to figure out if there is a workaround or just figure out an alternative. But for most people who are looking to create an effective, eye catching website, Sites should be able to keep you covered.

Using Themes
If you are not the type who is good at formatting documents or creating eye catching presentations then you are in luck because Sites has a bunch of built in themes that you can apply to your page which will change attributes such as page colors, fonts and styles. Once you apply a theme you can always change parts of the theme, so you are not stuck using all of the settings within that theme.

Figure 3.1 shows a page with a default image banner and text with a few pictures added. On the right side of the page you can see that the Themes panel is open, and it shows what types of themes you can apply to your webpage.

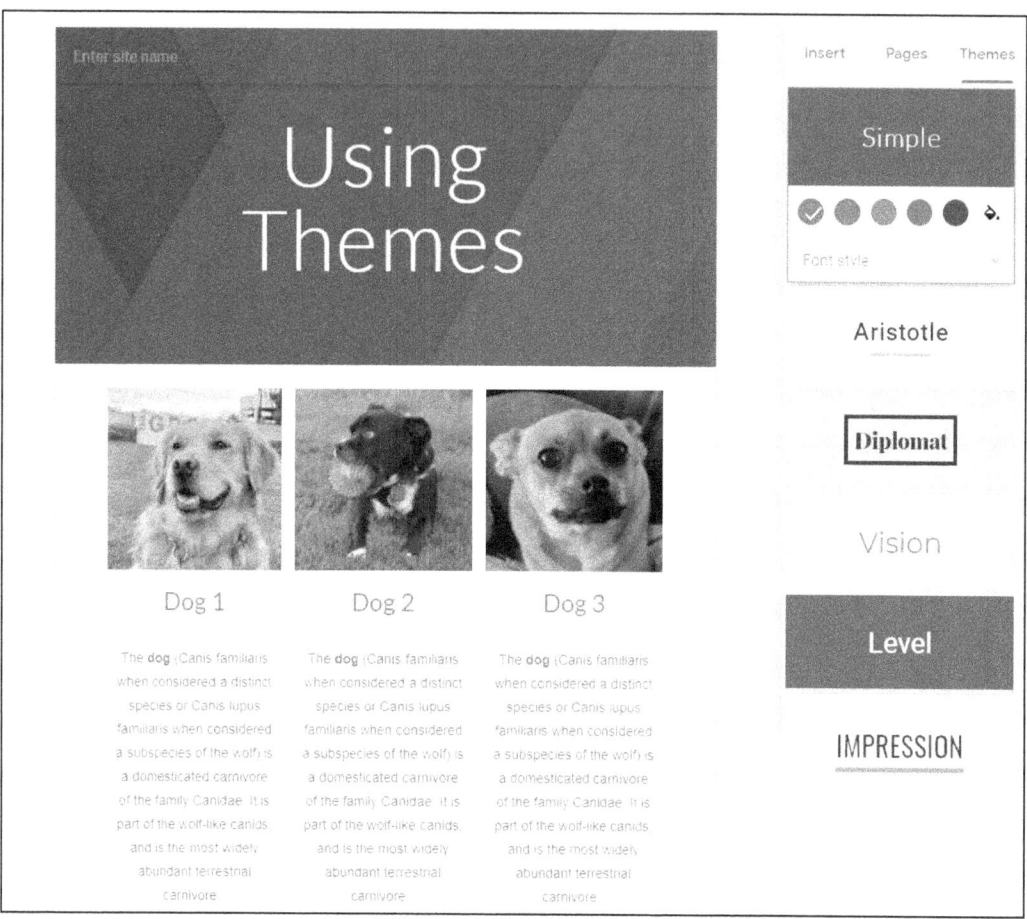

Figure 3.1

As you click on each theme, Sites will apply it to your page so you can see how it looks. Then when you are on that theme you can change its color or choose from different font styles that are included with that particular theme to suit your needs.

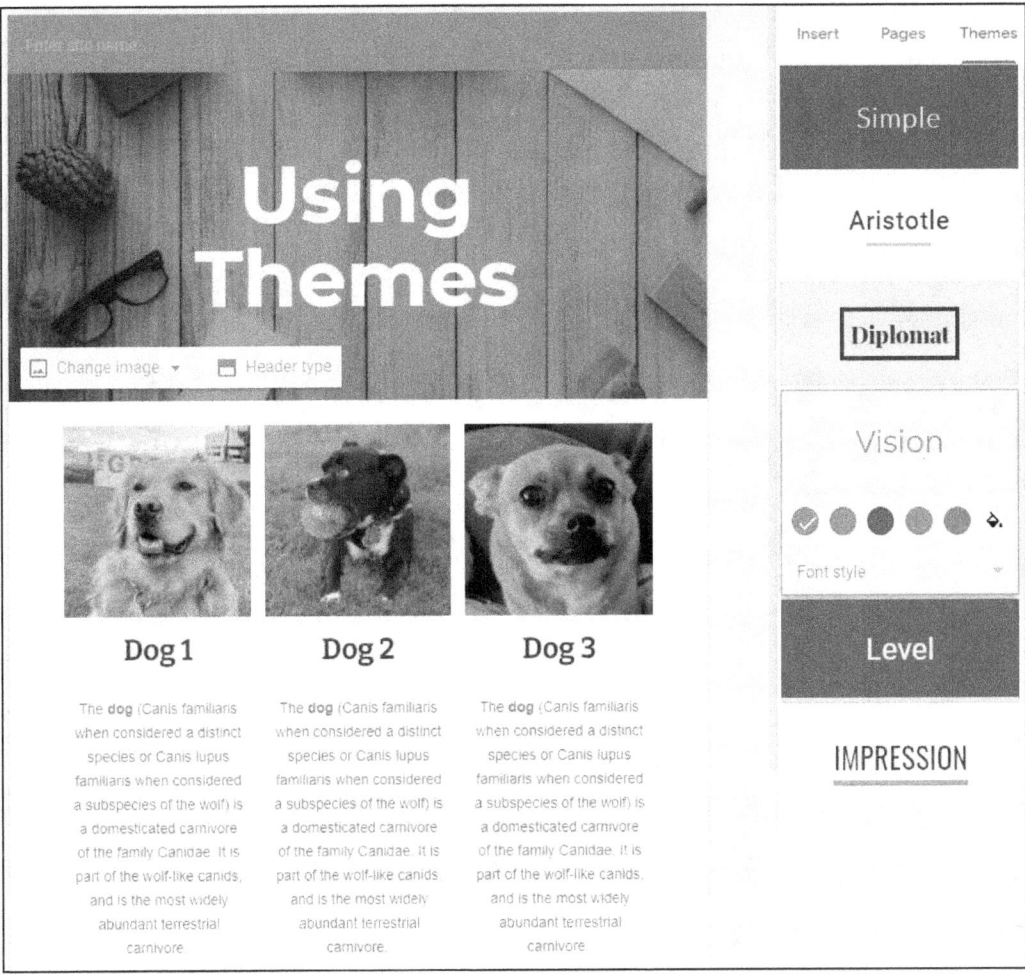

Figure 3.2

Once you have a theme used with your site then it will be applied to any new pages that you create. And if you choose a different theme then it will be applied to all of the pages within your site.

Adding Placeholders

When you are working on your website you will most likely be coming up with design ideas and changing your mind on how you want things to look as you go along. Sometimes you might come up with an idea but not know exactly where you are going with your idea and would like to leave a place on a page that you can come back to later once you figure out exactly what you want to do.

When you get into one of these situations you can simply add a placeholder to a page to remind you that you need to finish your design or add some content later once you have everything you need. Placeholders are just boxes that you insert at a particular place on a page and you can add these from the *Insert* menu simply by clicking on the *Placeholder* option.

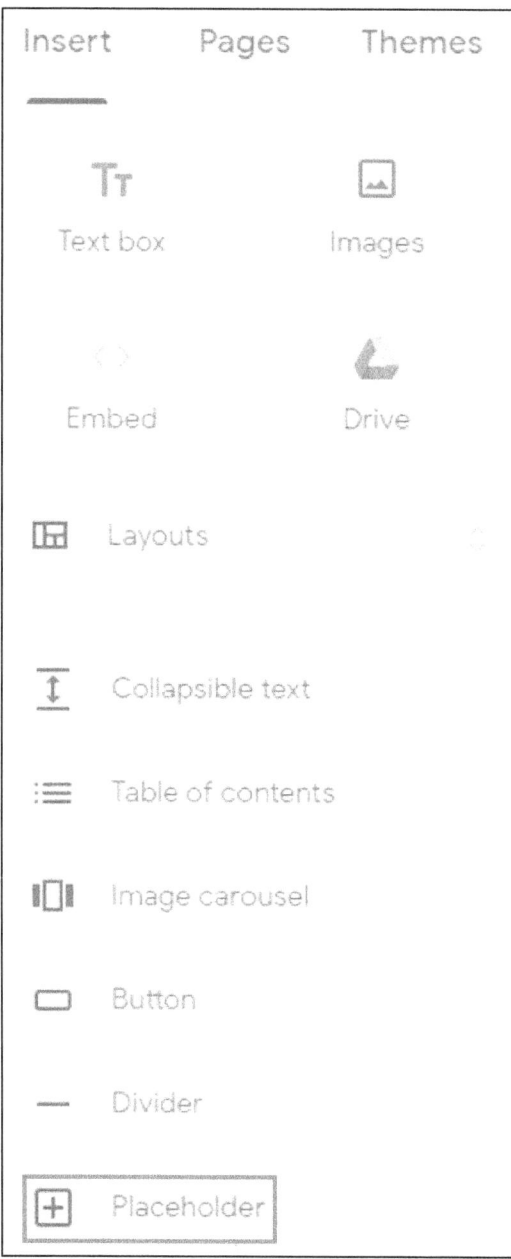

Figure 3.3

Once the placeholder is on your page you can drag it around if you need to move it to a different section on the page as well as delete it if you no longer need it.

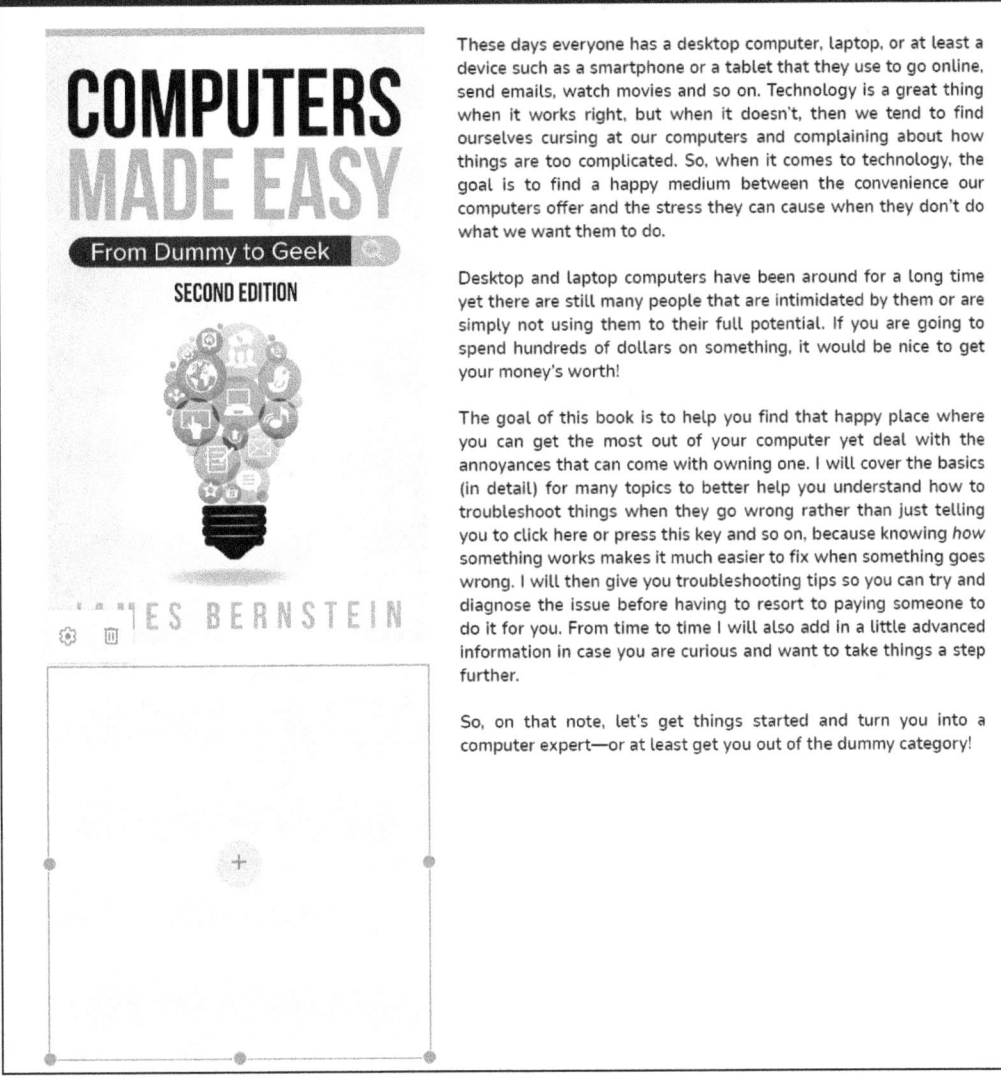

Figure 3.4

If you click on the settings gear icon you will be able to select what type of content you want to use with that placeholder. The default is to use any type of content, but this can be changed to other items such as images, documents, videos and so on. The only reason you would change the file type is if you were having others work on your site and only wanted them to be able to add certain types of content.

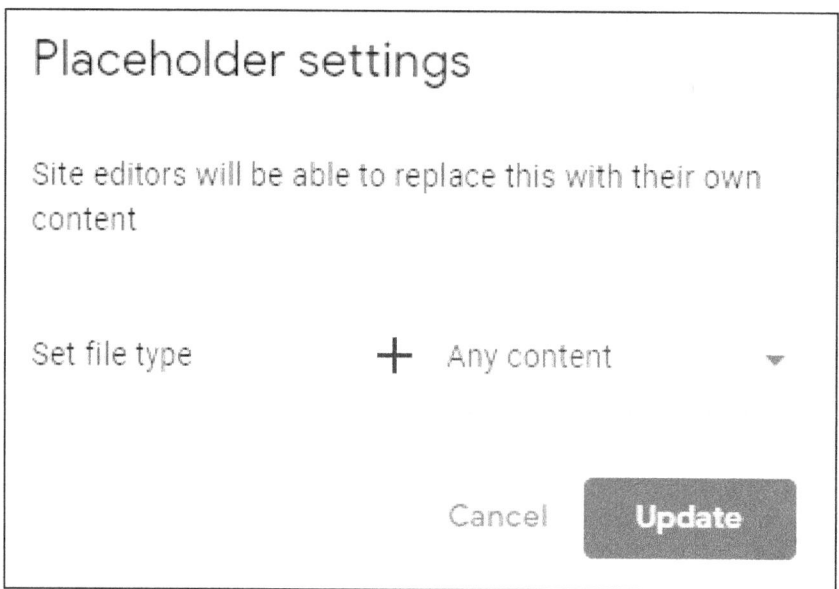

Figure 3.5

When you click on the + button inside of your placeholder, you will see the options you have in regards to adding content where this placeholder is located on your page.

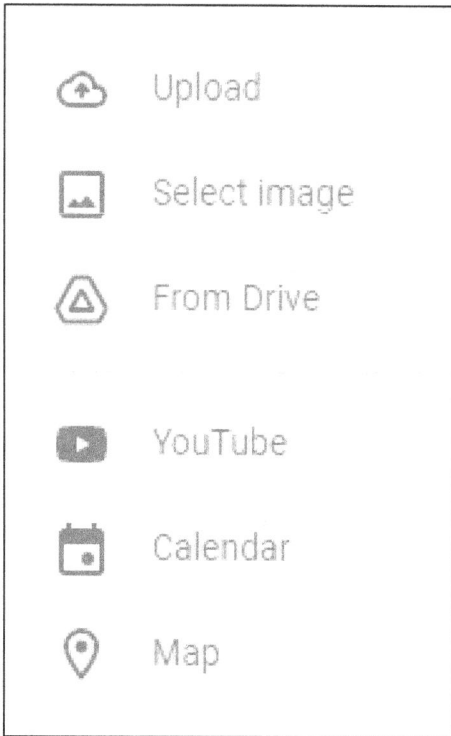

Figure 3.6

Adding Links to Text and Images

One thing you will be doing a lot when designing your website is adding links to text and images so your visitors will be able to navigate around your website and be able to easily get to other pages. You might also want to create links to other websites besides your own or maybe even to other websites that belong to you.

Adding a link to an image or text is pretty straightforward and when you click on either one, you will get some icons that allow you to perform various actions, and the icon you will want to click on will be the link icon.

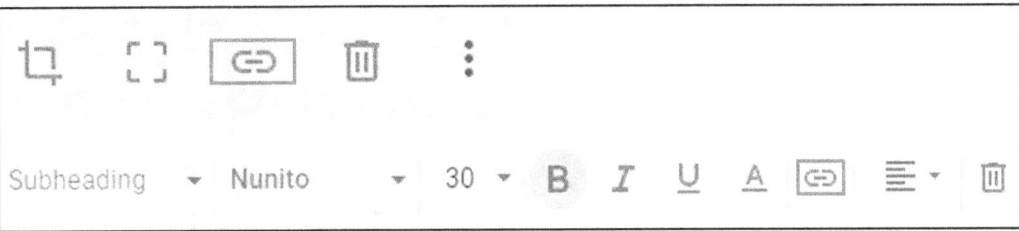

Figure 3.7

When you click on the link icon, Sites will show you a listing of your other pages assuming you want to link your image or text to one of the other pages. If that's the case, simply choose the page from your list that you want to link to and click on *Apply*. If you start typing the names of files you have in your Google Drive then you can also link those documents etc. to images and text within your website. Just remember that the files you link to your page will need to have the appropriate sharing permissions on them so others will be able to open them.

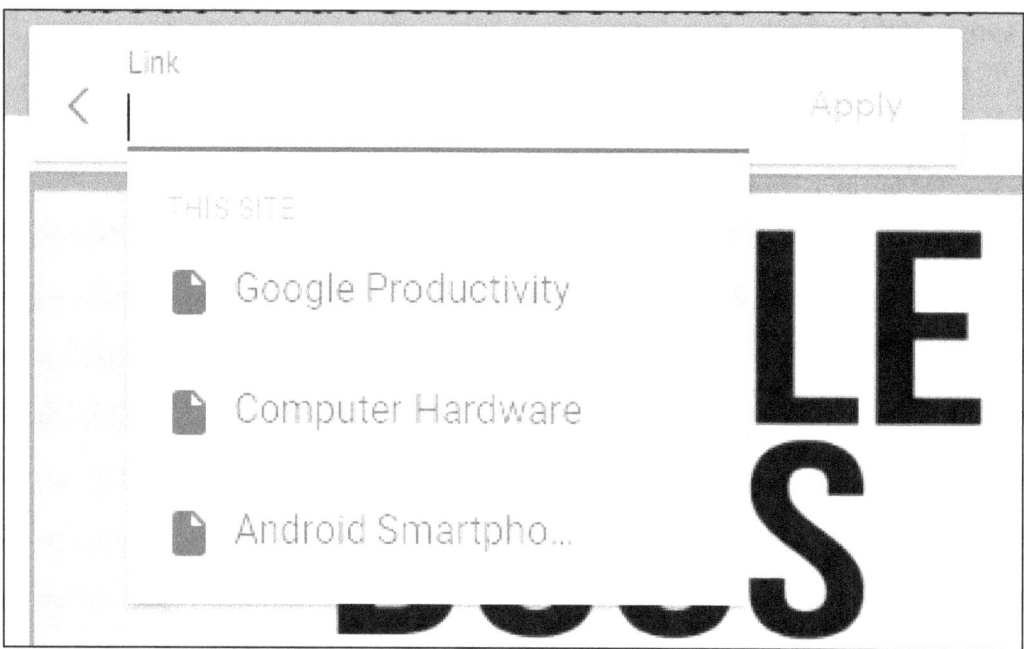

Figure 3.8

If you want to link to an external website then you can simply type in the website address (URL) or paste it in from the other website and click on *Apply*.

Figure 3.9

If you need to go back and edit or remove the link address you can simply click on the link icon again and make your changes.

When want to test out your links you will need to click on the Preview button, so your page is functioning in a "live" mode. Sites will make the pages from your links open in new tabs within your web browser.

For my text link, I want to add an email address link to my **Contact** section at the bottom of the page. You can add an email link using the same process as you do for a website link. Then when a website visitor clicks on the link it will open up their default email program with the email address automatically filled in.

The format you need to use to make this work is as follows:
mailto:YourEmailAddress

You will need to replace *YourEmailAddress* with the actual email address you want to use to receive emails from your site visitors. Figure 3.10 shows how my configuration looks.

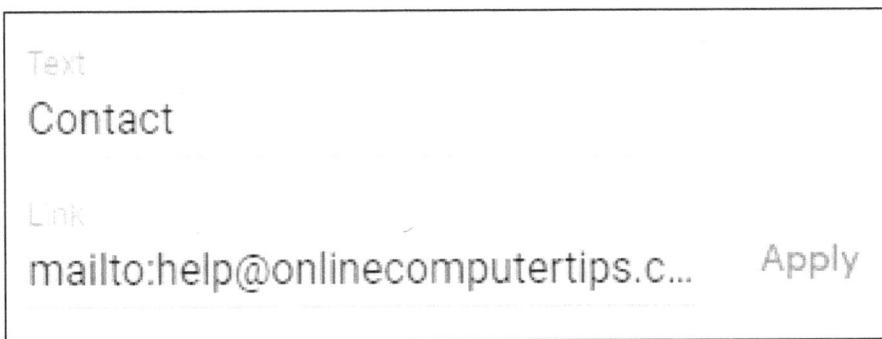

Figure 3.10

Now when I click on my text I have the option to change the text formatting as well as edit or delete my link.

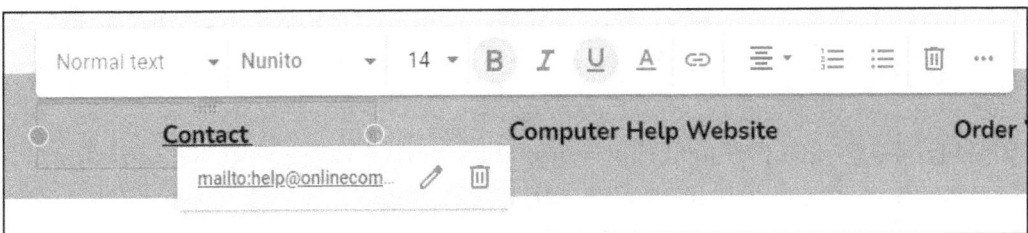

Figure 3.11

I will now add links to the two other text items at the bottom of my homepage and after that is complete, my text will be underlined indicating that they are clickable links.

| Contact | Computer Help Website | Order Your Copy Now! |

Figure 3.12

Be careful when using links that will show your email address because you might end up getting a lot of spam emails from bots that crawl pages looking for these types of links. Many sites will use a contact form instead (discussed in Chapter 4) with a Captcha security procedure that has to be manually completed by a real person before continuing.

Now that I have my contact and purchase text and links configured at the bottom of the page I will want to have this same information on every page of my site.

You might think that you would use the *Duplicate section* option that appears to the left of your section when you click on it but that will only duplicate the section on the same page, and I don't want to do that.

Figure 3.13

What I need to do is highlight the section itself and use the copy keyboard shortcut to copy the section. This shortcut is *Ctrl-C* for Windows and *Command-C* for Mac. Then I will need to go to the next page in my site where I want this section to be copied to and then paste it in by using *Ctrl-V* for Windows or *Command-V* for Mac.

The section should be copied to the same location on the page but if it is not then you can just click on it and drag it to the appropriate area.

Adding Clickable Buttons

One easy way to add some flair to your site is to add buttons for links that can take you to other pages on your site or even other sites. You can even have buttons that your visitors can click on to do things such as download a file or print an online form.

You can add buttons in Sites to link to the same types of items that you can with regular text and image links. When you click on *button* from the *Insert* panel you will be asked to name your button and then add the link that will be associated with that button.

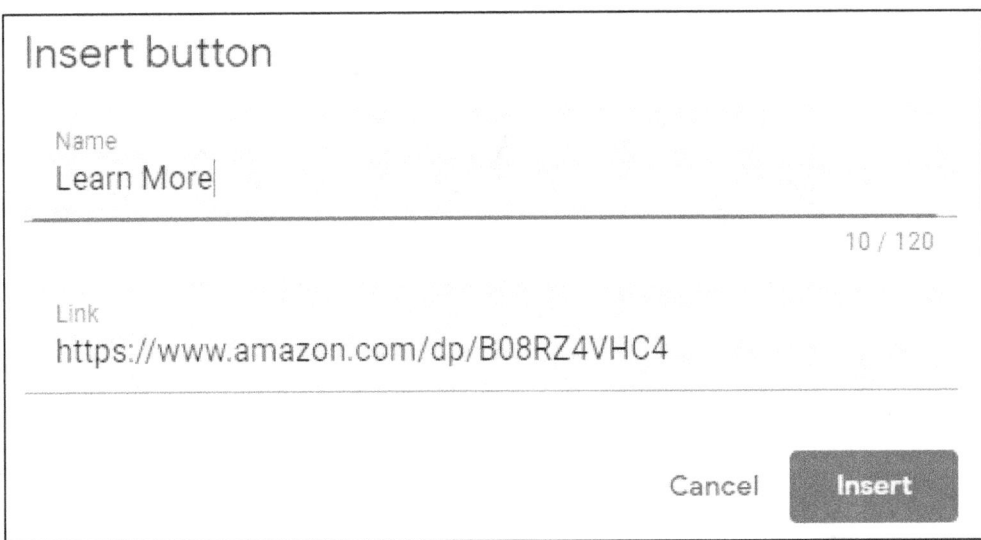

Figure 3.14

Depending on where your mouse cursor is, Sites might add the button in its own section or add it to the section that you are currently in. Figure 3.15 shows my button added to its own new section.

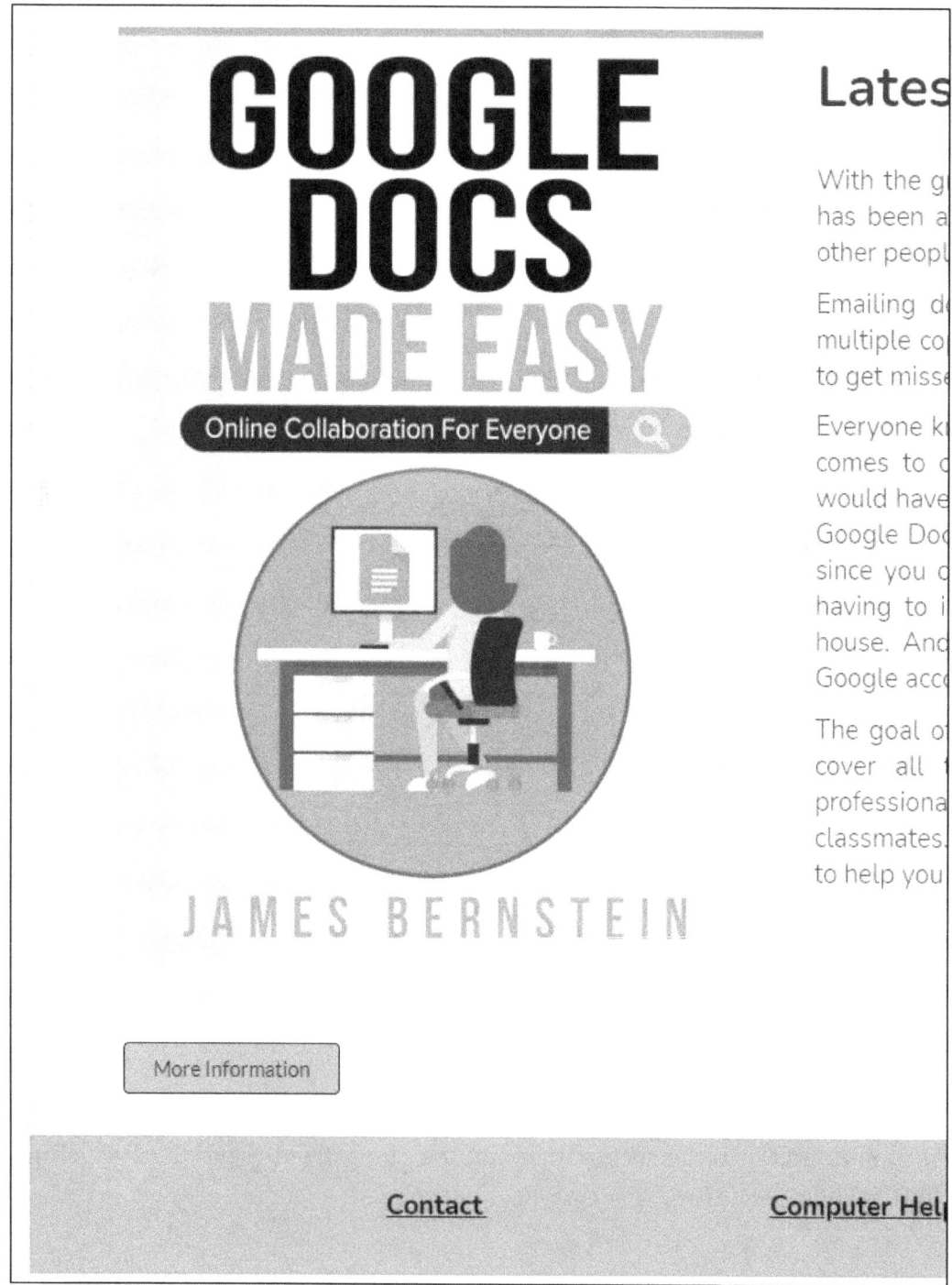

Figure 3.15

I can then drag it into a current text or image section and the button will change to fit that particular section which is really not the best way to add a button since it tends to make your button larger than it should be.

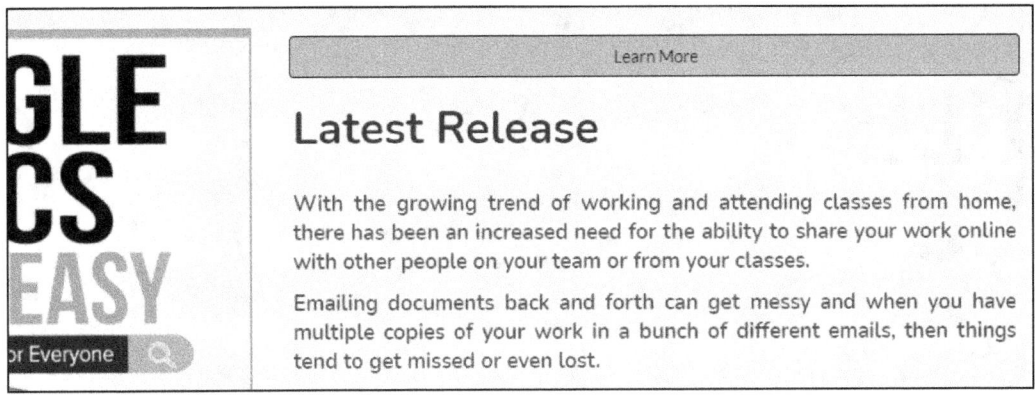

Figure 3.16

If I drag my button into the section with an image then it also resizes itself to fit that section.

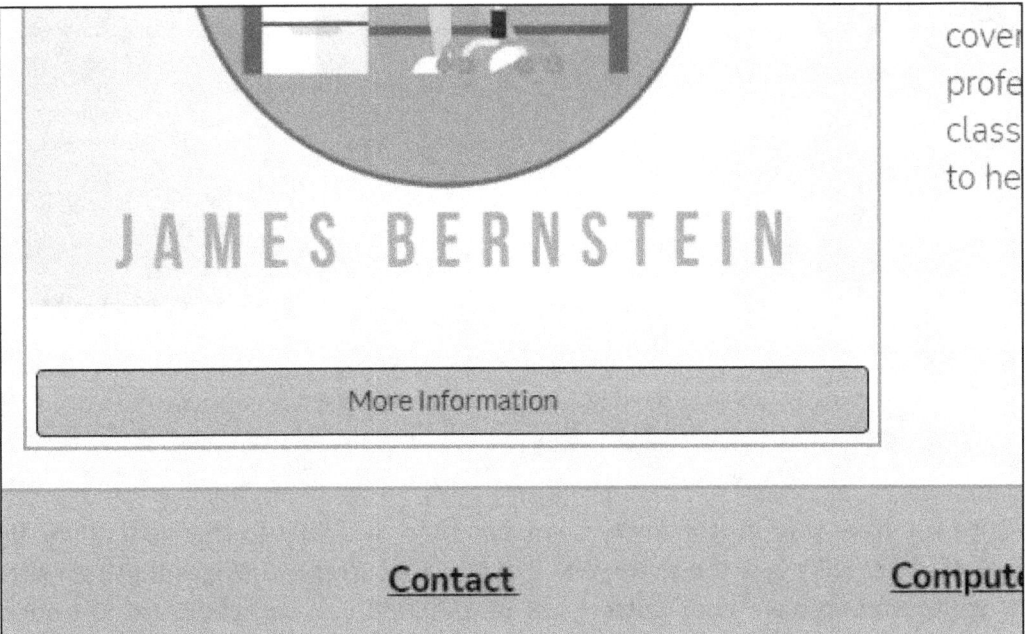

Figure 3.17

If you plan on using buttons you might want to place them in their own sections and then you can drag and drop the button anywhere you like within that section as seen in figure 3.18.

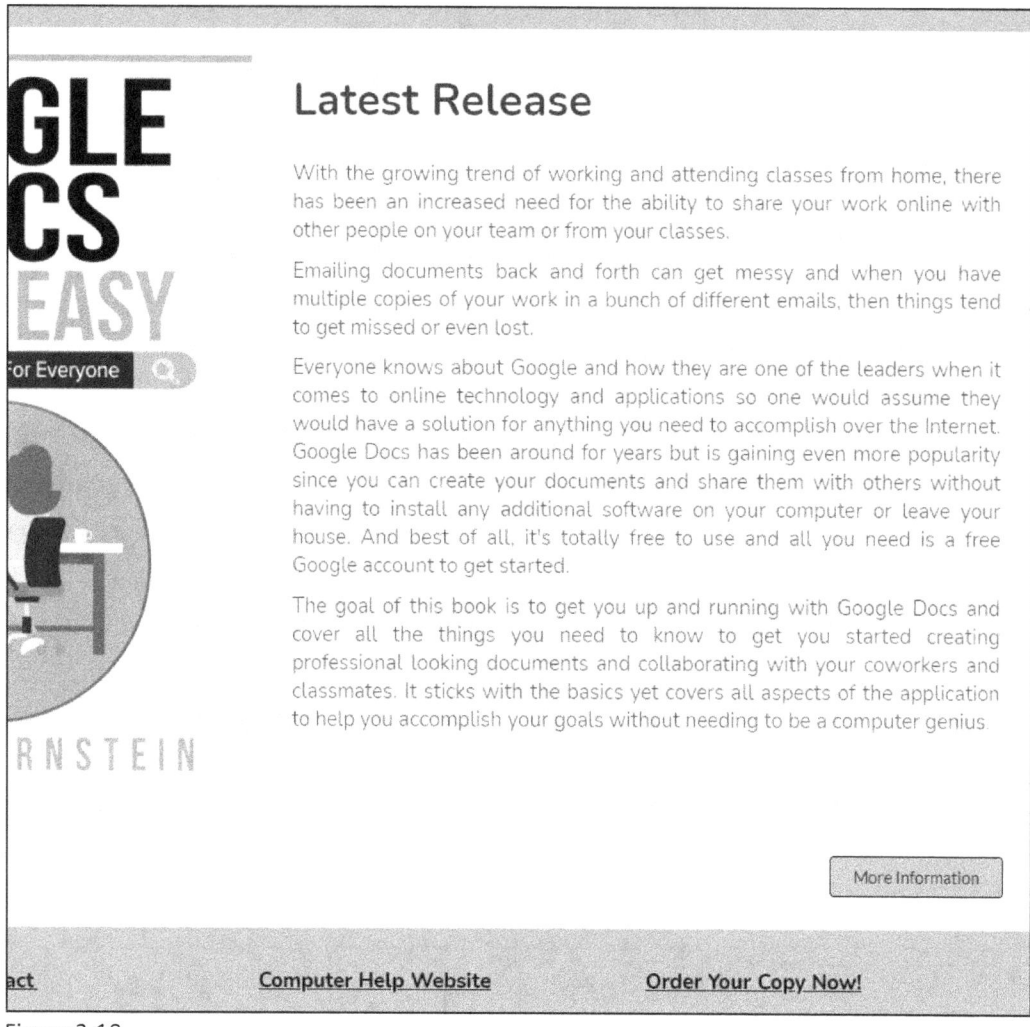

Figure 3.18

Once you have your button in place you can then click on it to change its style. By default, sites will apply the same style that you are currently using within your site. If you prefer to have your button just be outlined you can choose that option (figure 3.19) or have it only show the text (figure 3.20).

Figure 3.19

Figure 3.20

If you want to get fancy then you can download a button image online or create your own and then place it on the page as an image and then create a link from that image (figure 3.21). Just be sure to make it a transparent PNG file otherwise you will have a white background around the image and if you place it on something that is another color than white it will show the white box around your button.

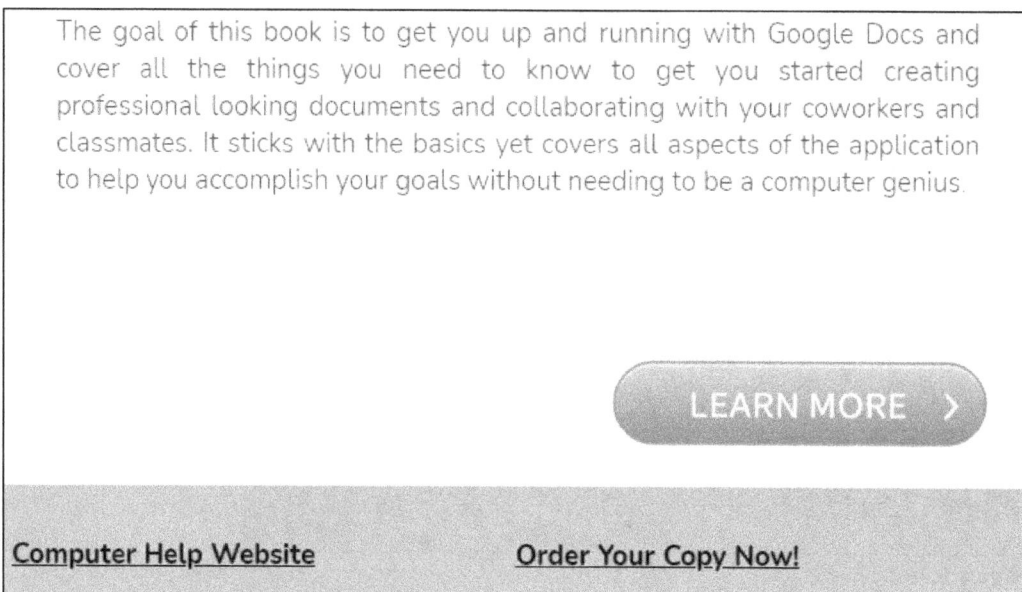

The goal of this book is to get you up and running with Google Docs and cover all the things you need to know to get you started creating professional looking documents and collaborating with your coworkers and classmates. It sticks with the basics yet covers all aspects of the application to help you accomplish your goals without needing to be a computer genius.

LEARN MORE >

Computer Help Website   **Order Your Copy Now!**

Figure 3.21

Using Dividers to Separate Your Sections

If you end up using a lot of sections on one page then your content might start to blend in together making it hard to see your page structure. One easy way to break up your page and make your sections stand out is to use dividers in between them.

Dividers are thin horizontal lines that you can place across your page to above or below your sections. You can add a divider from the Insert group within sites. Once you place a divider on a page, you can drag and drop it to a different section if needed. If you don't want the divider on your page anymore, then you can simply delete it.

Figure 3.22 shows one of my pages without a divider between the two book sections and figure 3.23 shows the same page with a divider added.

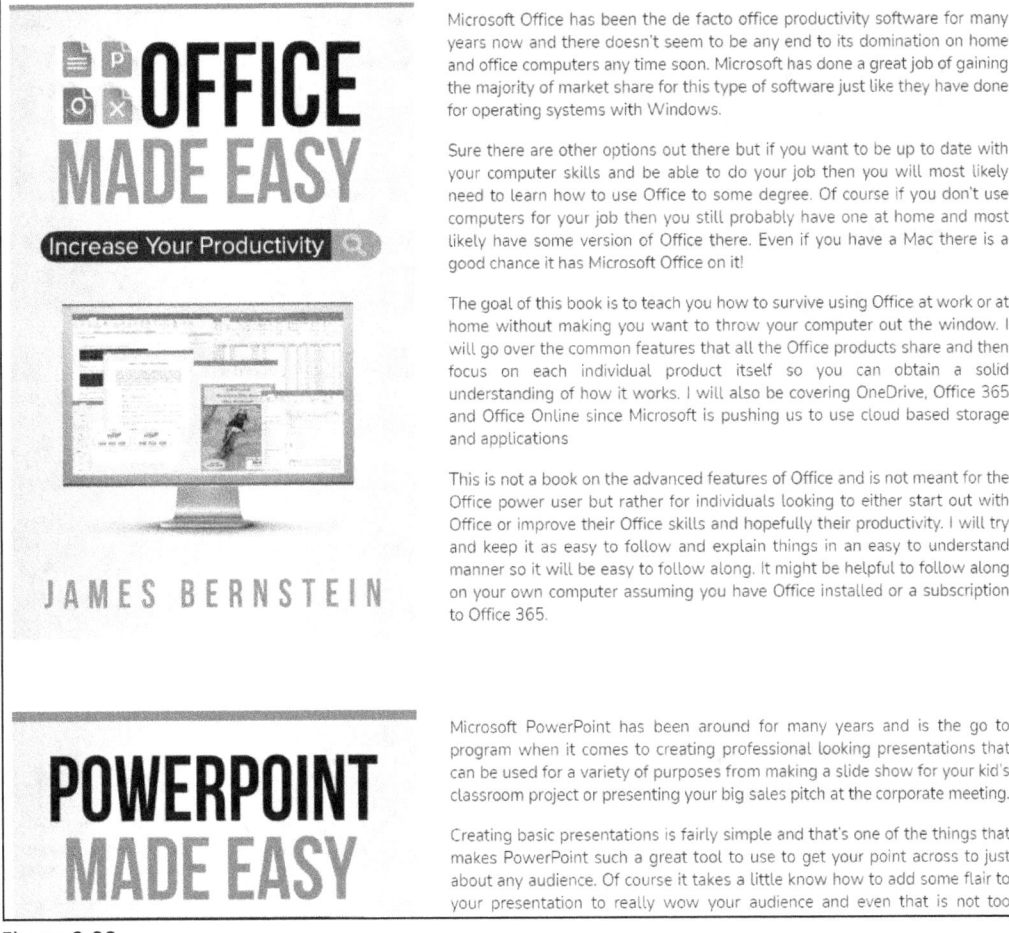

Microsoft Office has been the de facto office productivity software for many years now and there doesn't seem to be any end to its domination on home and office computers any time soon. Microsoft has done a great job of gaining the majority of market share for this type of software just like they have done for operating systems with Windows.

Sure there are other options out there but if you want to be up to date with your computer skills and be able to do your job then you will most likely need to learn how to use Office to some degree. Of course if you don't use computers for your job then you still probably have one at home and most likely have some version of Office there. Even if you have a Mac there is a good chance it has Microsoft Office on it!

The goal of this book is to teach you how to survive using Office at work or at home without making you want to throw your computer out the window. I will go over the common features that all the Office products share and then focus on each individual product itself so you can obtain a solid understanding of how it works. I will also be covering OneDrive, Office 365 and Office Online since Microsoft is pushing us to use cloud based storage and applications

This is not a book on the advanced features of Office and is not meant for the Office power user but rather for individuals looking to either start out with Office or improve their Office skills and hopefully their productivity. I will try and keep it as easy to follow and explain things in an easy to understand manner so it will be easy to follow along. It might be helpful to follow along on your own computer assuming you have Office installed or a subscription to Office 365.

Microsoft PowerPoint has been around for many years and is the go to program when it comes to creating professional looking presentations that can be used for a variety of purposes from making a slide show for your kid's classroom project or presenting your big sales pitch at the corporate meeting.

Creating basic presentations is fairly simple and that's one of the things that makes PowerPoint such a great tool to use to get your point across to just about any audience. Of course it takes a little know how to add some flair to your presentation to really wow your audience and even that is not too

Figure 3.22

Figure 3.23

As you can see, the divider is a very subtle effect but does make a difference when used to break up sections. As of now, there is no way to add a vertical divider using the built in Site tools.

Inserting Page Footers

You might have noticed when you had your mouse at the bottom of the page that you got a popup that says *Add Footer* and you might have been wondering what that was used for.

Figure 3.24

The Add Footer button is just a quick and easy way to add a footer section to the bottom of your page that will automatically get repeated on all of your other pages. It works the same way as adding a footer in Microsoft Word or Google Docs.

Figure 3.25 shows the footer creation process and as you can see it looks exactly the same as when you add a normal text section except the font is a smaller size by default. You can change the font formatting for your headers just like you can any other text and when you do, it will get updated on all of your pages. Figure 3.26 shows the results.

Figure 3.25

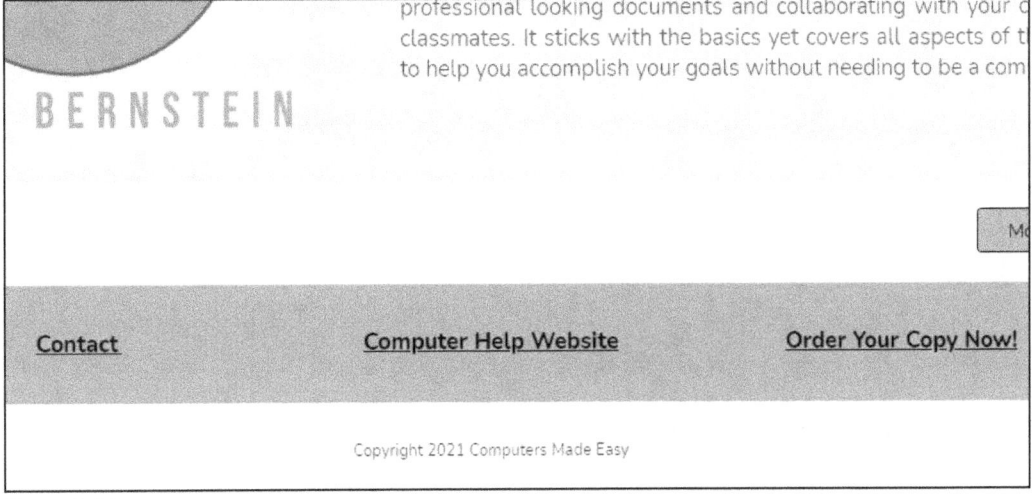

Figure 3.26

Image Carousels

Sites has a nice feature that allows you to configure a slide show of your images that can be cycled through automatically or manually by your visitors. You can add multiple images and then place the image carousel wherever you like on your page and then resize it to make it fit properly.

The *Image Carousel* option can be found in the *Insert* panel and when you click on it you will have the option to insert images from your local computer or your Google Drive, Google Image search, URL of an image, or you can add a photo from your Google Photos assuming you use it.

Once you decide where your images are coming from, all you need to do is add them to your carousel and then click on the *Insert* button. For my example, I will be creating an image carousel for all my book covers that I will place in the top image banner on the home page.

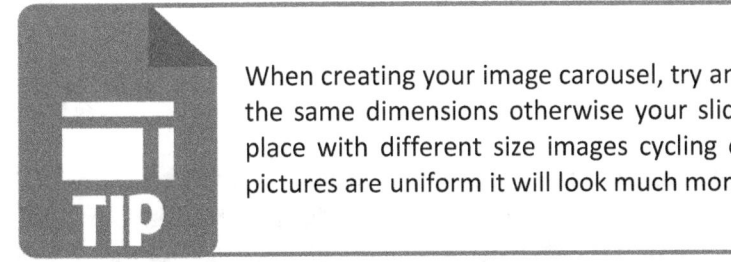

Figure 3.27

> When creating your image carousel, try and use pictures that have the same dimensions otherwise your slide show will look out of place with different size images cycling on the screen. If all the pictures are uniform it will look much more professional.
>
> **TIP**

Figure 3.28 shows the placement of my image carousel and how it will look on my homepage.

Figure 3.28

When you are in the insert images dialog box (figure 3.29), you will see that there is a gear icon that will take you to the carousel settings. From here you can change a few options to fine tune how your slideshow will look.

Figure 3.29

The *Show dots* option will display a row of dots under your images to show that there are multiple pictures in your slide show. You can disable this feature if you do not like the way it looks. If you take a look at figure 3.30 you will see these dots and also some left and right arrows that appear when you place your mouse over the image. These arrows allow you to manually cycle the pictures forward and backward at your own pace.

Figure 3.30

The *Show captions* option will allow you to place text under each one of your images as shown in figure 3.31.

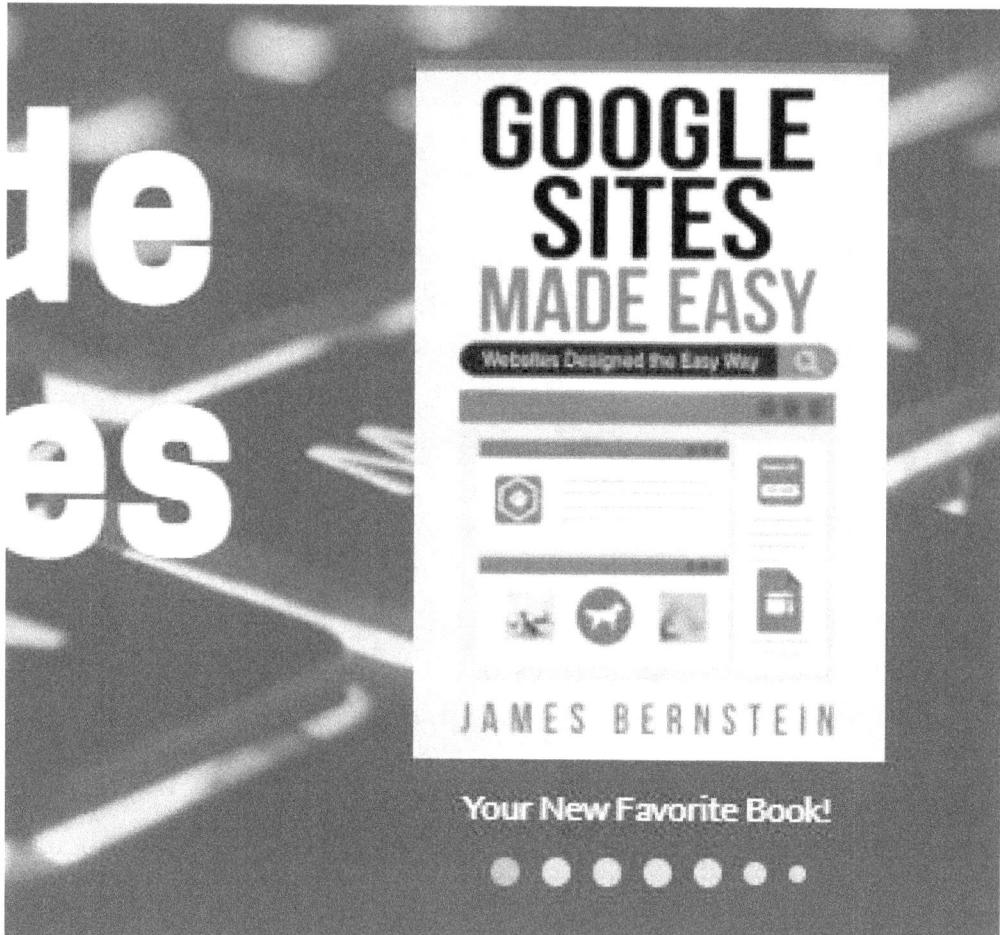

Figure 3.31

To edit this caption text you will need to click on each specific image in the carousel settings and then on the caption button to add the text as seen in figure 3.32. Just be sure not to make your text too long otherwise it will get cut off. Also be sure to click the *Update* button because if you click out of the box it will go away without saving your changes.

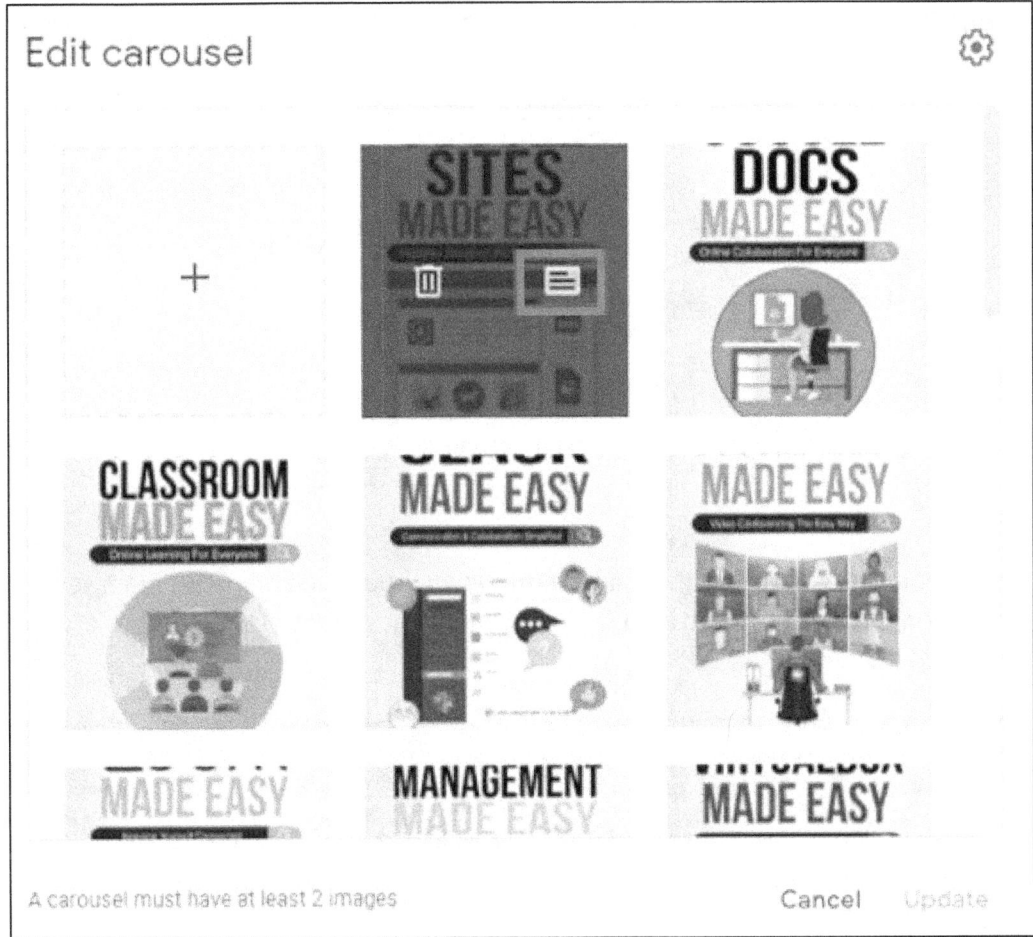

Figure 3.32

The *Auto start* option will make your slide show play automatically when someone goes to your website and lands on that page. If it's not checked then the visitor will have to scroll through the images manually using the arrow buttons. The *Transition speed* setting can be adjusted to determine how fast the images change when you use the Auto start option.

Adding Collapsible Text (Drop Down Menus)

If you have a need to display a listing of items but don't want those items cluttering up your page then you can add a collapsible text section that allows your visitors to click on the main subject heading and then see the list of items under that heading.

When you add collapsible text you will have a spot for the larger main subject text and then under that you will be able to add your listing of items. For my list, I will put **Available Titles** for the main header and then type in the title of each one of my books in the section underneath that.

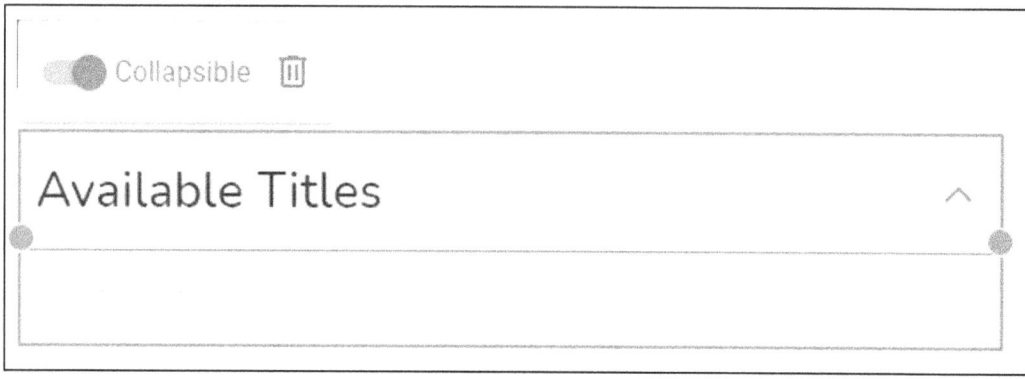

Figure 3.33

Now when I preview my page I can see that I have the Available Titles main section showing but in order to show all the book titles underneath I will need to click on the down arrow to the right.

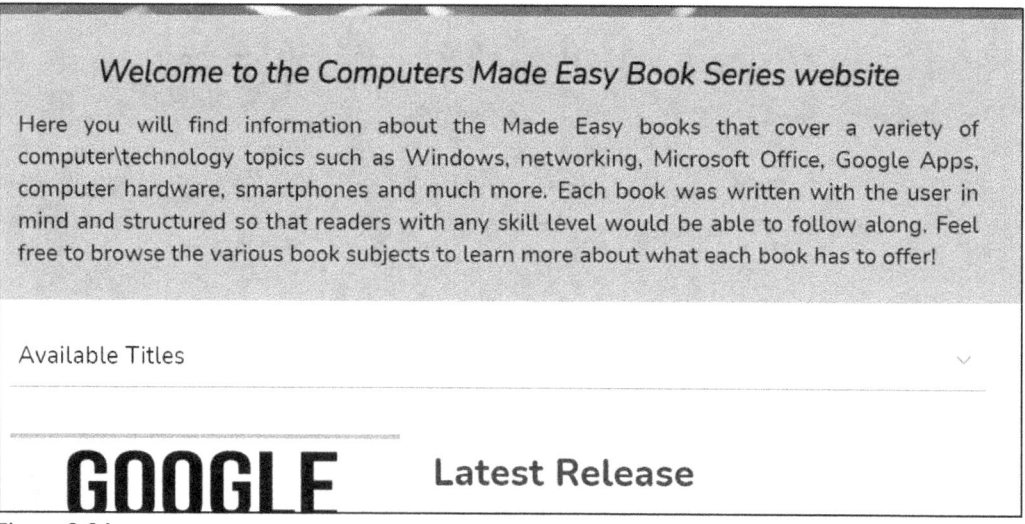

Figure 3.34

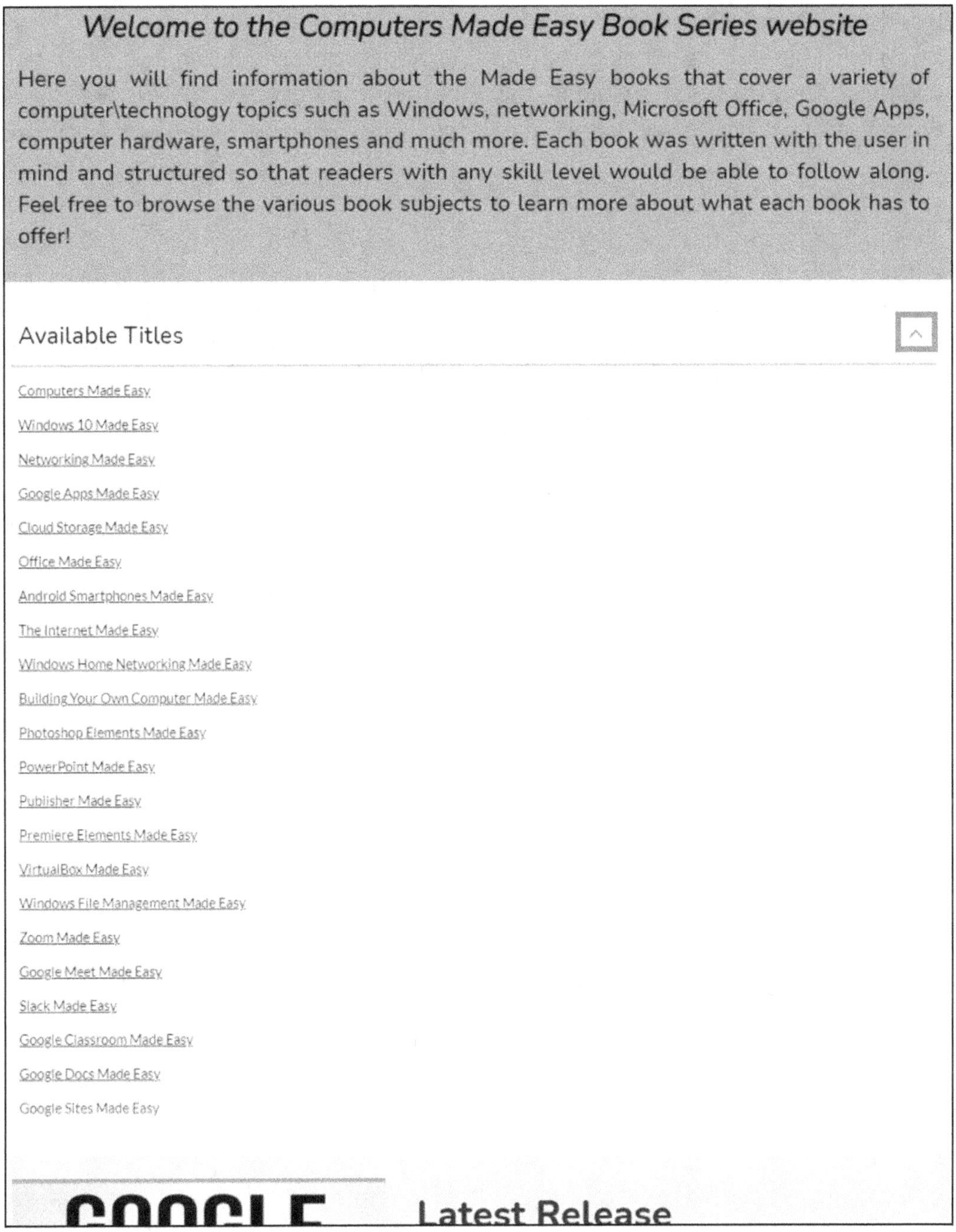

Figure 3.35

Then if I want to hide the book titles I can click on the arrow which has changed to an up arrow. I also made each book title a clickable link that will take the visitor to a page where they can get more information about the title and buy it if they desire.

Inserting a Google Document

If you have been using other google apps\products before getting into Sites then you most likely have some Google documents stored in your Google Drive. These documents can be Docs documents, Sheets spreadsheets, Slides presentations and so on.

Sites will allow you to insert these types of files directly into your website so your visitors can access them and view the information contained in these files. You will insert these files from your Google Drive and there are a couple of ways you can do this. Once again, just be sure that you have the appropriate sharing permissions set on any documents\files you want to use on your website.

You can go to the *Insert* panel and choose what type of file you want to insert, or you can double click to bring up the wheel menu and then choose the *From Drive* option (figure 3.36). Each method will work differently so you can try them both and see what works the best for you.

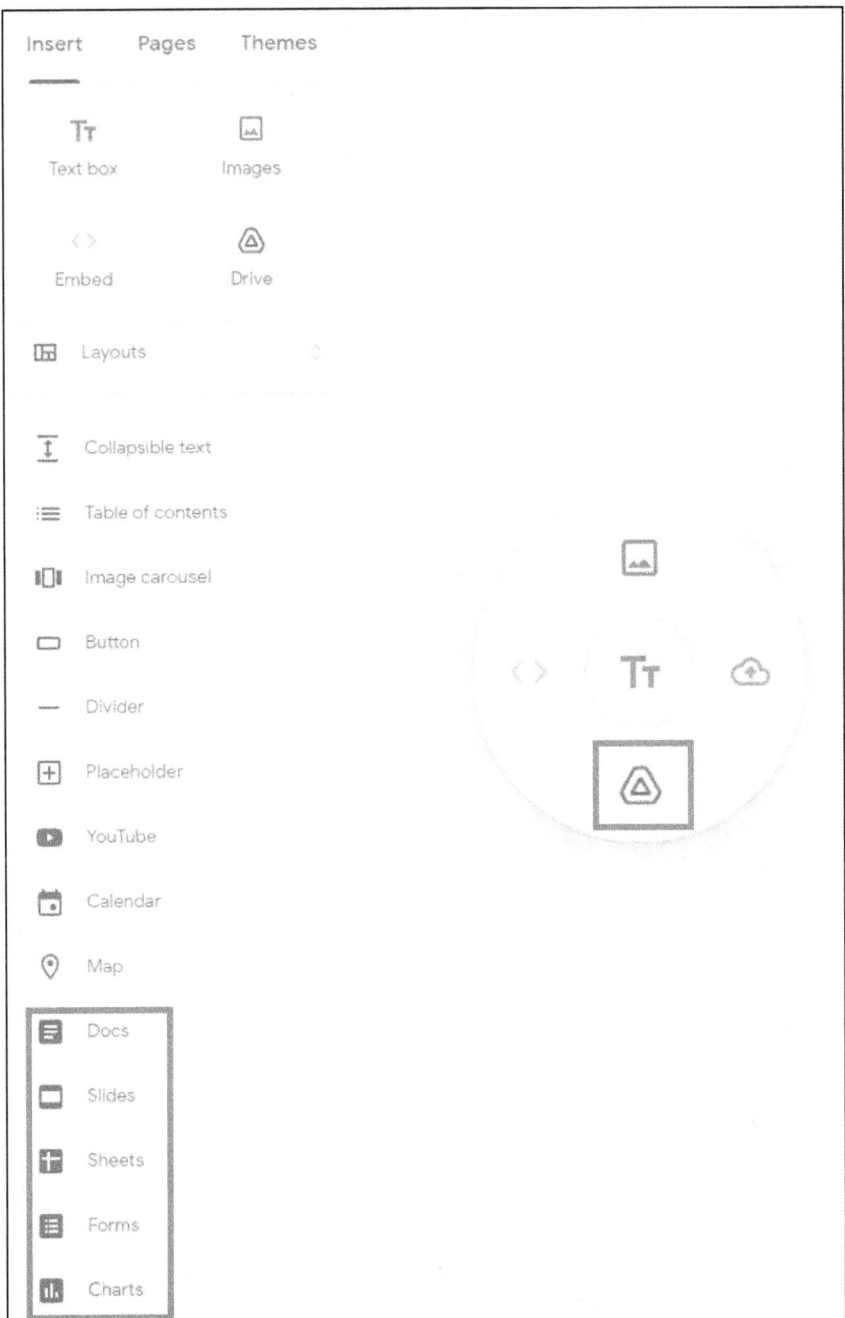

Figure 3.36

If I were to click on the Docs item in the Insert panel then Sites would bring up any Google Docs that I have stored in my Google Drive as seen in figure 3.35. Then I can simply click on the one I want to have inserted into my page.

Figure 3.37

When the document is inserted into my site, my visitors will be able to read that document and scroll through it right on the page itself. They will not need to download the file first.

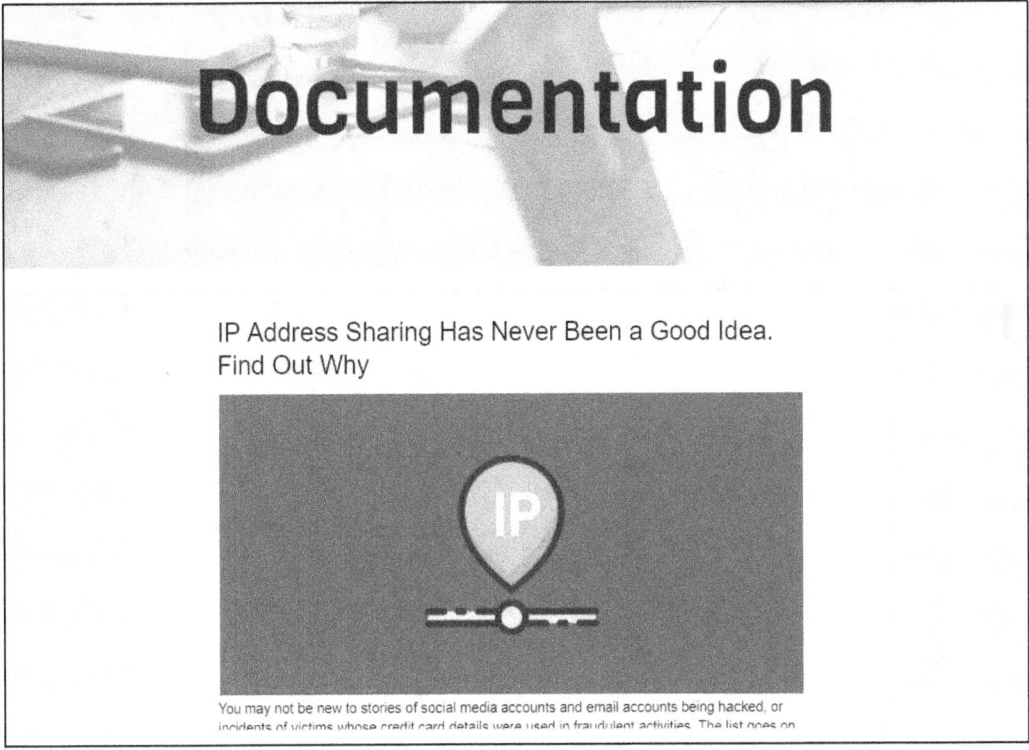

Figure 3.38

If I were to use the menu wheel and choose the insert from Drive option then I would be shown all of the file types (as well as folders) in my Google Drive and not just Docs files like in the sample above. Now I can insert other types of files besides Docs files since they will all be available to insert. I can also view my files by category such as shared with me, recent, starred as well as files I have synced with my computer.

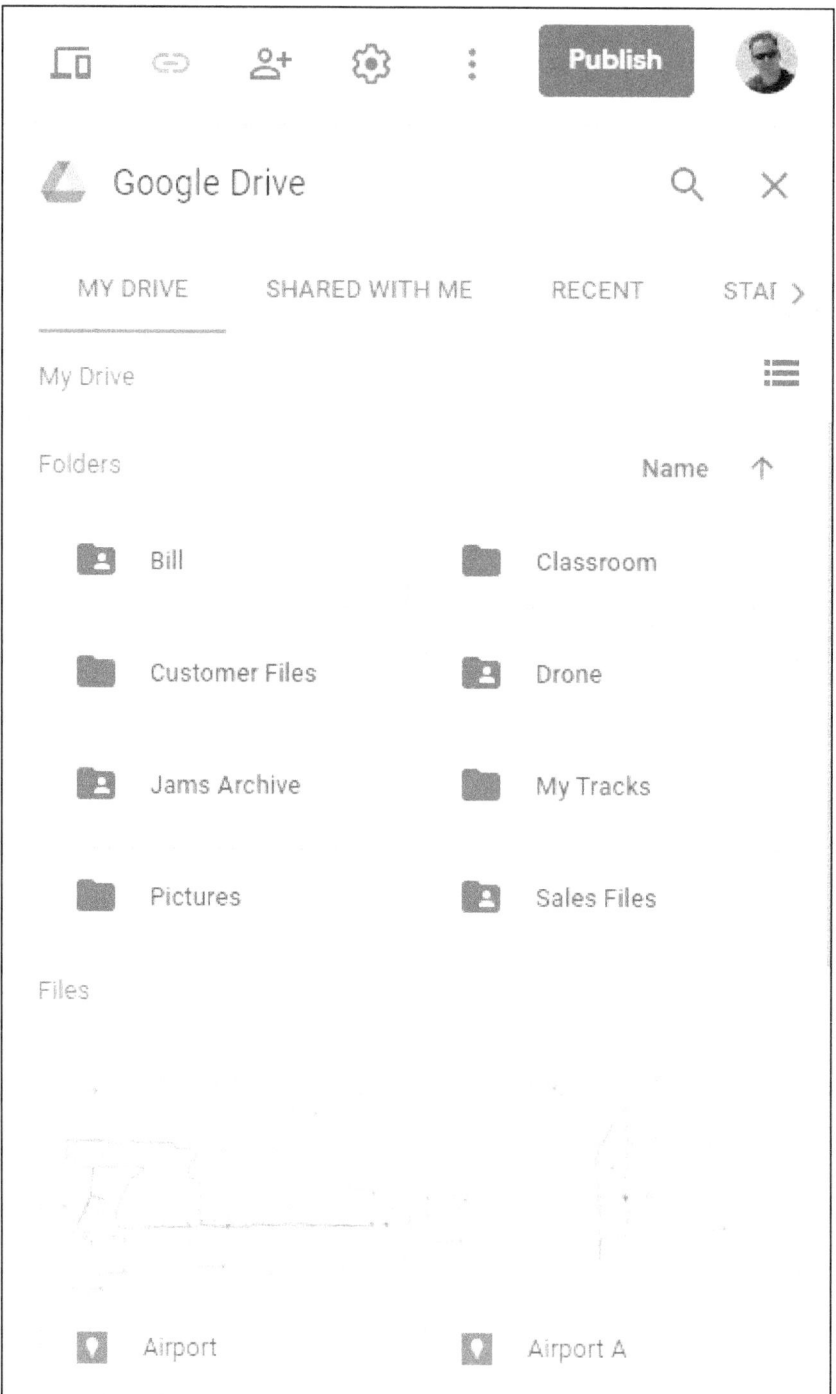

Figure 3.39

If you are interested in learning more about consumer and small business cloud storage then check out my book titled **Cloud Storage Made Easy**.
https://www.amazon.com/dp/1730838359

Adding a Map to Your Page

If your website will contain information about your business location or maybe a point of interest then you have the option to place a map on a particular page to help guide your visitors to that location.

You can add a map to your page from the Insert panel and when you do so it will prompt you to specify the location of your map. You can type in something broad such as a state or get more detailed such as a city or an actual address itself.

You can also scroll and zoom around the map and then drop a placemark on a specific location if you like. If you have created any custom maps with your Google account then you can add one of those as well using the *My Maps* section.

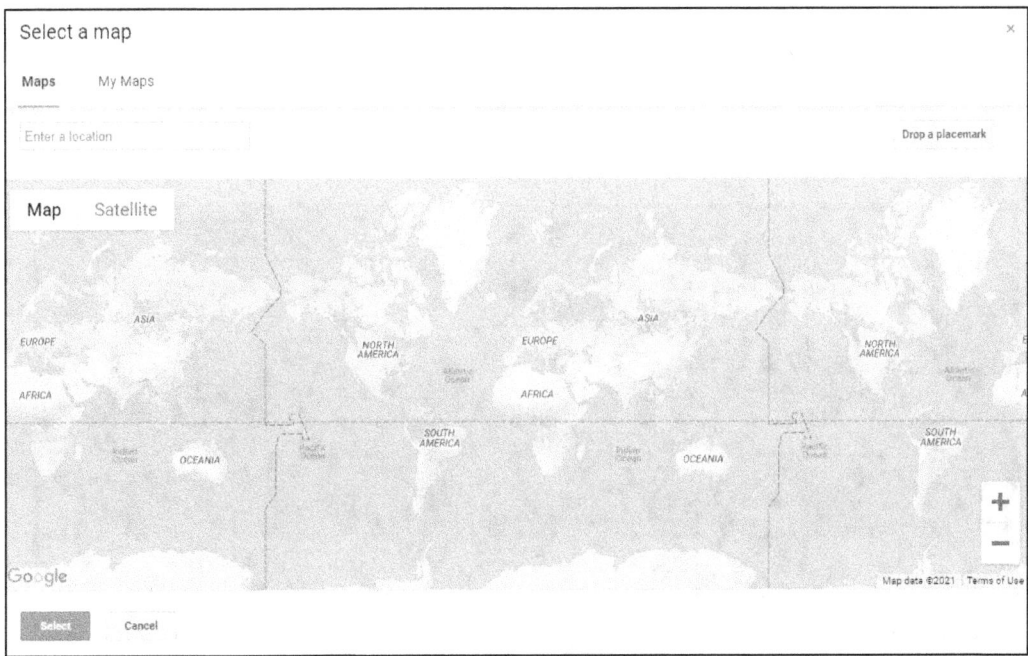

Figure 3.40

For my example I will use a real bookstore that I searched for in the location box and Sites will add a red pin at the location of that address as seen in figure 3.41.

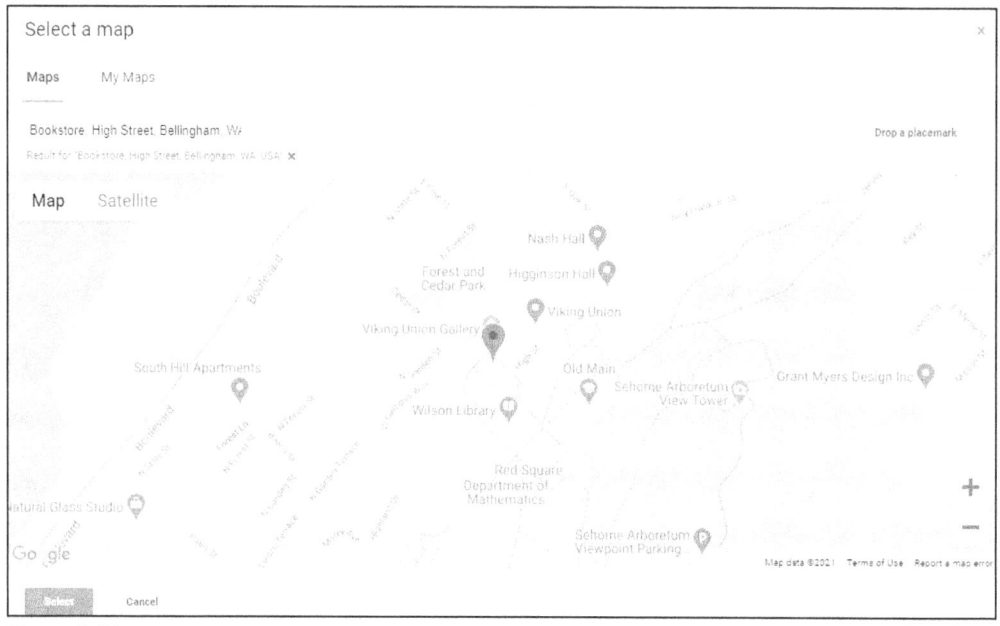

Figure 3.41

If I want to see what the satellite view looks like then I can click on the *Satellite* button.

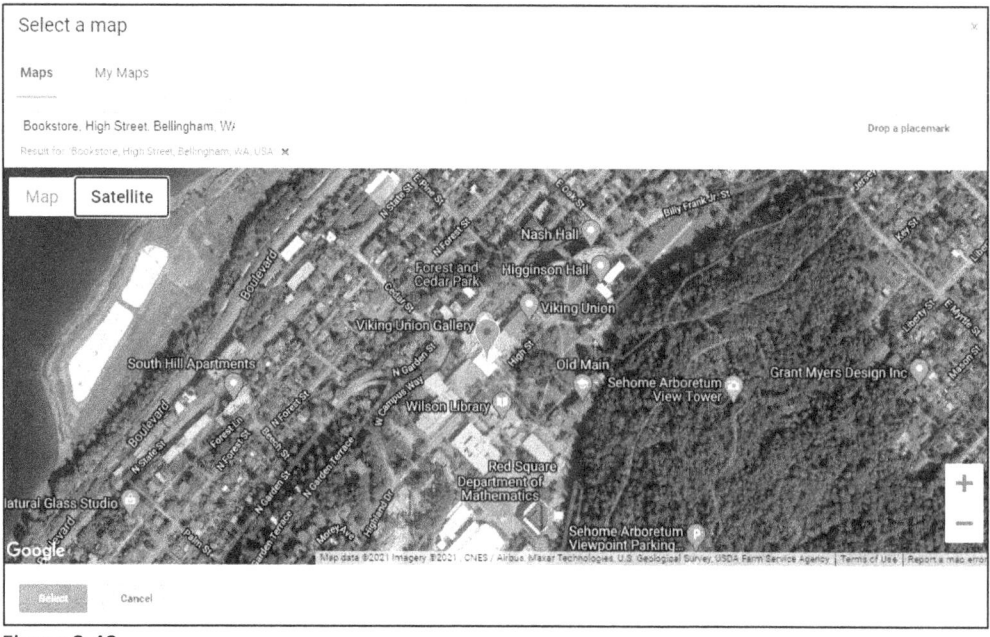

Figure 3.42

When everything looks good I will click on the *Select* button and the map will be added to my page in a new section with a default size.

Figure 3.43

If I don't like the default size then I can click on the map and resize it or even move it to a location.

Figure 3.43

Embedding Content

Sites has a feature that will allow you to add live content from other sources to your page so you can share additional content that your visitors might find useful. This is similar to how I added a Google document to my site earlier in this chapter.

The embed option will let you insert a link to another site or specific code that you can obtain from many sites right into one of your pages. The process is similar for each but how you get the information for each type will vary.

To start the embedding process you can double click where you want the content to be on your page to bring up the wheel menu. Then you will click on the *Embed* option to bring up the *Embed from the web* dialog box.

Figure 3.45

If you choose the By URL option you can then type in the address for a website you would like to have displayed on your page and click on the *Insert* button. I will insert my computer help website into my Documentation page.

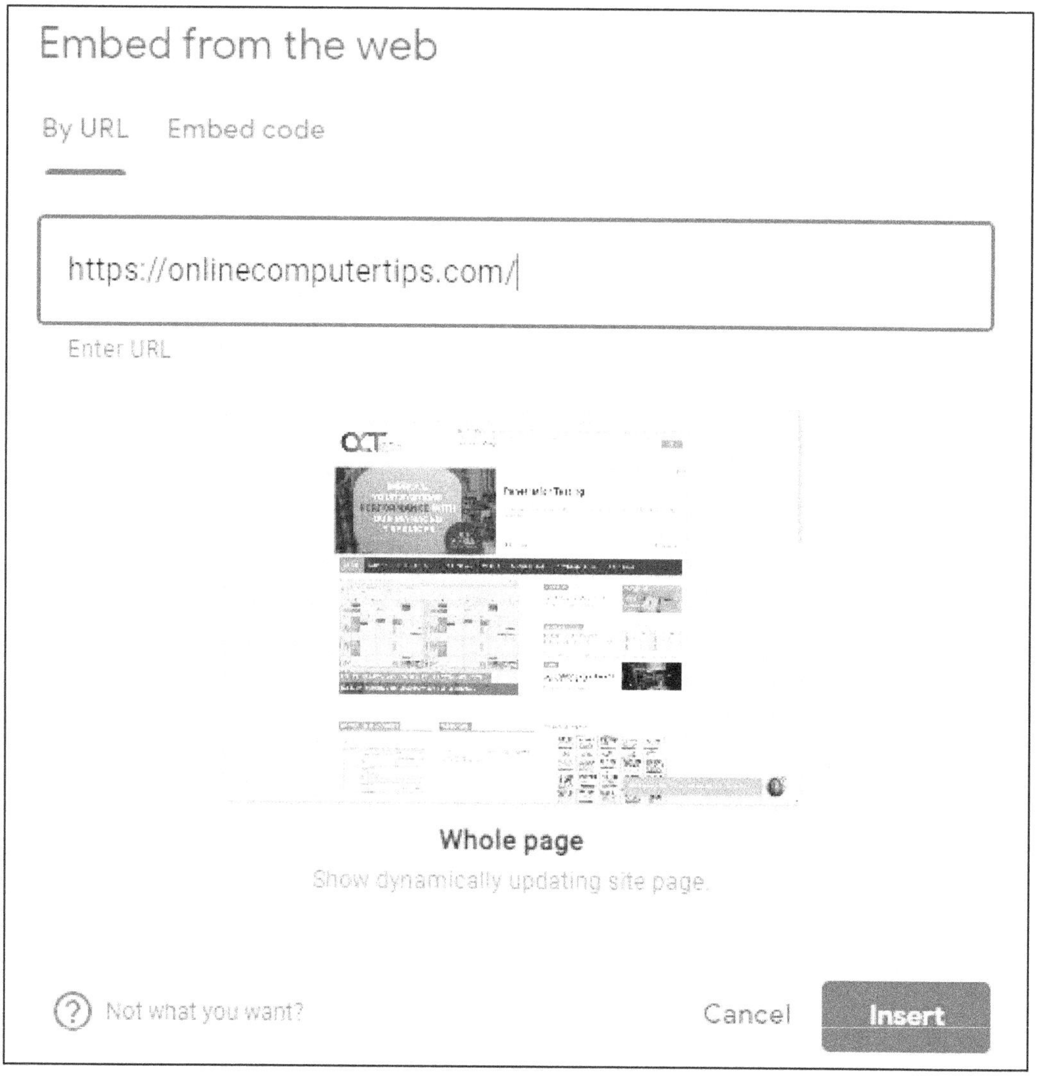

Figure 3.46

Figure 3.47 shows my website underneath the Google doc that I inserted earlier in the chapter. I can now click around my computer help website from within my book website so it's like two sites in one!

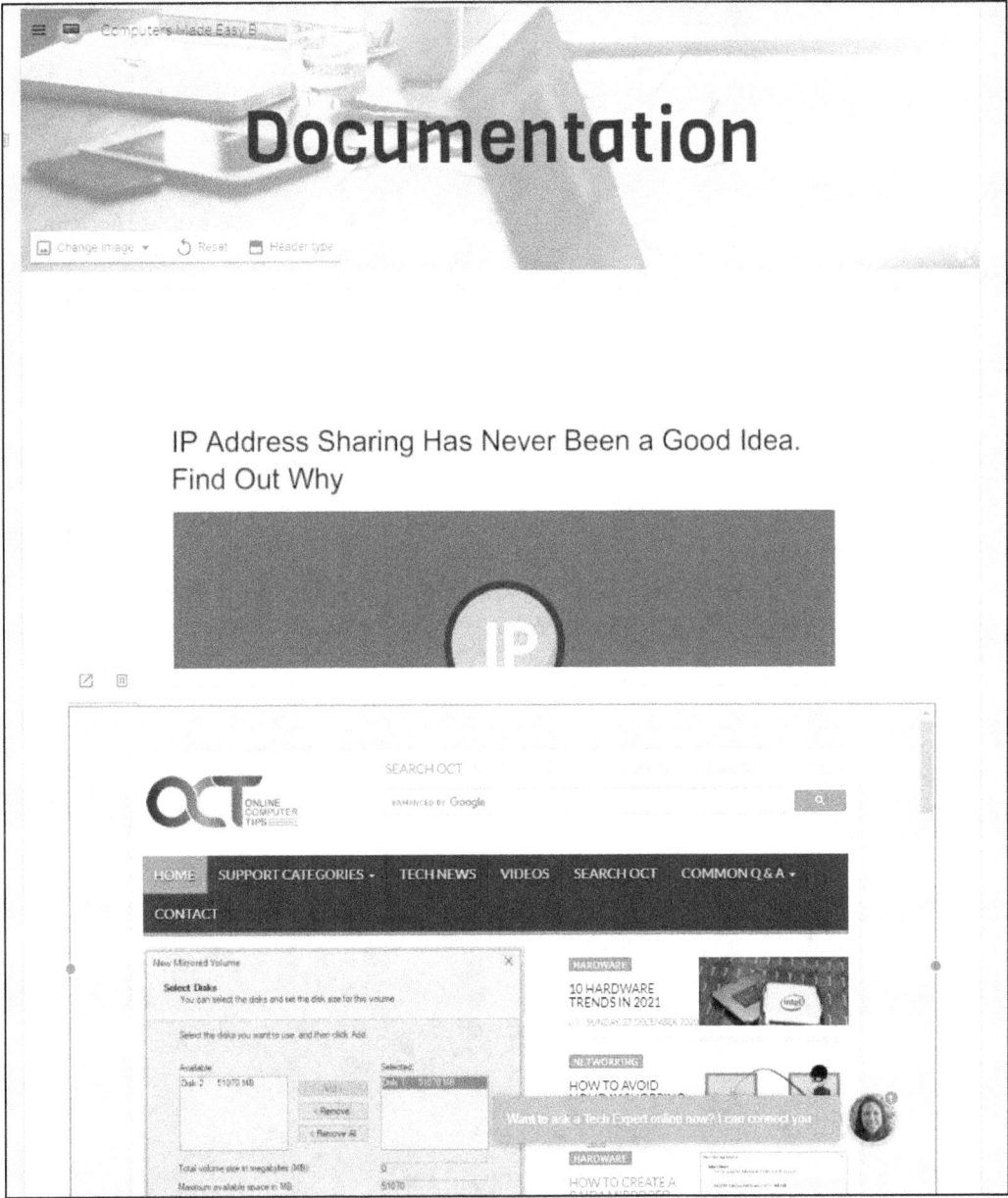

Figure 3.47

The other embedding option you have is to use embedded code from another site. This can be used when trying to add something like a news feed or Twitter feed that gets updated in real time.

For my example, I will get the code for my Twitter feed and then paste it into the *Embed code* section and then click on *Next* as seen in figure 3.48.

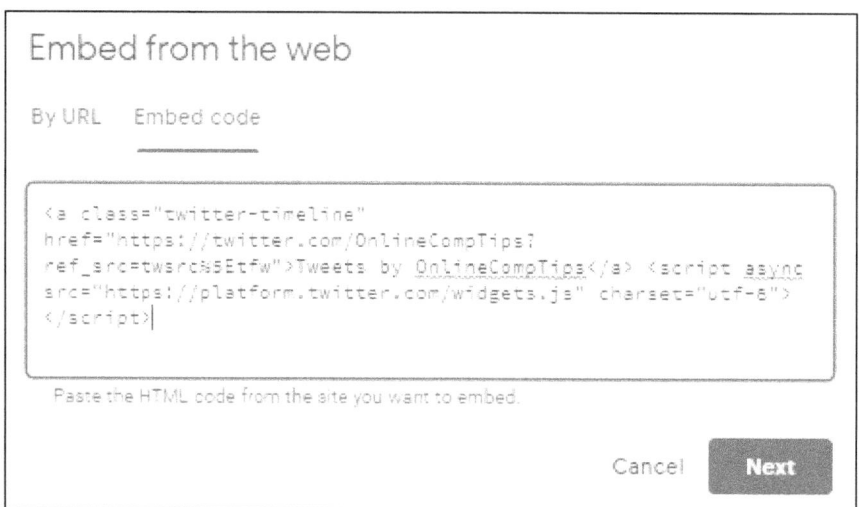

Figure 3.48

Figure 3.49 shows a preview of how my Twitter feed will look and if everything looks ok I can click on the insert button.

Figure 3.49

Now I have my real time Twitter feed embedded into my site so my visitors can see our tweets without having to go to the actual Twitter website.

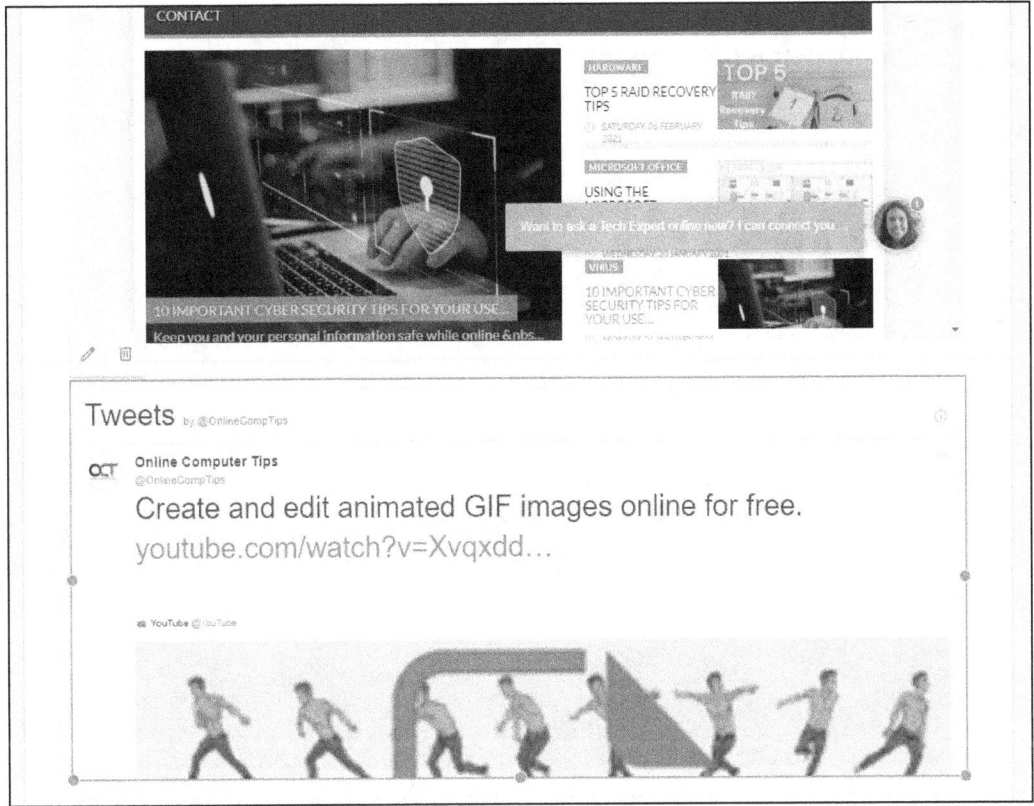

Figure 3.50

If you want to embed your Twitter feed into your website then all you need to do is copy the address of your Twitter page and paste it into the embed box located here to get your embedded code. https://publish.twitter.com/#

Adding Text to Your Images

Now that you know how to add images and text to your pages I wanted to take a moment to show you how to add text captions to your images. By doing this you can easily add a description or saying to your images to help explain what they are about.

Once you have your image in place on the page you can type in some text in any other section of that same page. Then all you need to do is drag the text to the top or bottom of the image to have Sites display the text as a caption for that image. Figure 3.51 shows a book cover image with some text that says **#1 Best Seller** underneath the bar that says Contact.

Figure 3.51

If I drag the text onto the top or bottom of the picture then Sites will align the text with the image as if it were part of the image itself. Figure 3.49 shows how it looks when I drag the text to the bottom of the image and then center it.

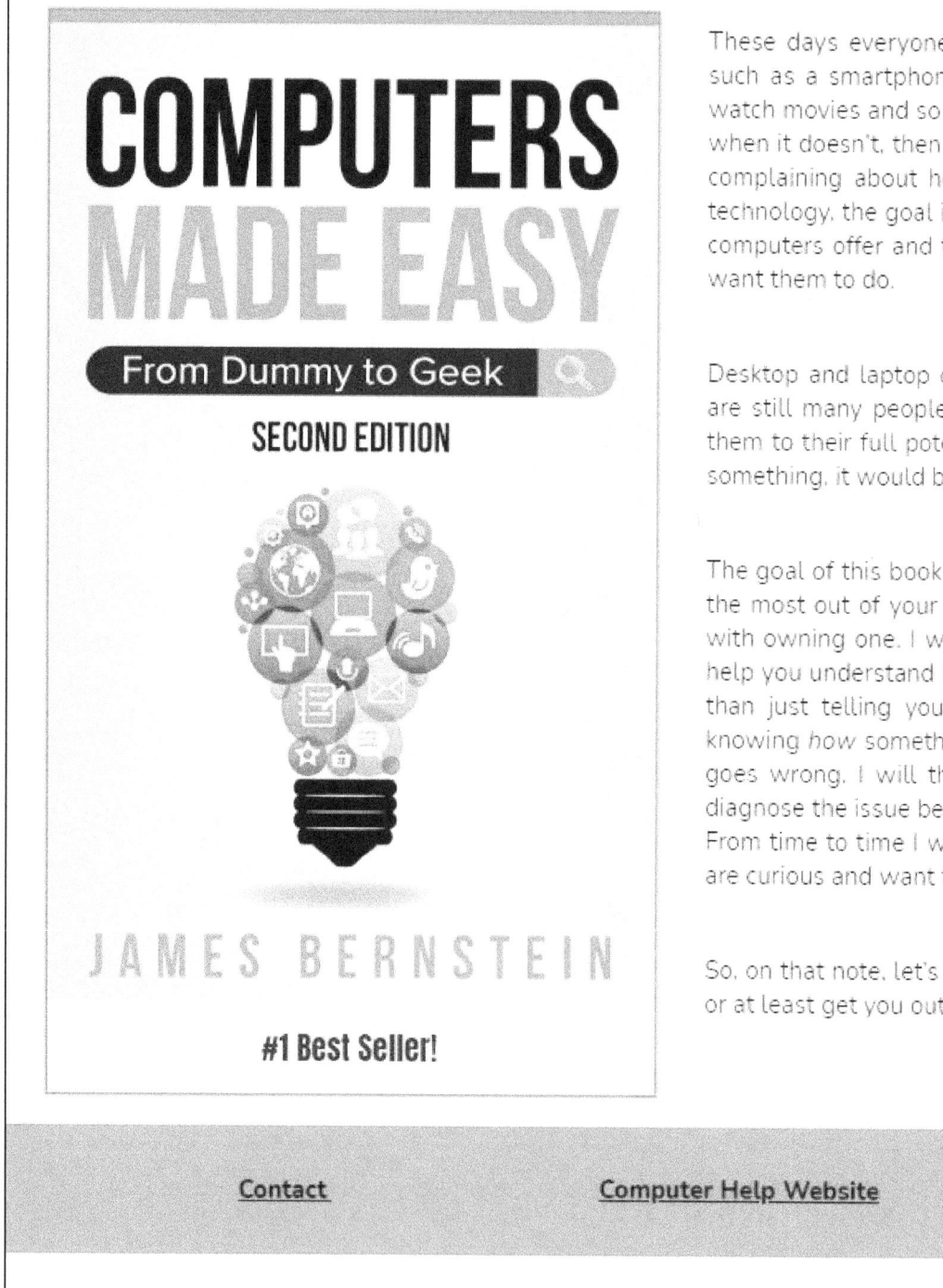

Figure 3.52

Insert YouTube Videos or Videos From Your Drive

It's very common to have playable videos show on websites to do things such as demonstrate how a product works or promote some sort of entertainment like a band etc. With sites, you have the option to embed a YouTube video on a page or even a video you took yourself and have stored in your Google Drive.

I discussed embedding websites and Twitter feed earlier in the chapter and you can also do the same with YouTube videos, but the good part is you don't need to go out and get the embed code. All you need to do is click on the *YouTube* choice in the *Insert* panel and find the video you want to add to your page.

If you use the *Video search* option, you will have a choice to search for a particular video or topic and insert the one you want into your page by highlighting it and clicking on the *Select* button. If you have your own YouTube videos then you can click on *Uploaded* to view the videos associated with the Google account you are using Sites with.

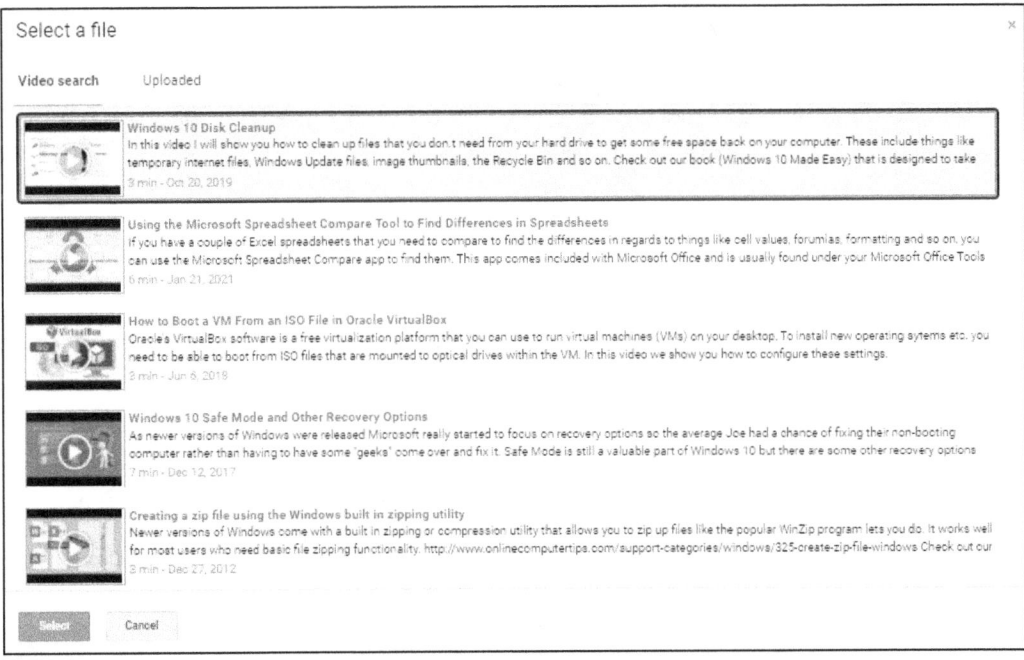

Figure 3.53

Once you choose a video it will be placed within a section on your page. You can then resize the video or drag it to another location on your page. Then when a visitor is on that particular page they can play the video from within that page itself.

Figure 3.54

If you have videos stored on your Google Drive then you can add them to a page as well. To do so you will need to double click on your page to bring up the wheel menu and then choose the *From Drive* option.

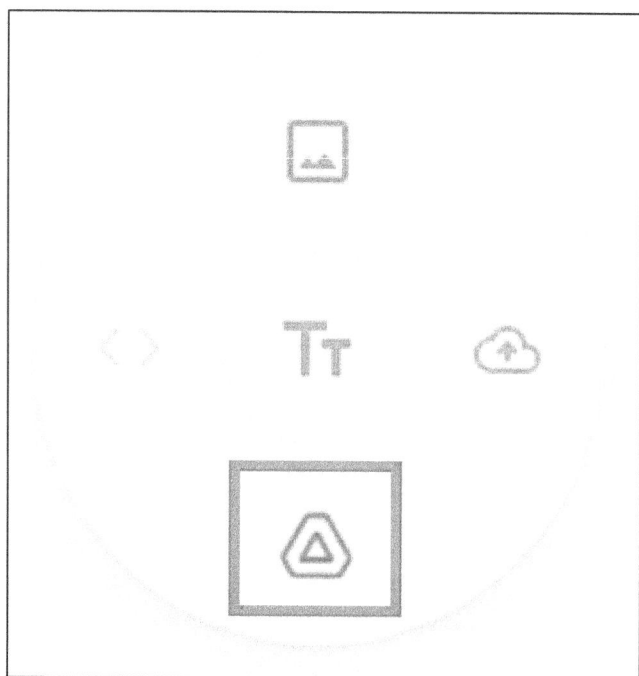

Figure 3.55

Next, you will need to navigate to the location in your Drive where you have the video stored and click on the one you want to use and then click on *Insert*.

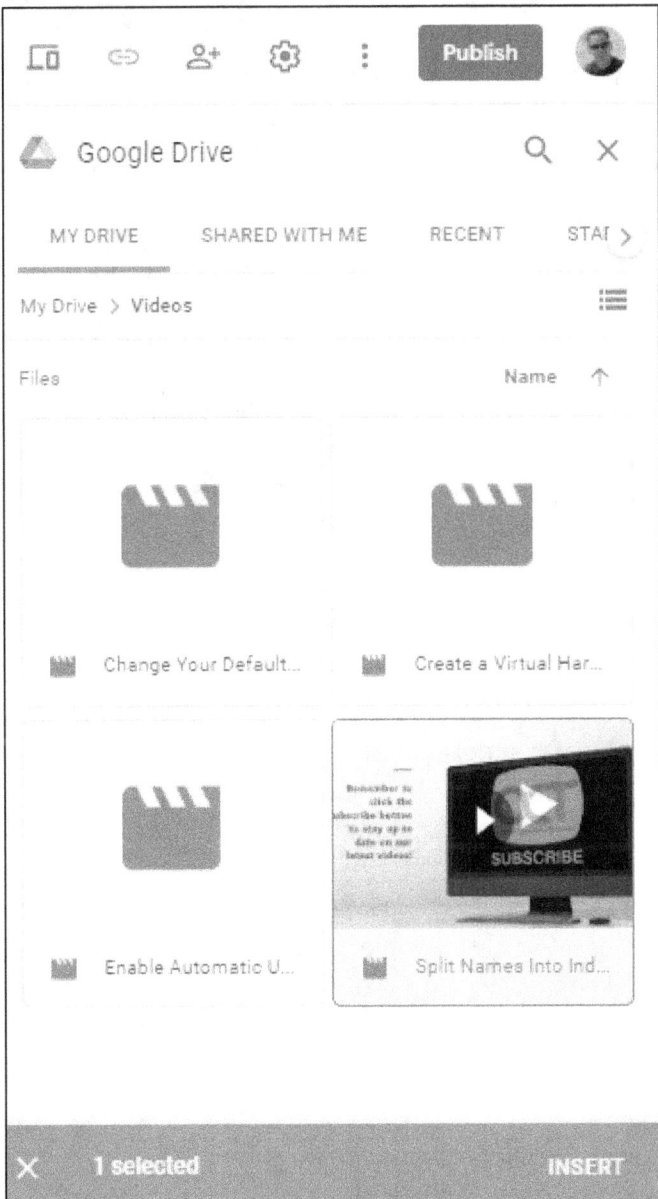

Figure 3.56

Then you can drag your video where you would like it to go and resize it as needed just like you can with a YouTube video. Once again, you will need to make sure the sharing permissions on the videos are set correctly just like any other type of file you use from your Google Drive.

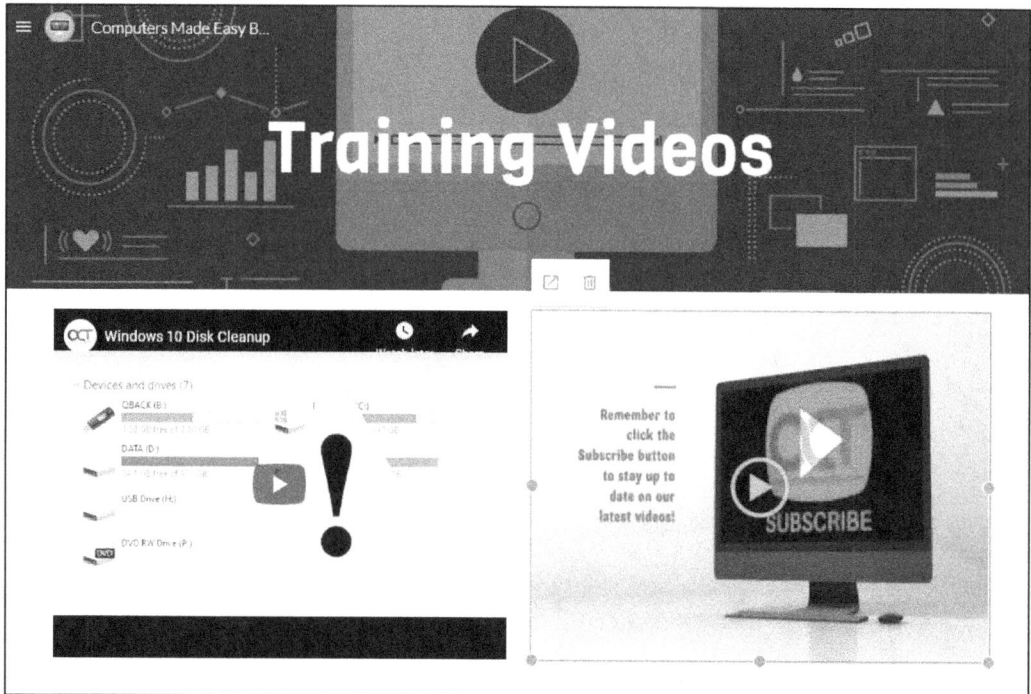

Figure 3.57

Adding a Table of Contents

If you have a lot of information on a page that is broken into sections then you can add a table of contents to the top of that page with clickable links that your visitors can use to take them to a particular section within that page.

You can create your table of contents first or you can add one to an existing page that already has the content in place. For my example, I will add a table of contents to some existing text on a page. The first thing I will need to do is click on *Table of contents* from the *Insert* panel to have Sheets place my table of contents section at the top of the page.

Figure 3.58

Next, I will highlight the text that I want to be in my table of contents and change the text style to *Heading*. I will then do that for all the other section headings that I have on my page.

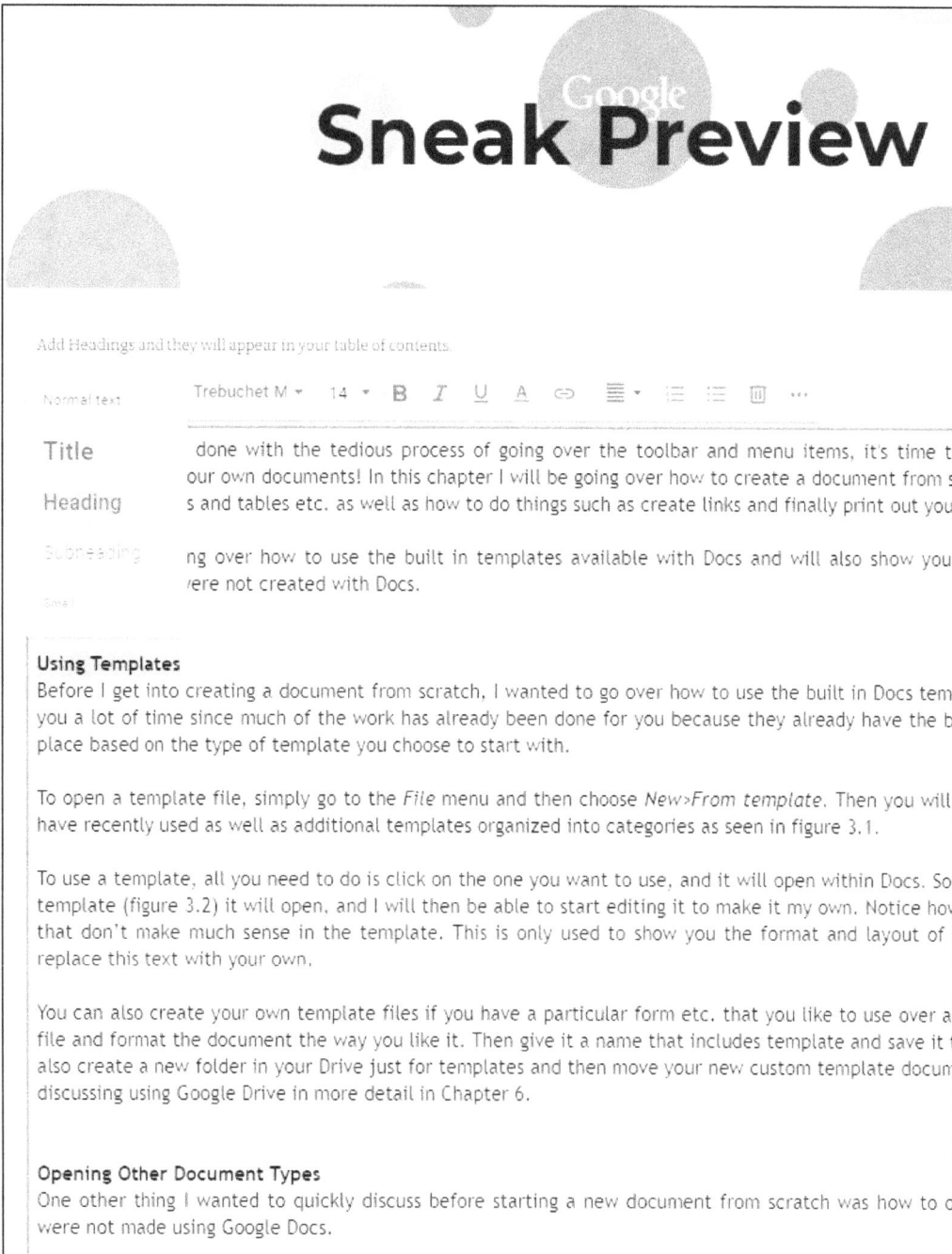

Figure 3.59

Now I have a table of contents that was created from the text I highlighted and changed to Heading and when a visitor clicks on a particular line they will be taken directly to that section on the page. I also added a section background to make things stand out a little better.

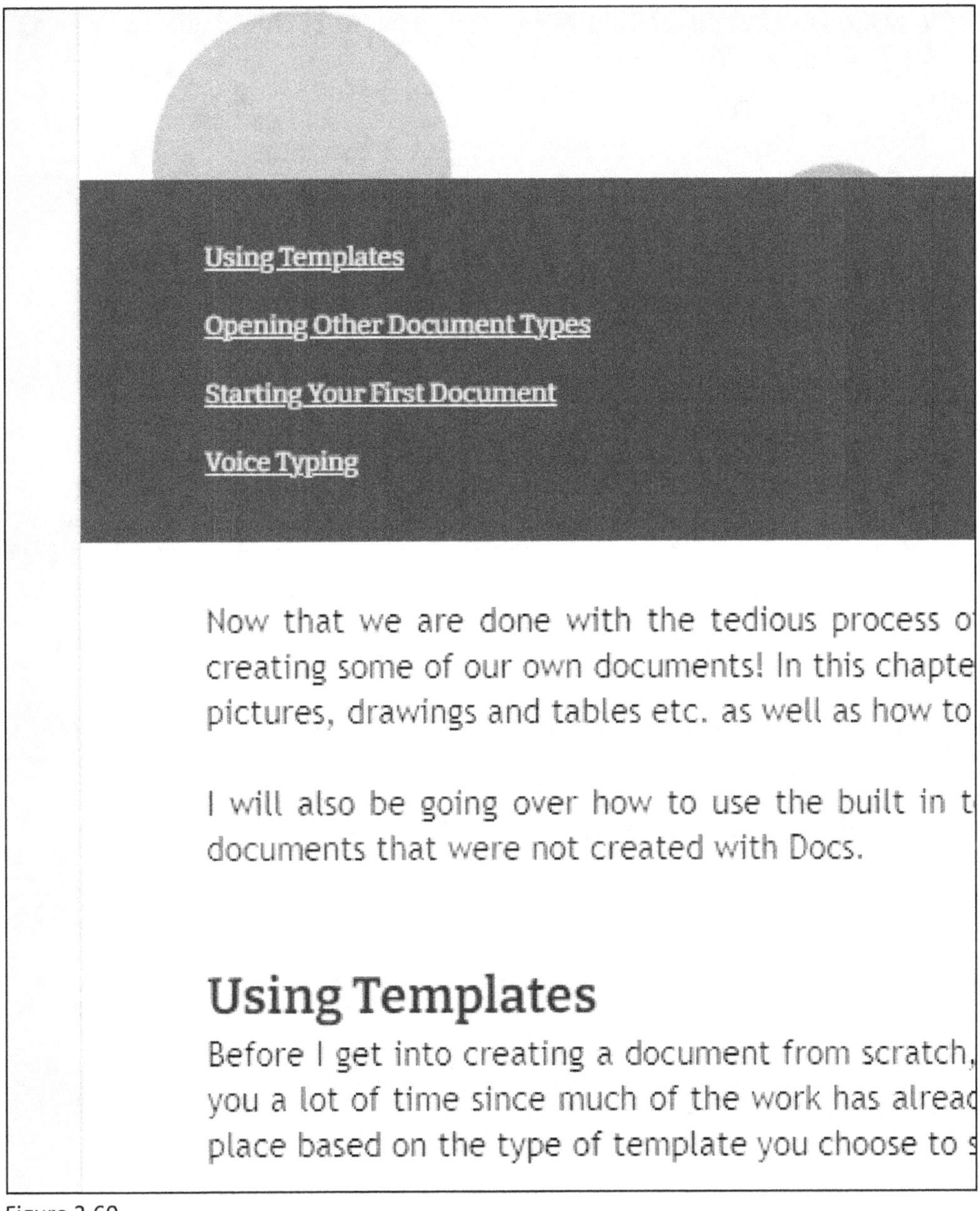

Using Templates

Opening Other Document Types

Starting Your First Document

Voice Typing

Now that we are done with the tedious process o
creating some of our own documents! In this chapte
pictures, drawings and tables etc. as well as how to

I will also be going over how to use the built in t
documents that were not created with Docs.

Using Templates
Before I get into creating a document from scratch,
you a lot of time since much of the work has alread
place based on the type of template you choose to s

Figure 3.60

Inserting a Google Calendar

If you are using your website to host events or want to notify your visitors of upcoming events then you can insert a Google Calendar that will update itself as you add more items to that calendar.

Once again you will need to go to the Insert panel and this time choose *Calendar* from the list. You will then be shown all of the calendars that you have associated with your Google account as well as generic calendars such as holidays etc. From here you can choose the calendar you want to use on your site and then click *Insert*.

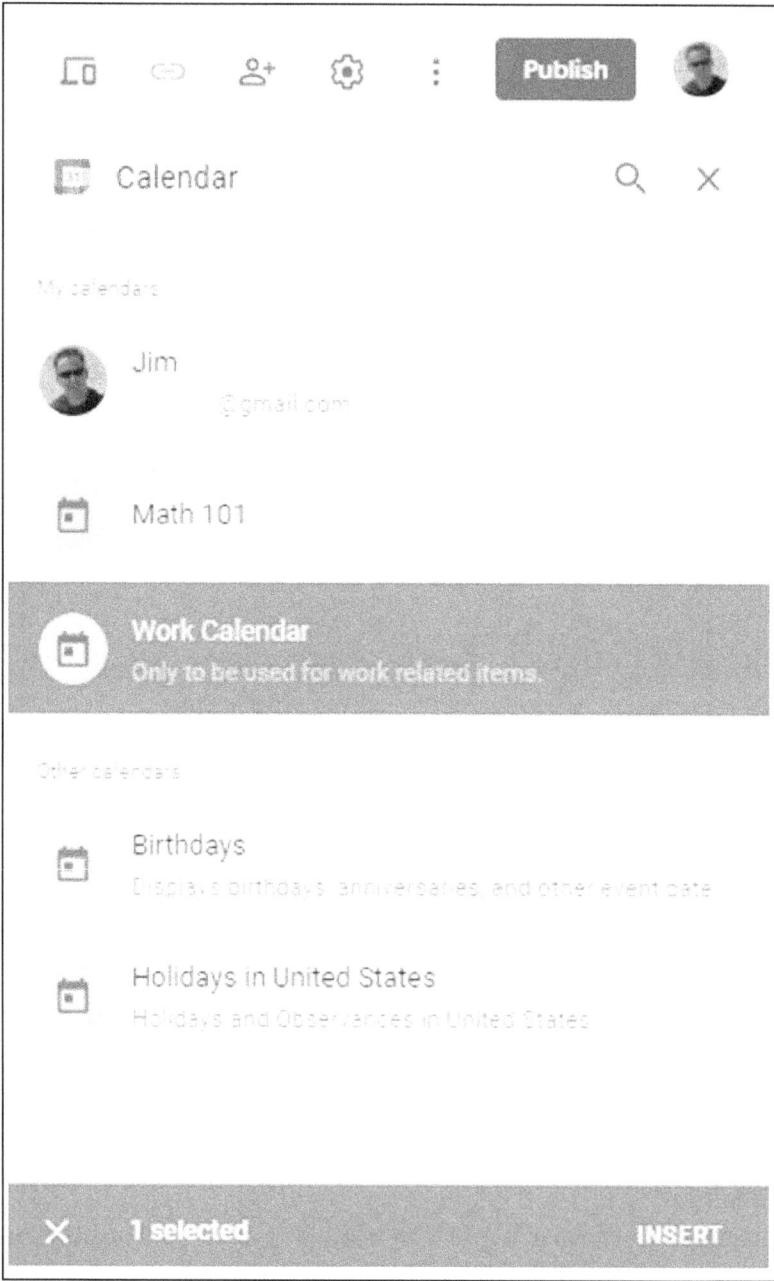

Figure 3.61

When you preview or publish your page you will be able to change the view from week to month to agenda. Then you can click on a certain event to see its details.

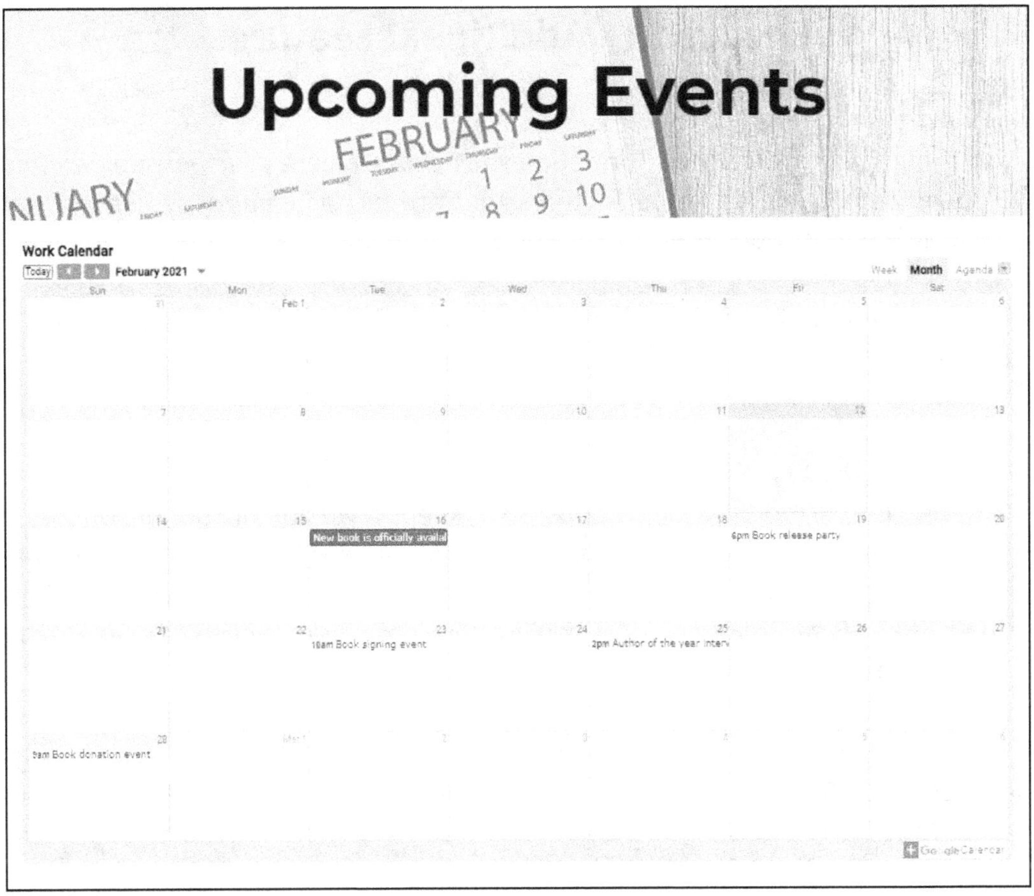
Upcoming Events
FEBRUARY
Work Calendar
Today
February 2021
Week
Month
Agenda
Sun
Mon
Tue
Wed
Thu
Fri
Sat
New book is officially availal
6pm Book release party
10am Book signing event
2pm Author of the year interv
9am Book donation event

Figure 3.62

Chapter 4 - Additional Features

Now that I have covered the information you need to create your website I wanted to spend some time on some features that are not as commonly used or not necessarily part of Google Sites.

You may or may not find yourself using these features but it's a good thing to know that they are there and how to use them in case you change your mind later on.

Site Version History

Just like with most other Google apps, Sites keeps a version history of your work in case you need to revert back to an earlier version. You might have noticed that there is no save option like you might be used to with your other programs. This is because Sites saves your work as you go along so you don't need to worry about manually saving it.

Just because you don't have to save your work doesn't mean that you can't go back to an earlier version in case you decide you liked the work that you did earlier. Using Version History you can review older versions of your site and then make that version the current version if needed.

To see all of the saved versions of your website you can click on the three vertical dots next to the *Publish* button and then choose *Version history*.

94

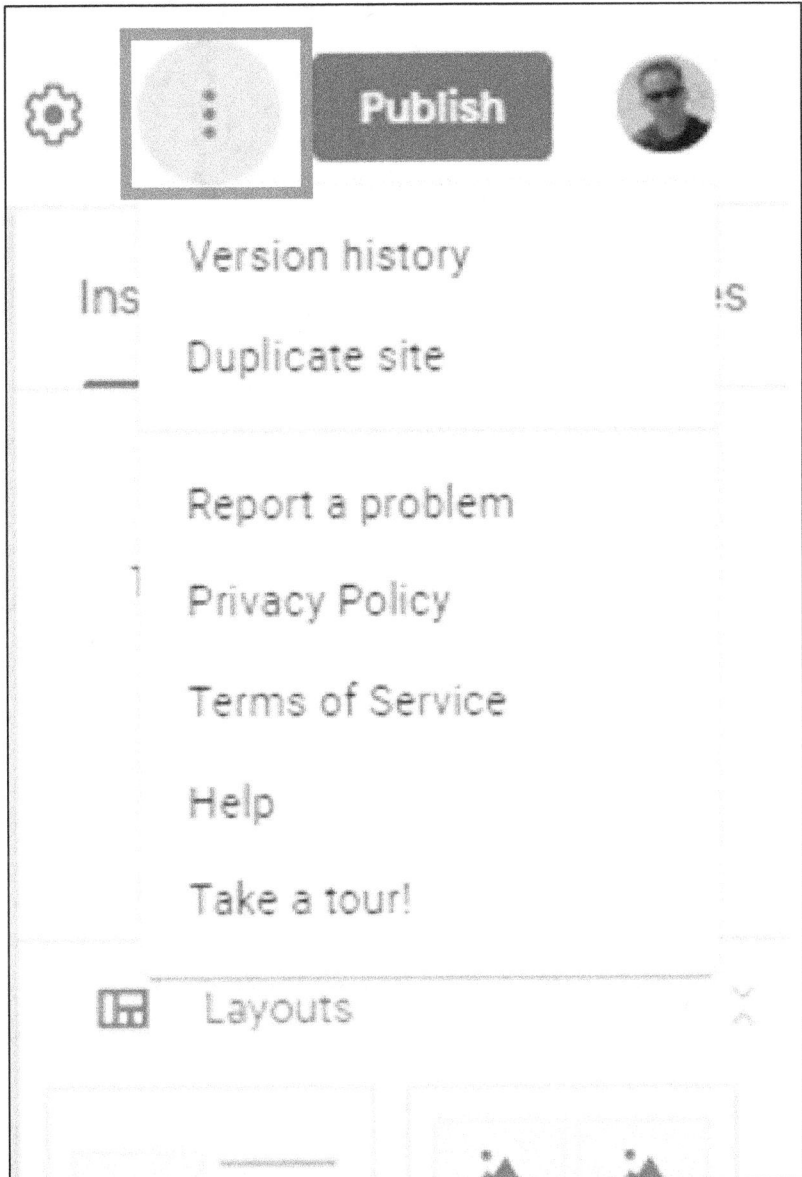

Figure 4.1

You will then be shown all of your saved versions with their respective date and time. To view a specific version simply click on that version and you will see how your site looked on that date. You can also click the small arrow next to a particular date to see all the versions for that date.

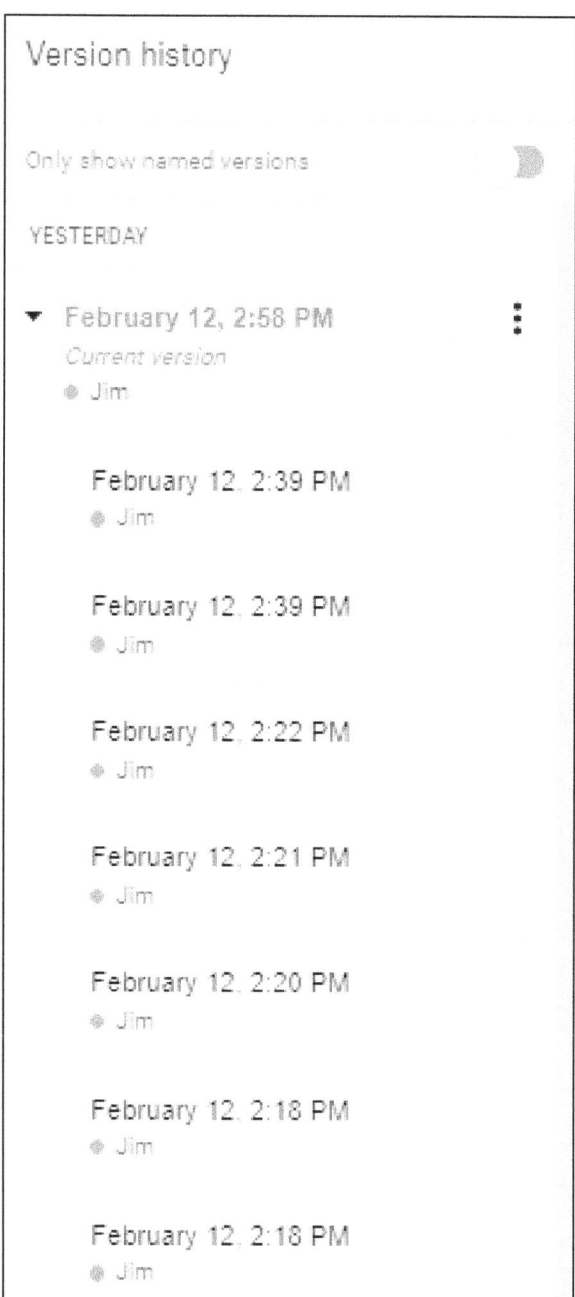

Figure 4.2

If you want to make an older version the current version then click on the three vertical dots next to that version and choose *Restore this version*.

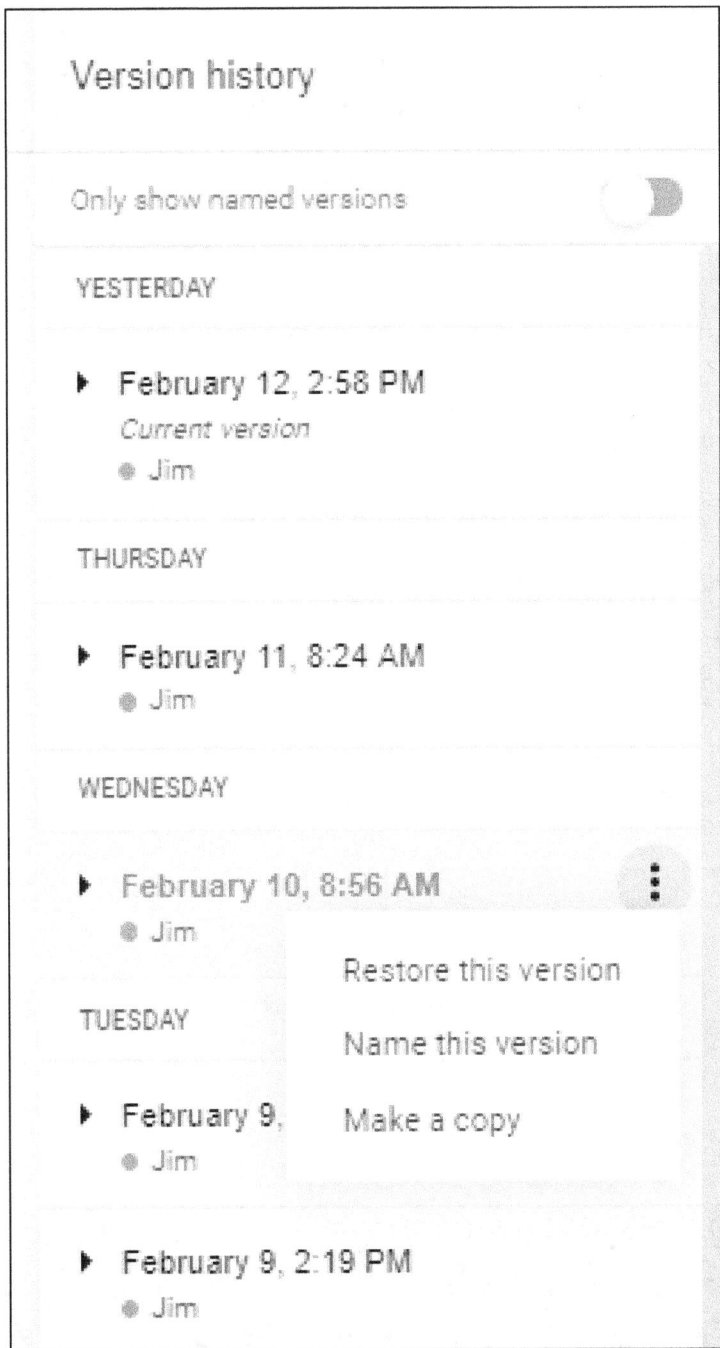

Figure 4.3

You can also name a version to make it easier to find that version if you need to go back to it. The *Make a copy* option will copy that version allowing you to make changes without disturbing the original.

Searching Your Website

Once you have a lot of content posted on your website you may find yourself needing to look for something and end up not being able to find it very easily. Fortunately, you can search your site if needed but the downside is that your site will have to be published before you can do so. I will be discussing the publishing process in Chapter 6.

Once your site is published you can then access it with your web browser, and you will notice a magnifying glass at the upper right corner of the page. This is where you will go to perform searches on the content from your website.

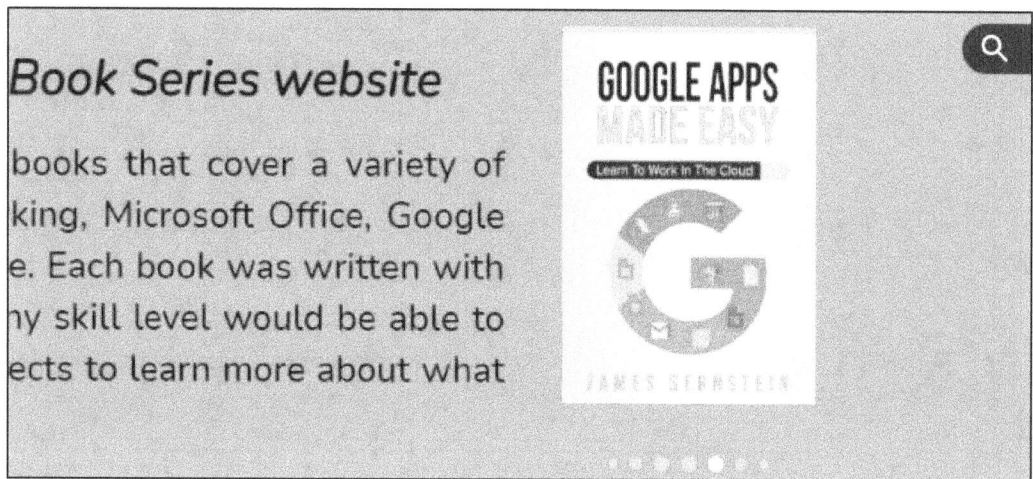

Figure 4.4

When you click on it you will be presented with a search box where you can type in a word or phrase that you would like to find within your website.

Figure 4.5

For example, if I were to search my site for the word windows I would be shown the results of my query and would be able to click on any of the results to be taken to that page. The search will be performed on page names as well as the contents of the pages themselves.

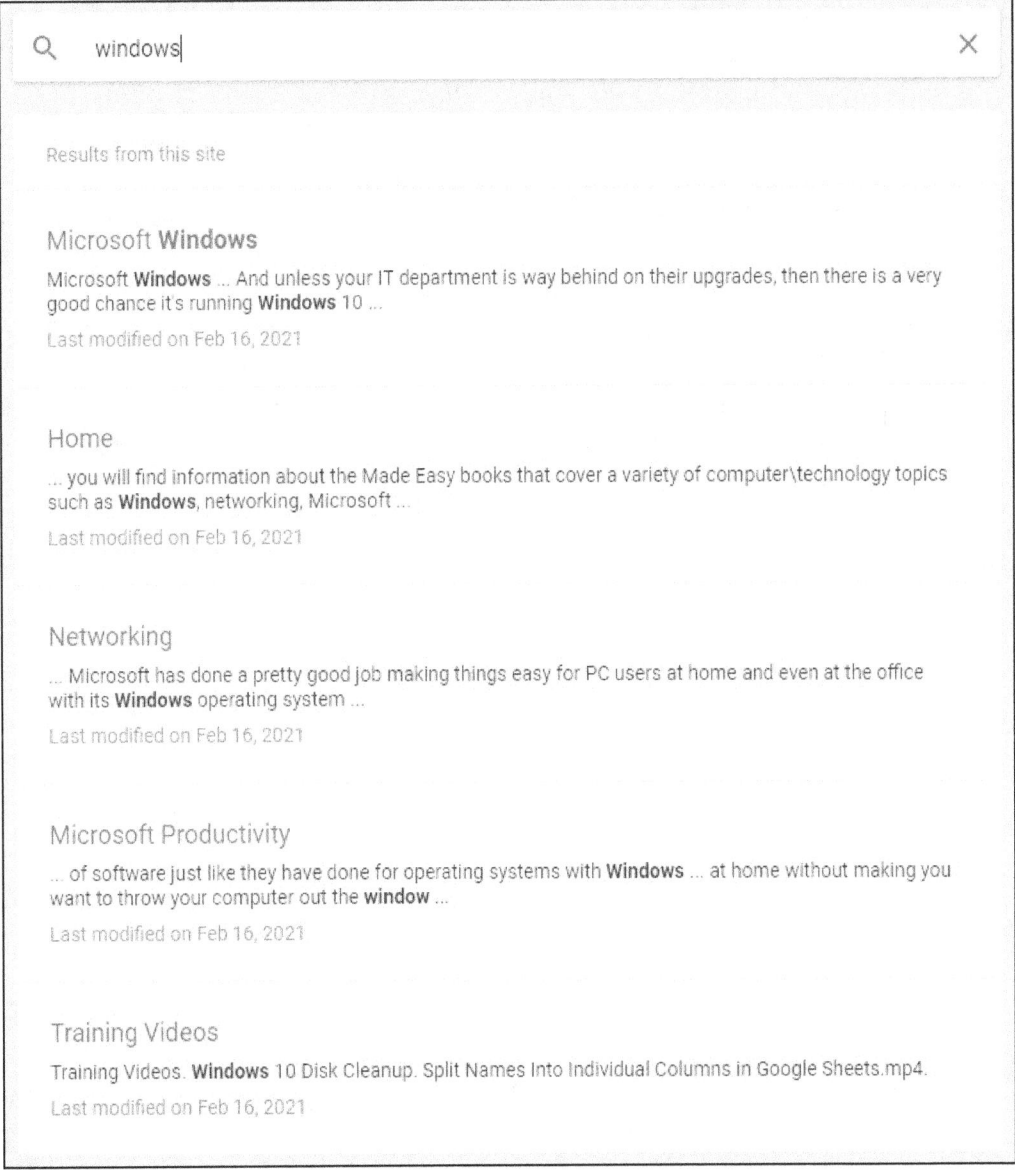

Figure 4.6

Using an Animated Header Image

Since your website will be a live entity and not something such as a book where it's the same (static) at all times, you can add a little flair to your pages by adding an animated header image. What I mean by that is you can have a picture that contains movement and almost looks like a video.

When you use these types of animated images, they simply cycle the same animation over and over and you can't do things such as pause or stop them. You might have heard the term "animated GIF", and these are the types of files that you can use on your pages.

You add animated images to your pages the same way that you add standard images to a page. The tricky part is finding one that will fit your image header and look like it was made for your page. There are apps and websites that will let you create your own animated image files if you want to take the time to learn how to do so.

If you don't want to make your own animated image files then you can do an online search for animated GIF files somewhere like Google Images for example. If you take a look at figure 4.6 you can see that I did a Google Image search for **animated gif computers** and it found a bunch of results and actually labeled the results that are GIF files at the lower left corner of each image preview. If I were to click on a particular preview then it would show me the animated image so I can see how it looks.

Figure 4.7

One thing to keep in mind when searching for images online is that if you don't have the rights to use an image or it's not offered as royalty free then technically you are using it illegally. So always try and find sites that offer images that are free to use for your site.

Another thing to keep in mind when using animated images is that Sites will crop them to make them fit your banner size so you might need to find a way to resize them or perform your own custom cropping before uploading them to your site. There are many online tools that will let you upload your GIF file and then edit it and then let you download the edited version.

Duplicating Your Site

Your website is technically a file stored in your Google Drive and just like other files such as documents and spreadsheets, you can duplicate your Sites website if you ever have a reason to do so. Figure 4.7 shows my Google Drive files and as you can see I have my book website highlighted and it's displayed just like any other file in my Drive.

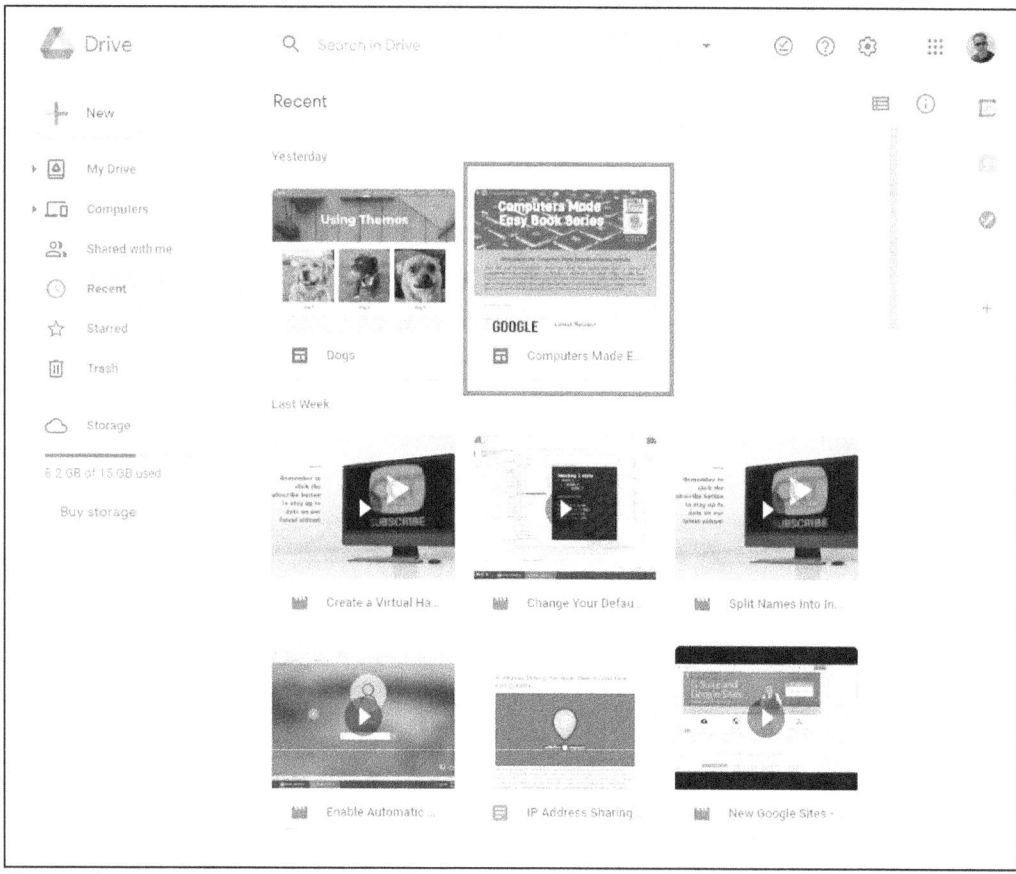

Figure 4.8

If you want to duplicate your site then you can simply make a copy of it from your Google Drive like you would any other file or you can do it right from Sites itself by clicking on the three vertical dots next to the *Publish* button and clicking on *Duplicate site*.

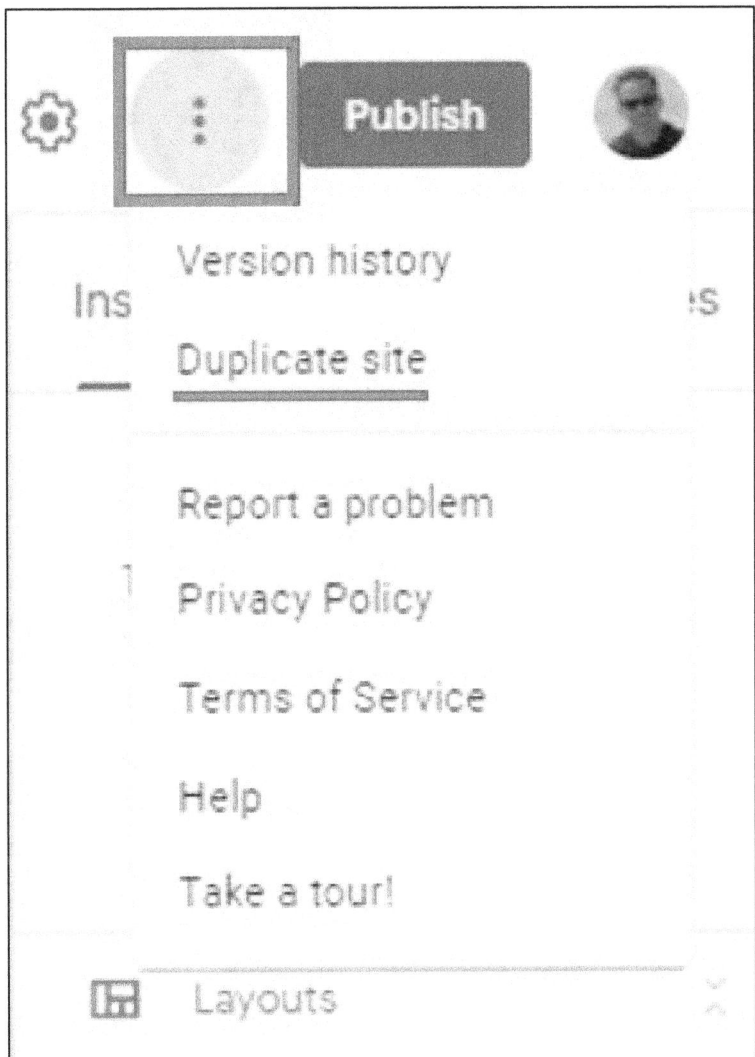

Figure 4.9

Then you will be prompted to name your duplicated site and decide where in your Drive you wish to save it. If you are sharing your site with other collaborators you can then choose to have your duplicated site shared with the same people by checking the box that says *Share with the same editors*.

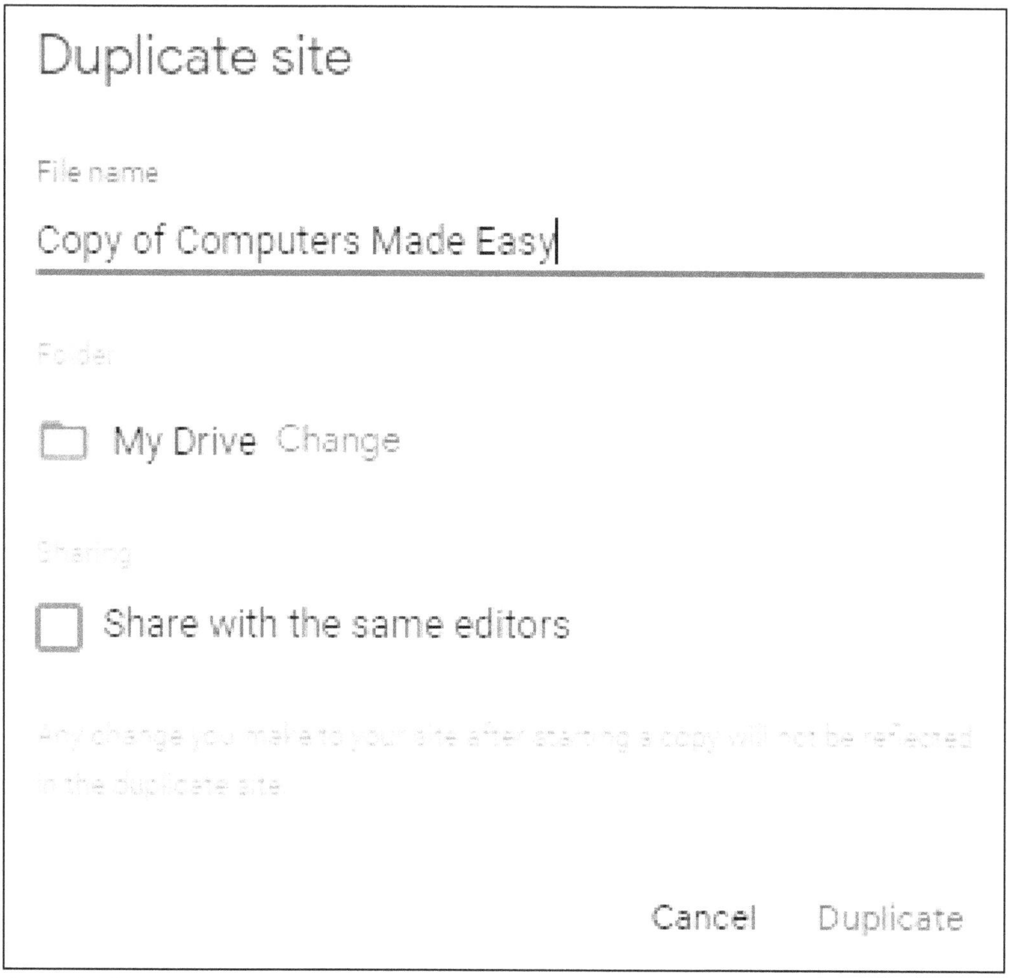

Duplicate site

File name

Copy of Computers Made Easy|

Folder

□ My Drive Change

Sharing

□ Share with the same editors

Any change you make to your site after starting a copy will not be reflected in the duplicate site

Cancel   Duplicate

Figure 4.10

After duplicating my site I can then go back to my Google Drive and see the newly created copy of my site stored there with the original.

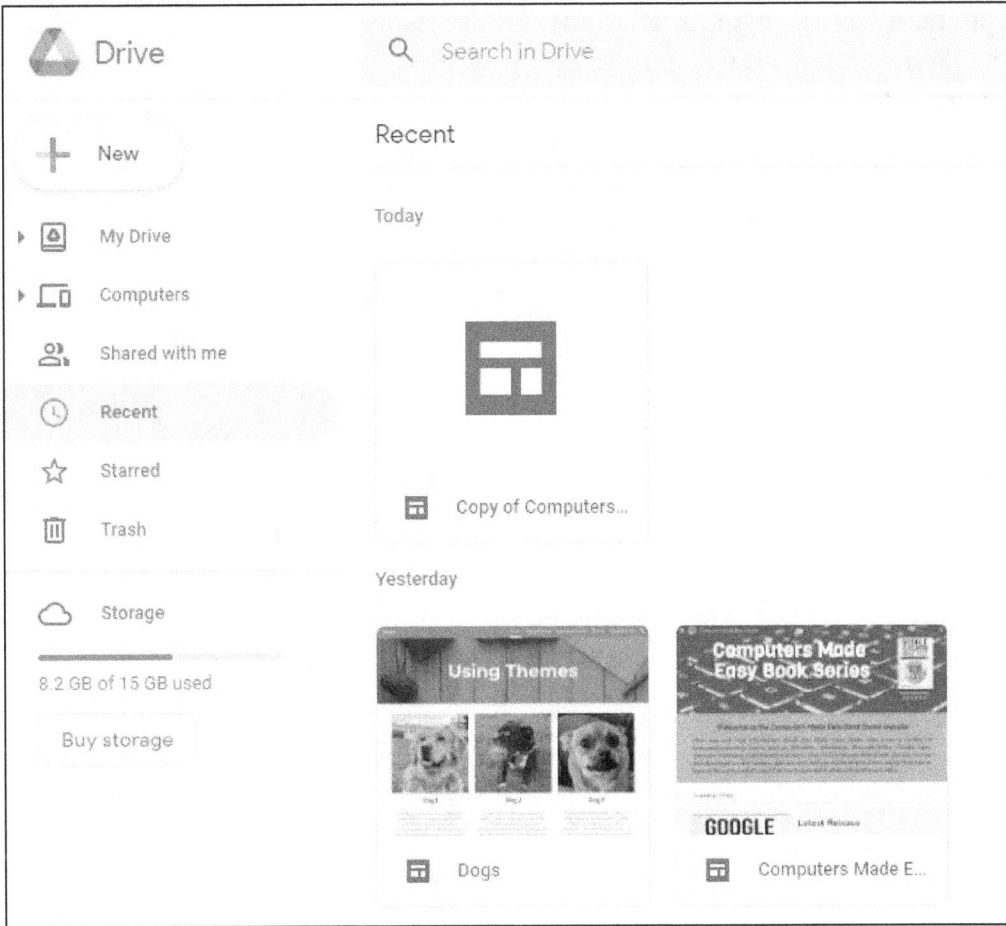

Figure 4.11

When you duplicate a site, be sure that you are working on the copy that you want to be working on, otherwise you will have your updates made in the wrong file.

Creating Announcement Banners

If you want something to stand out on your site or maybe offer a special limited time deal on some of the products you are selling then using an announcement banner is a great way to "advertise" your special deal.

You can easily add an announcement banner to just your home page or to every page on your site with just a few clicks. To get to the announcement banner configuration you will need to click on the settings gear icon up near the Publish button.

From here you will need to go to the *Announcement banner* section and enable the banner with the *Show banner* slider. Next, you can choose a color for your banner and then type in the message that will be shown on your banner.

The *Button label* section is what your visitors will click on to take them to this special deal or whatever page you want them to go to when they click on it.

You will then add the URL\Address for the destination page in the *Link* section.

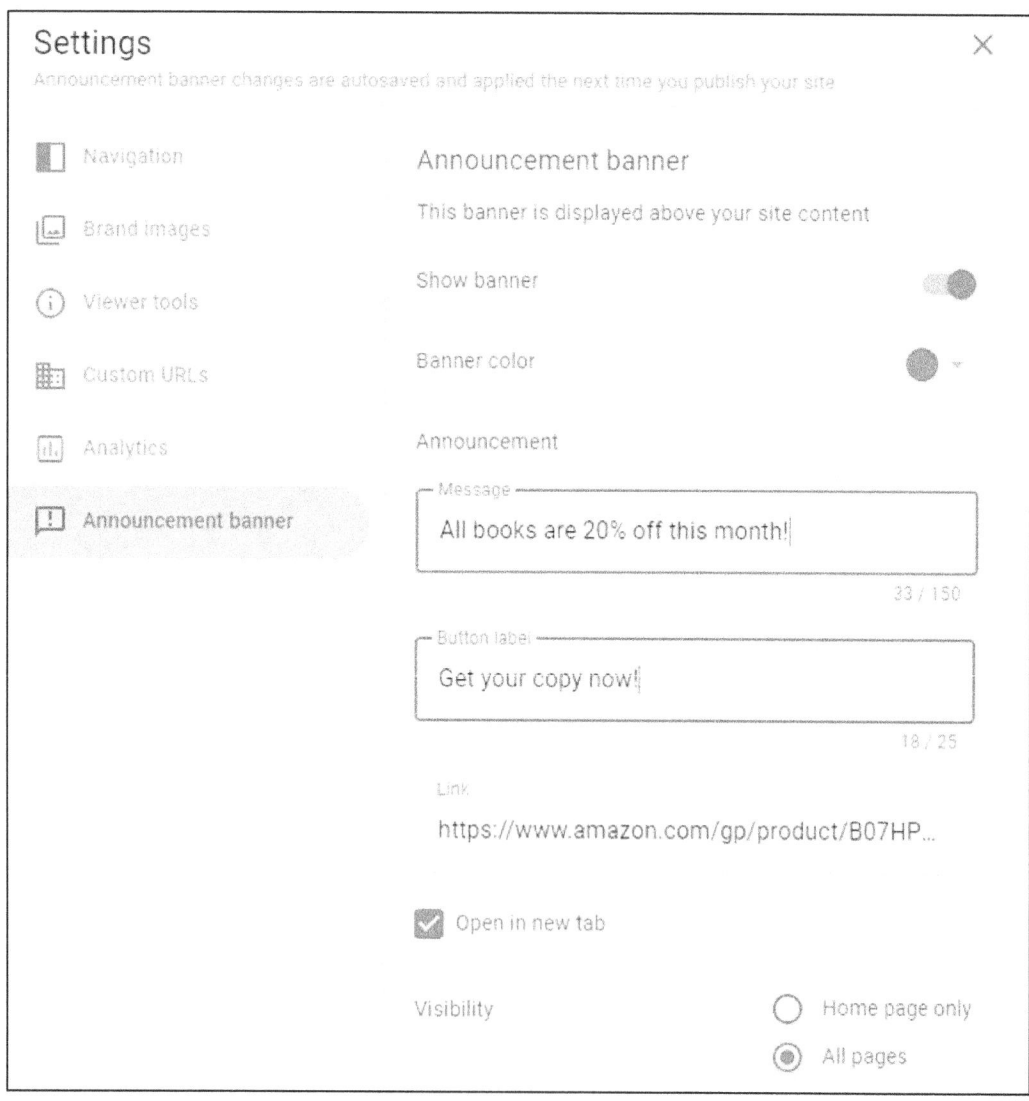

Figure 4.12

If you want the destination page to open in a new browser tab rather than change the existing tab the visitor is in the check the box that says *Open in new tab*.

The *Visibility* section is where you can configure the banner to be placed on just the home page or on all of the pages on your site.

Figure 4.13 shows my home page with the new banner on the top in yellow and figure 4.14 shows a closeup of the banner.

Figure 4.13

All books are 20% off this month!   Get your copy now!

Figure 4.14

Finding Free Images For Your Site
You might have remembered me saying once or twice in this book how you need to be careful when using images that you find online because if you don't own them then you aren't technically allowed to use them on your website.

There are stock photo sites such as Depositphotos and Shuttershock that you can subscribe to and download pictures from that you can then use on your website or in other publications.

You can also use the Google Image search and go to the *Tools* option under the search box and change the usage rights to *Creative Commons licenses* to find pictures you can use for free.

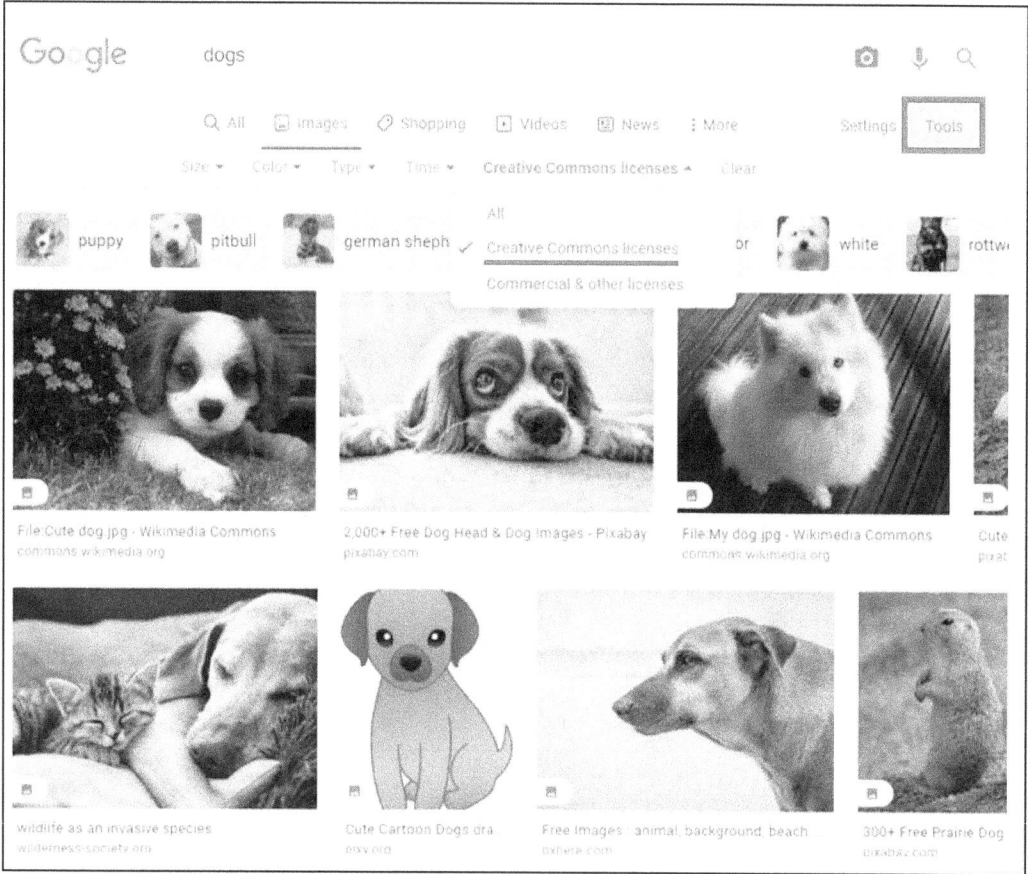

Figure 4.15

Bing Images also has a similar option that will display free to use images.

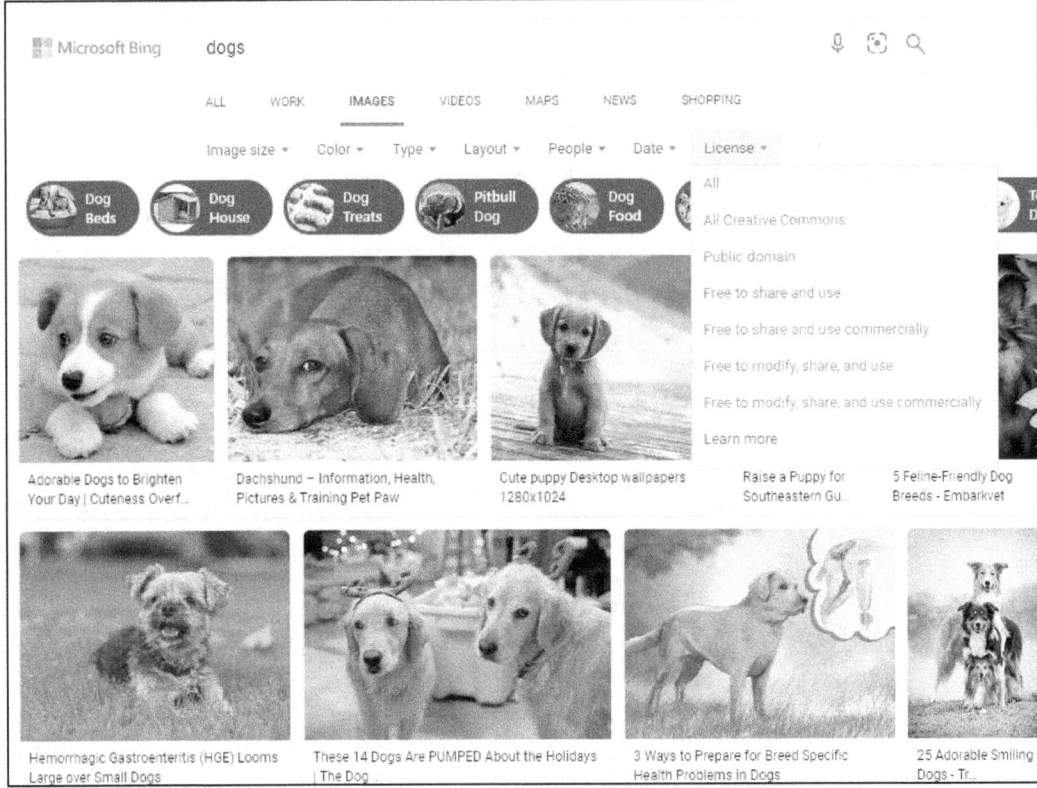

Figure 4.16

If you want to find some more professional, higher quality free to use images then you can give sites such as **pexels.com** and **unsplash.com** a try and see what kind of images you can find there.

Embedding Facebook Content

I discussed how to embed your Twitter feed into your website in the last chapter which was very straightforward but now I would like to tell you about how you can do the same thing and more with your Facebook account.

Facebook will not only allow you to embed your timeline but also specific posts or comments as well as like and share buttons. For my example, I will be going over the Page Plugin option that lets you embed your Facebook timeline onto your website as I did for my Twitter discussion. If you would like to try out some of the other Facebook plugins then you can check them out and see how they work for you.

The first thing you will need to do is go to the Facebook Developer Social Plugins site.

https://developers.facebook.com/docs/plugins

From there you will click on Page Plugin on the left hand menu and enter your Facebook page URL (address). You can then fine tune how big your content will appear on your site using the width and height boxes. There are some other checkbox options below that where you can configure some other display settings.

Figure 4.17

Once everything looks good you can click on the *Get Code* button at the bottom of the page and then go to the *iFrame* section and copy the code.

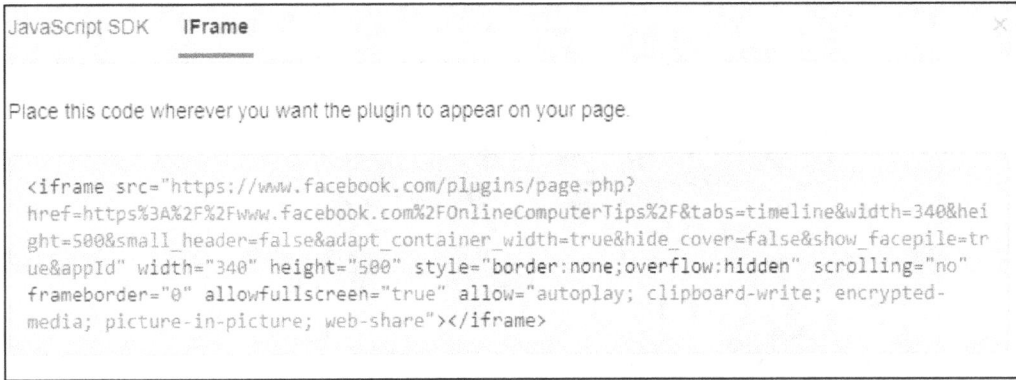

Figure 4.18

You will then double click on the page you want to embed the code on to bring up the wheel menu and click the *Embed* option once again. From there you will click on *Embed code* and paste in the code you just copied.

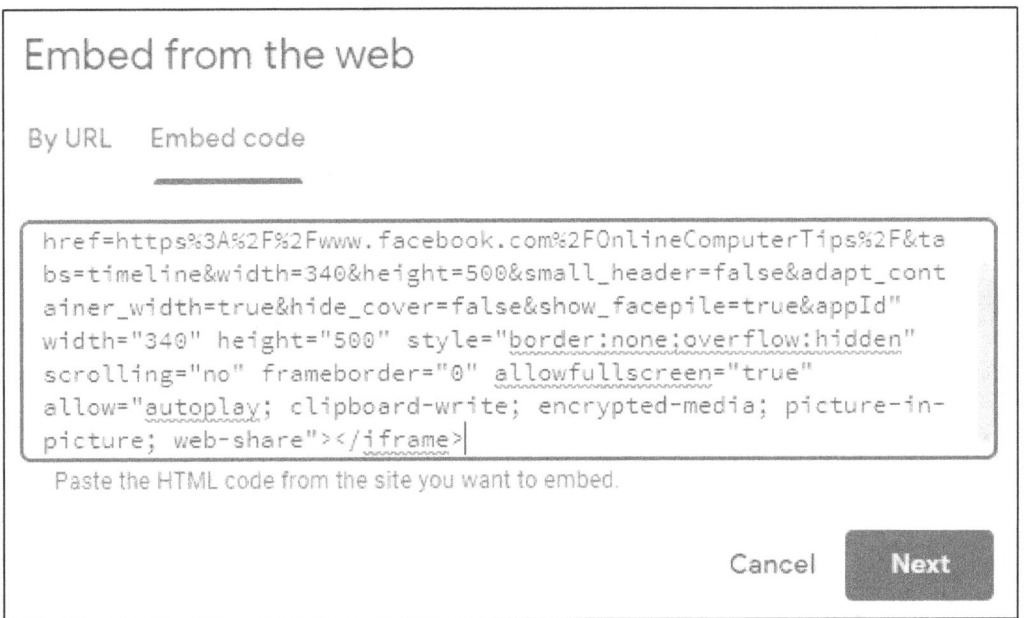

Figure 4.19

When you click on *Next* you will then be shown a preview of how your embedded Facebook page will look and if you like what you see you can then click the *Insert* button.

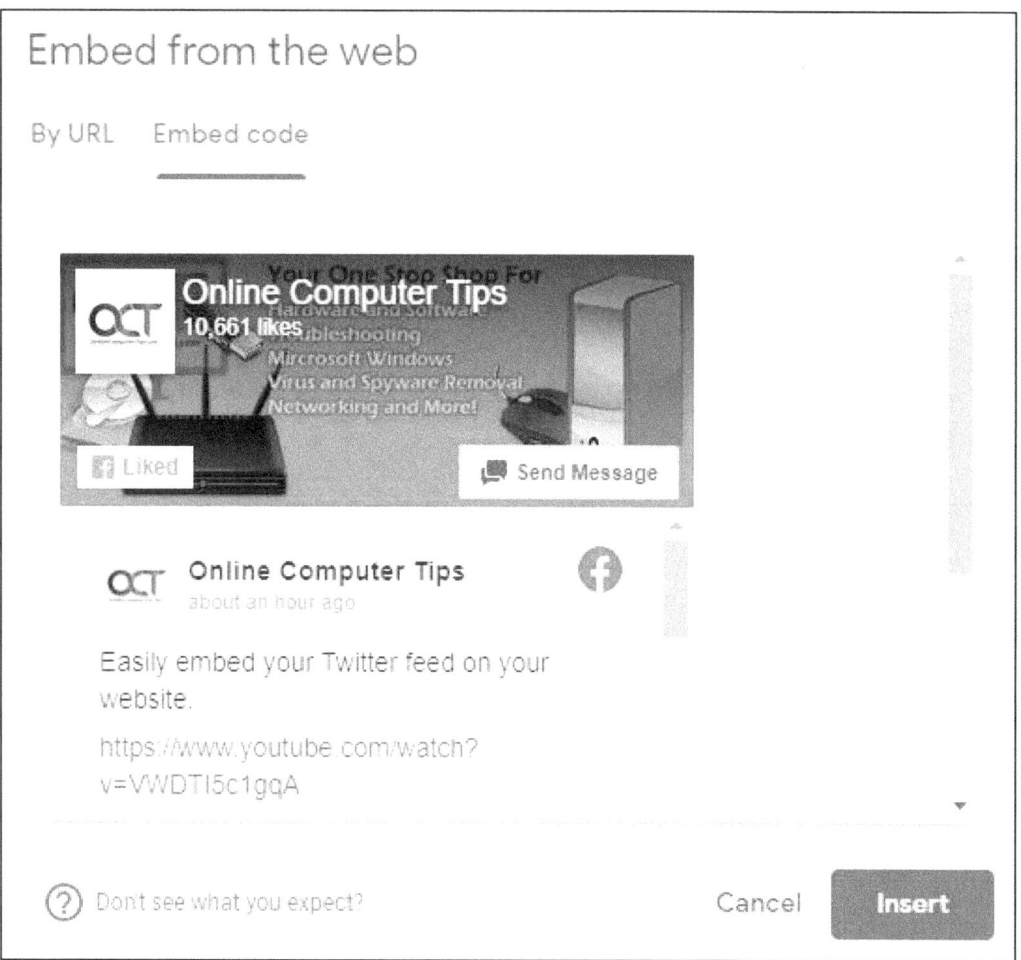

Figure 4.20

Once the code is on your page you can move and resize your Facebook timeline, so it looks right for your page.

Figure 4.21

Creating a Contact Form

If you don't want to give out y our email address for your visitors to contact you with then you can create a contact form using Google Forms and then insert it into your website. This way your visitors can fill out the required information and then you will be able to see their entries.

If you go to Google Forms at **https://docs.google.com/forms** you can either start from scratch with a new form or use a template that best matches what you are trying to accomplish such as the Contact information template shown in figure 4.22.

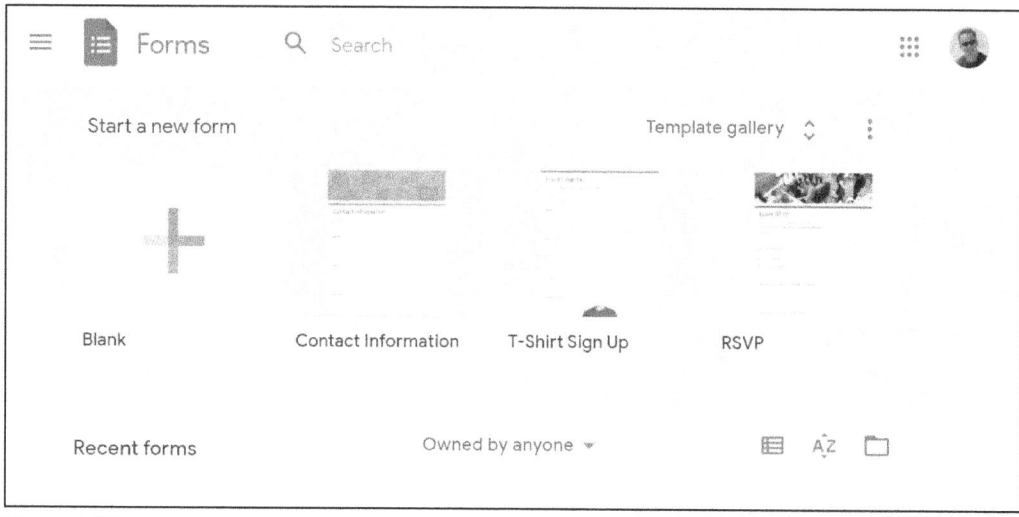

Figure 4.22

I am going to create a new form and name it Contact Us. I will then click the **+** icon to add a new section for the visitor to type in their name. I will use the *Short answer* question type since that best fits what I am trying to accomplish.

Contact Us

Form description

Your Name   Short answer

Short answer text

                              Required

Figure 4.23

I will then add another section for their email address and use the Short answer choice. Finally, I will add a third section for their question or comment and use the *Long answer* type so they will have room to type their question. If you want some or all of the sections to be mandatory then you can change the slider next to *Required* so its enabled.

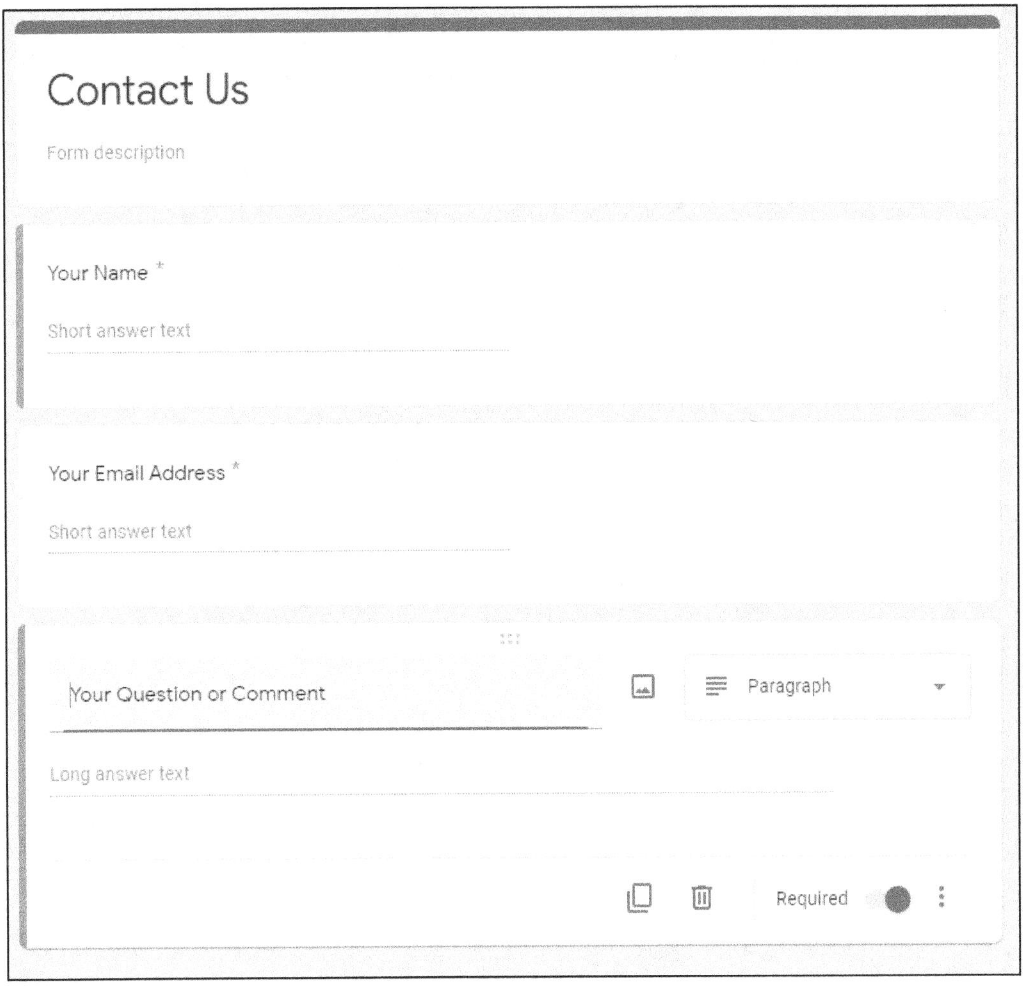

Figure 4.24

Once you have your form ready to go you can go to the *Insert* panel back in Sites and then click on *Forms* and then select the form that you have created and click on *Insert*. Just be sure to create the form using the same Google account that you created your site with, so it shows up as a choice here.

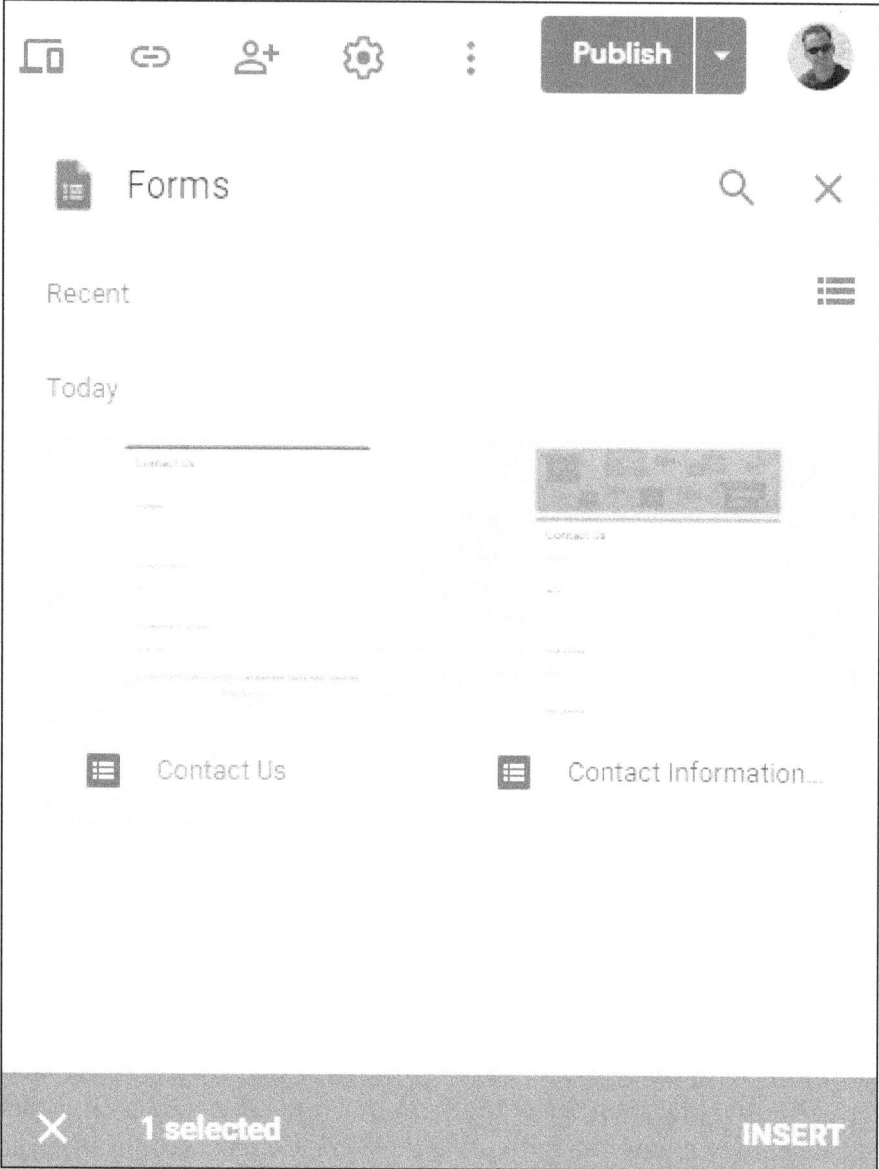

Figure 4.25

Now I have my form inserted onto my page and I can then move it and resize it just like any other section I would use within my site.

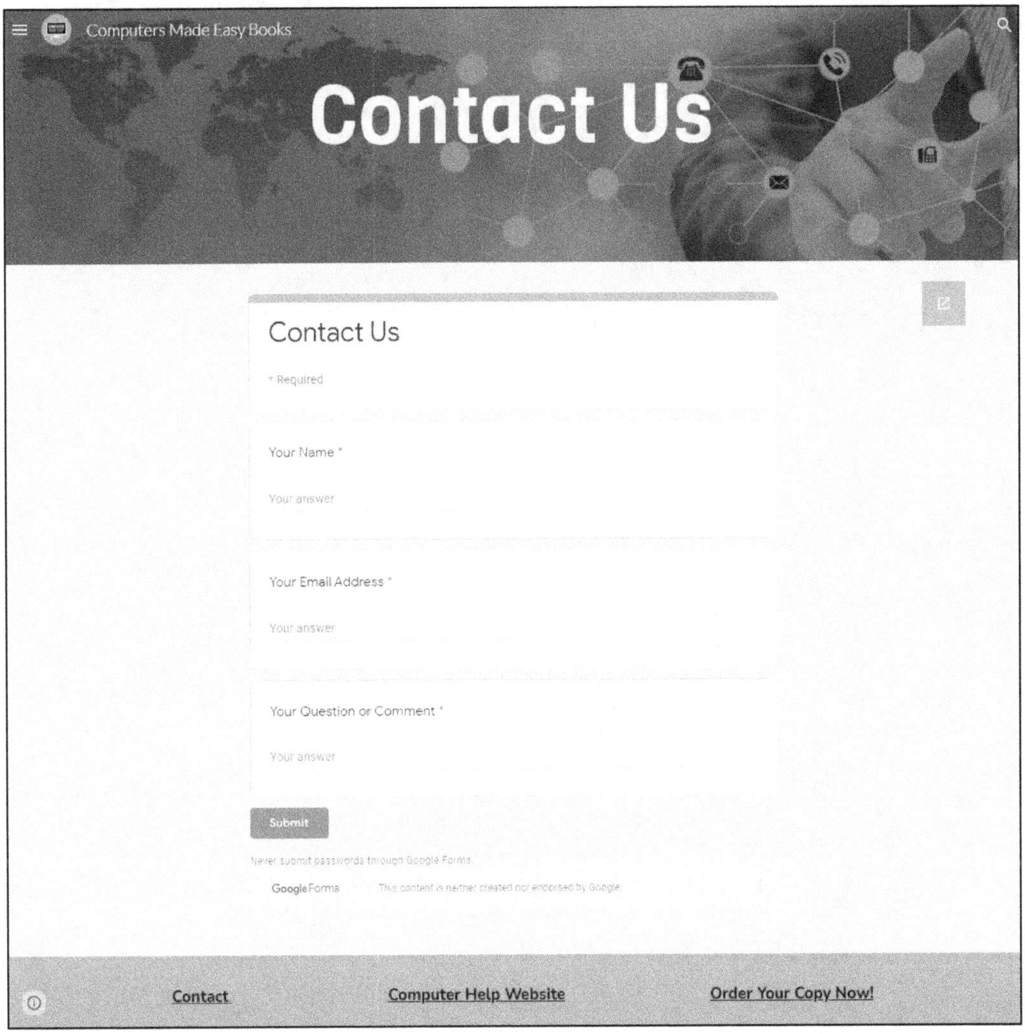

Figure 4.26

Now when someone fills out your form and clicks on the *Submit* button, Google Forms will keep track of their form submissions and you can go back and see them under the *Responses* section of your form within Google Forms.

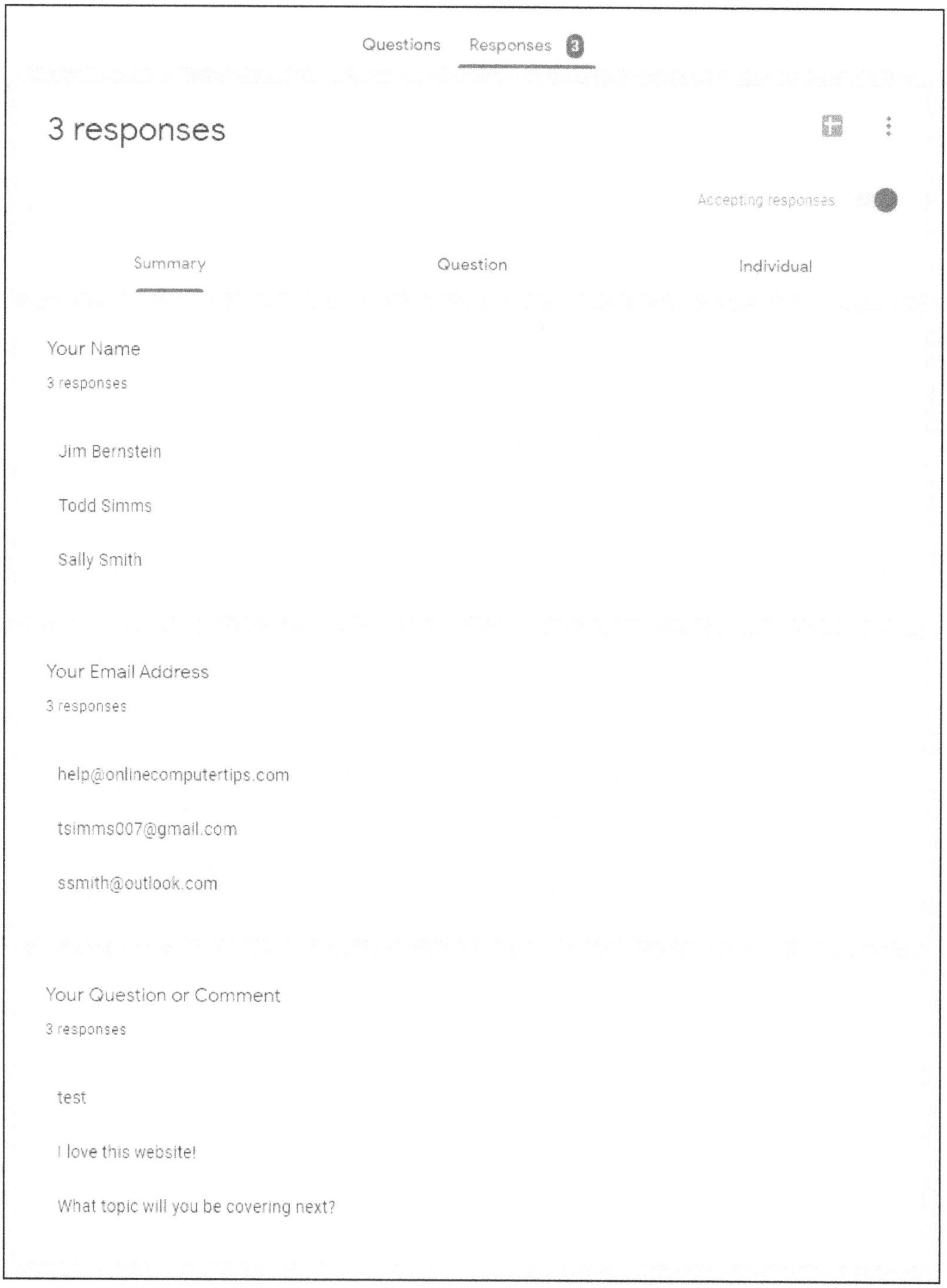

Figure 4.27

If you would like to be notified each time someone fills out and submits their information from your form you can click on the three vertical dots at the top right of the form as seen in figure 4.27 and put a check mark next to *Get email notifications for new responses*.

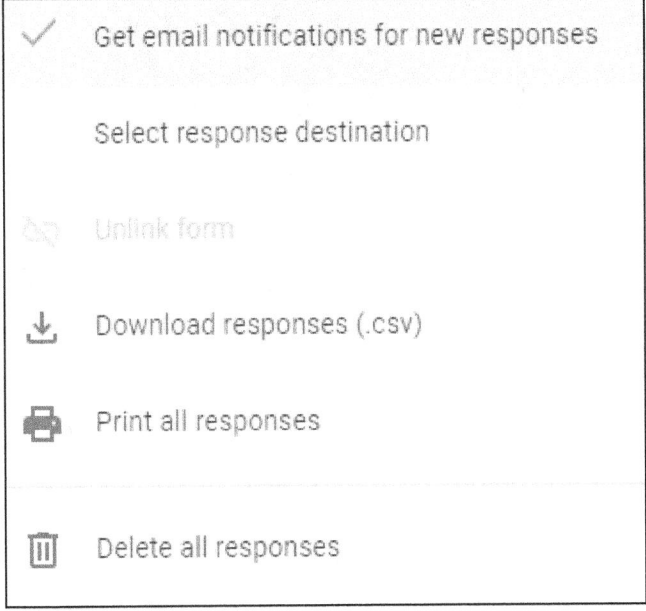

Figure 4.28

When you receive an email notification about your form in your inbox it will look similar to figure 4.29 and you can then click the *View Summary* button to be taken to your responses.

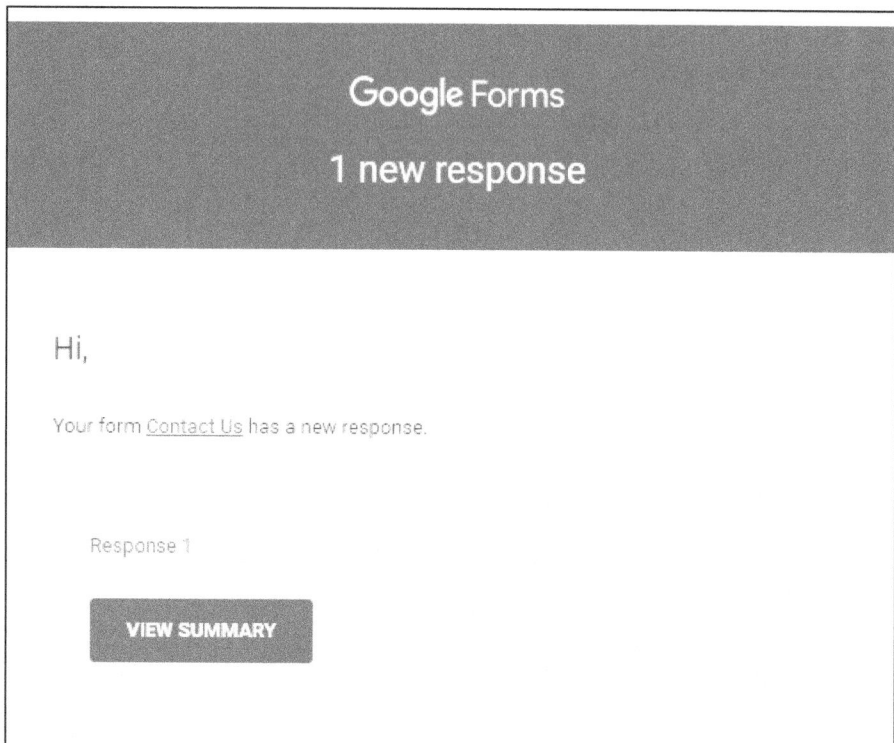

Figure 4.29

Chapter 5 – Google Drive

Since I have been talking about Google Drive throughout this book I thought it would be a good idea to devote a chapter to the topic since you will most likely be using Google Drive quite a bit if you plan on being a serious Google Sites or Apps user.

Introducing Google Drive

Since many of the Google Apps in addition to Sites rely on storing documents in the cloud, you really should have a solid understanding of how Google Drive works since this is the place you will most likely be using to store the files that you use with many of your other Google Apps.

Everyone has heard of Google, and they seem to be getting their hands more and more into other areas of technology, so it only seems appropriate that they would be involved in the cloud storage business. (And they have been involved in the cloud storage business for some time now.)

The cloud storage service provided by Google used to be just called Google Drive, but recently they have changed the name to rebrand their cloud storage solution to Google One. Now they offer family plans and even things like special hotel pricing as a way to entice you into signing up. In other words, the new Google One name includes more than just online storage, but you can also combine things like Google Photos and Gmail to simplify your Google services. Even though the newer name is Google One, they still call the storage portion of the plan Google Drive, so that is what I will be focusing on for this chapter.

The Google Drive Interface

If you haven't already figured out how to get into your Google Drive app then it's pretty simple to do. If you open your web browser and go to the Google home page you can get to it from what they call the Google waffle icon (figure 5.1). You can also drag the Drive icon closer to the top if it's something you plan on using all the time. You can also access Google Drive from **https://drive.google.com/** and if you are logged into your Google account it will take you right to your files and folders.

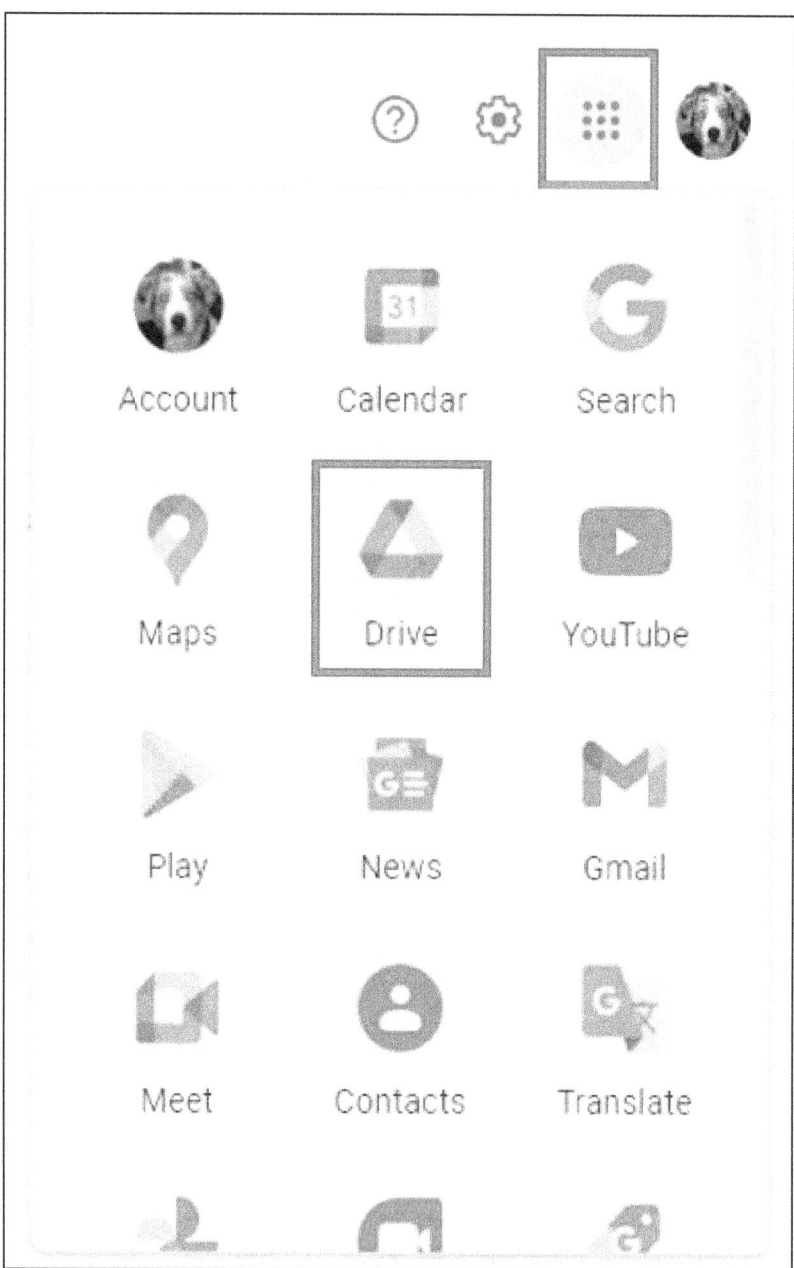

Figure 5.1

Once you open Drive you will see any files and folders that you have created as shown in figure 5.2. If you are new to Drive then you most likely won't have any folders and might not even have any files yet. I will be going over how to create folders and upload files in the next section.

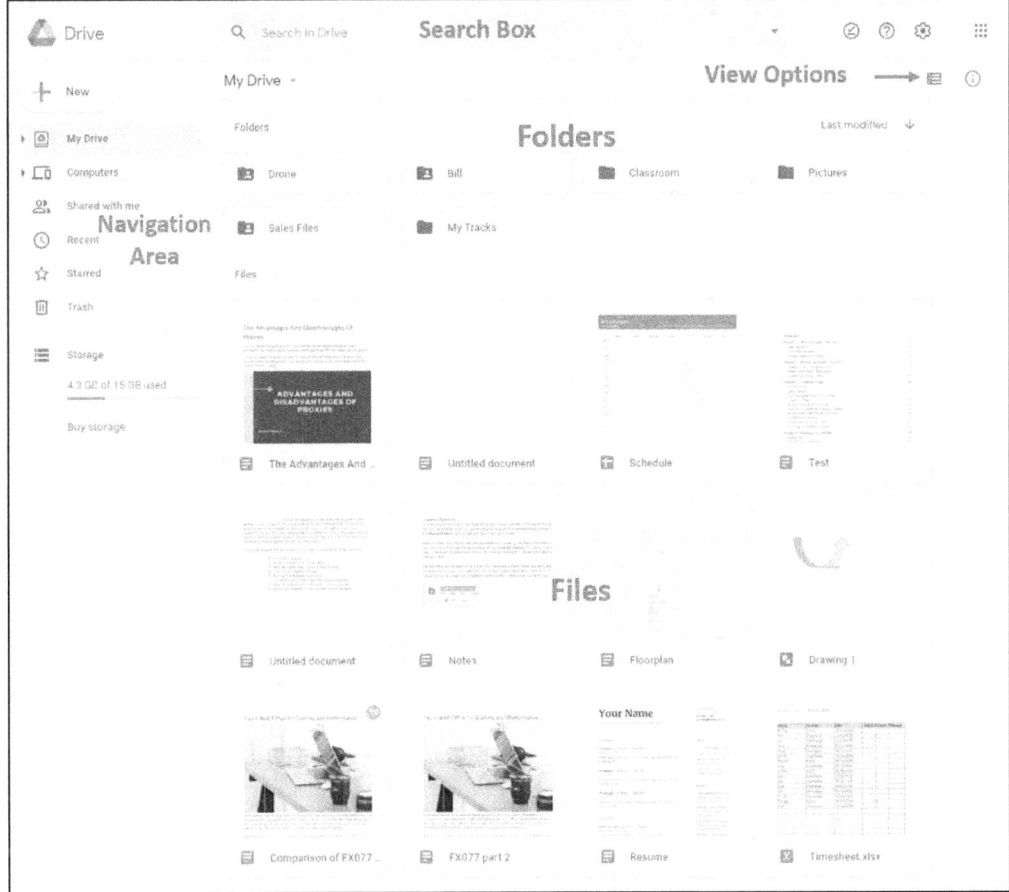

Figure 5.2

At the top of the Drive interface is a search box where you can search for files using a word or phrase. You can even search by email address to find files that were created or shared by a particular person.

If you don't like the thumbnail view for your files then you can click on the *view options* button to change it to more of a list\details view as seen in figure 5.3. Then you can click on the column name to sort by name, owner, modified date or file size.

Figure 5.3

The navigation area has several components and here is what each one of them does.

- **New** – If you want to create a new folder or upload a file from your computer then you can do so from here (figure 5.4). I will show you a couple of ways to do this in the next section. You can also start a new Google Docs, Sheets, Slides, or Form file from here and it will be saved right to your Drive. There are some other apps that you can open from the *More* menu choice as well.

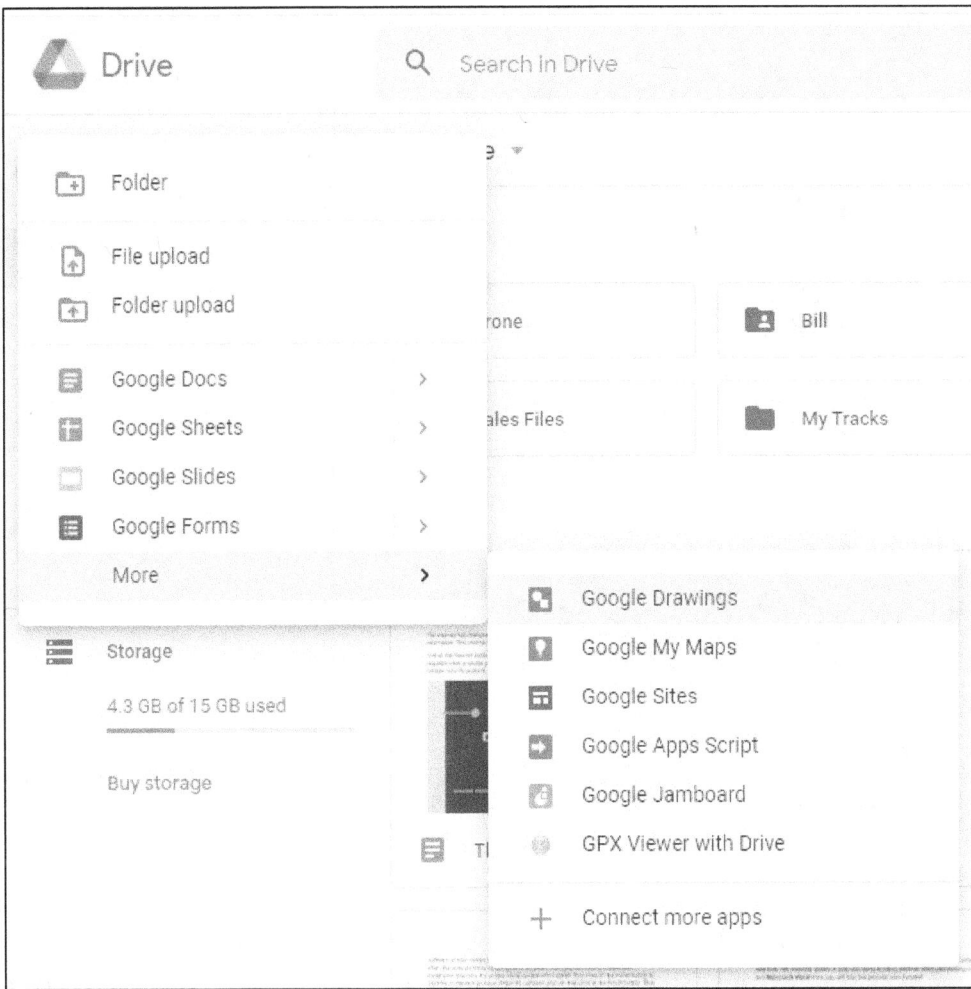

Figure 5.4

- **My Drive** – The My Drive section is the default view which we saw in figure 5.2. If you click on the down arrow next to My Drive then you will be shown your folder list underneath the My Drive icon and you can access any one of them from here.

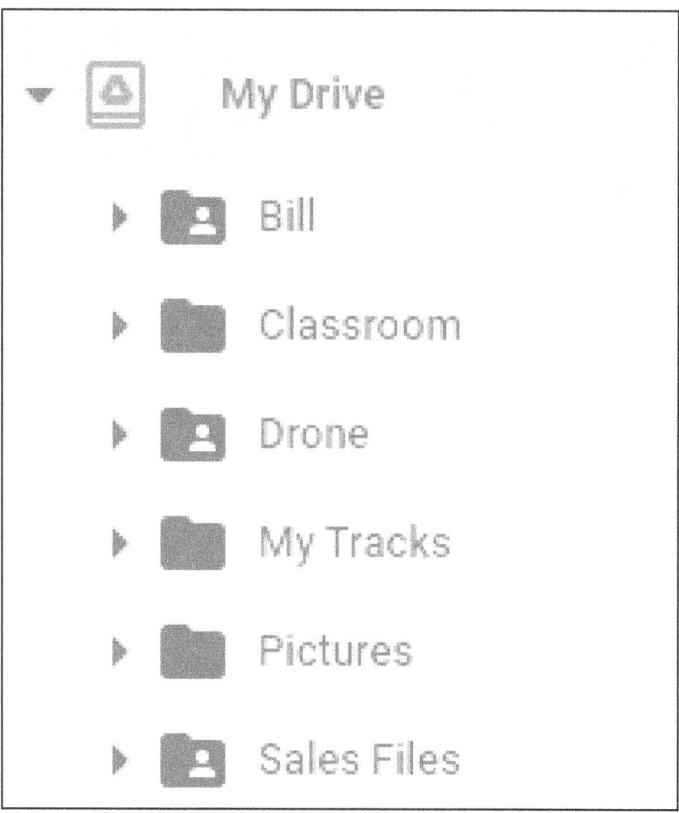

Figure 5.5

- **Computers** – If you use the Drive desktop client to sync your files between your computer and your Drive account then your computer will be shown here. If you have never used the desktop client then you won't have this choice shown. I will be going over the Drive client later in this chapter.

- **Shared with me** – This section gives you a quick way to access files that have been shared with you by other people.

- **Recent** – Here you will find files that you have recently worked on. So rather than have to go find where you have them saved you can just open them from here. Think of this as a shortcut to your recently used files.

- **Starred** – If you have files that you use all the time or that you want to be reminded of then you can star them so they will show up here. Think of starred files as favorites\bookmarks that you use in your web browser. To add a file to your starred section simply select that file in Drive and go to the three vertical dots at the top right of the window and choose *Add to Starred*.

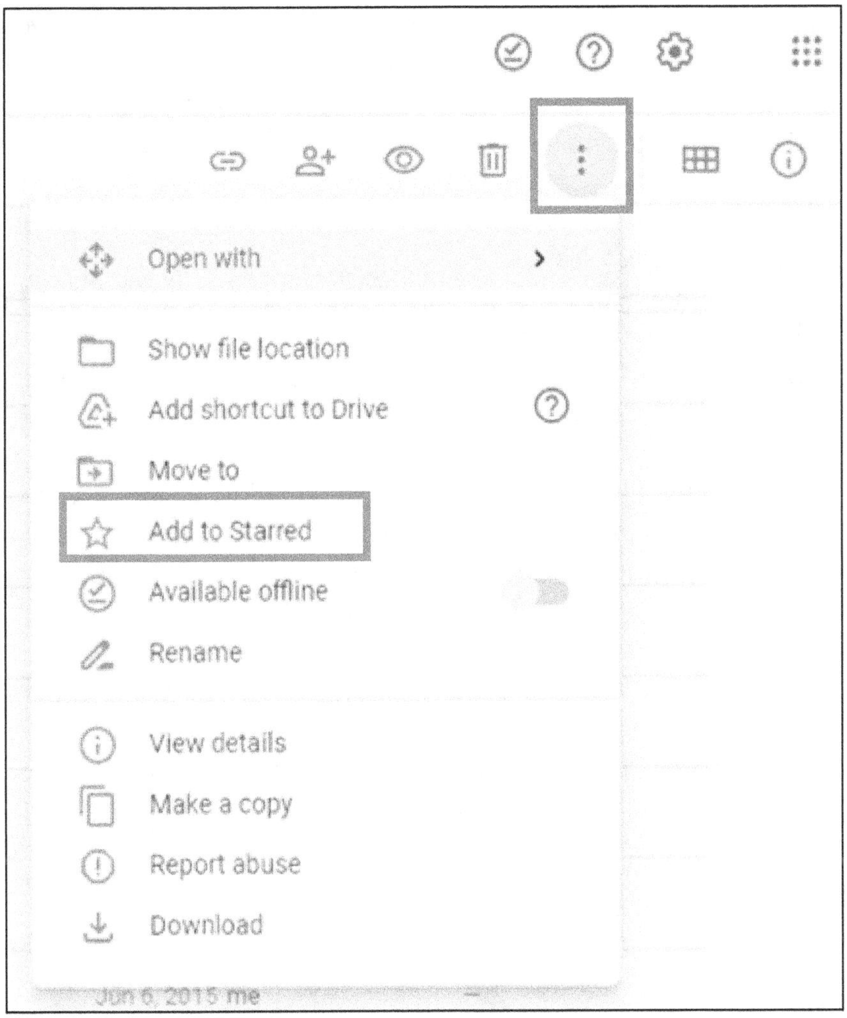

Figure 5.6

- **Trash** – When you delete a file, it will go to your Trash similar to how files go to the Recycle Bin in Windows when you delete them. You can recover files from the trash if needed by right clicking on them and choosing *Restore*.

Google is always changing how they do things with their apps and just about everything else including how long you can keep items in the trash. You used to be able to keep them forever but now they say they will automatically empty files from your trash after 30 days so keep that in mind. As of now I have items older than 30 days in my trash but that might soon change!

- **Storage** – Here is where you can see how much of your free online storage you are using as well as what files are taking up what amount of space. Google will give you 15GB of space for free but if you need more then you will need to sign up for one of their subscription plans or just make another Google account.

Creating Folders and Uploading Files

As you should know by now, when you create a new Google document or spreadsheet etc., it is automatically saved in your Drive and now you should know that you can go to the *New* button and create a new document from there that will also be saved in your drive.

If you plan on keeping your files organized then you should consider creating folders to help you do this. Once you create a folder you can then save new documents into that folder or move existing documents into that folder (and other files).

To create a new folder, click on the *New* button (or right click in a blank area) and choose *Folder*. Then give your folder a name and click on *Create*. You will then have your new folder shown with your other folders ready to be used.

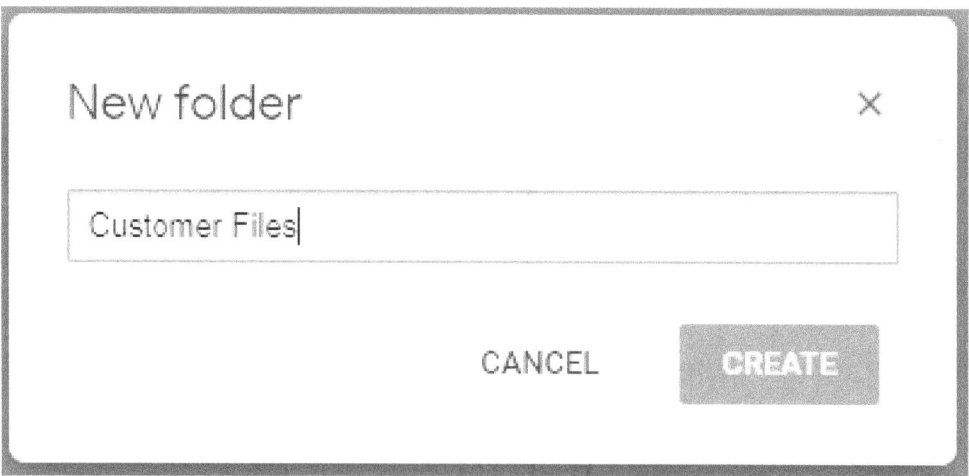

Figure 5.7

To upload a file or folder from your computer click on *New* and can then choose the *File Upload* or *Folder Upload* option and then browse to that file or folder on your local computer and choose *Open* (for files) or *Upload* (for folders).

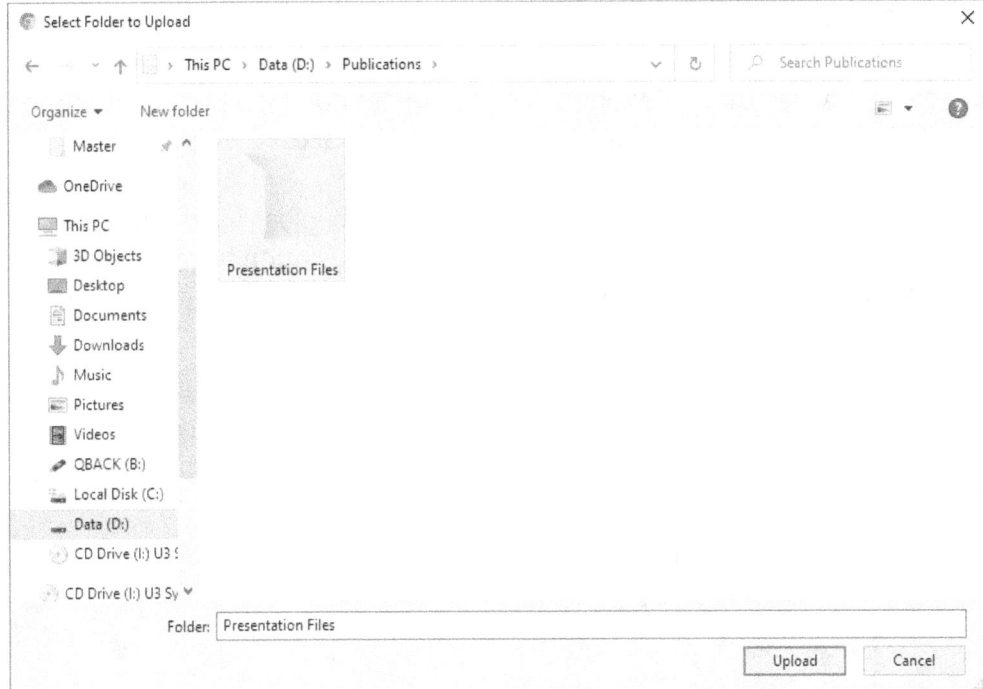

Figure 5.8

Another way to upload files and folders into Drive is to use the drag and drop method like you would use when working with the files and folders on your desktop computer. All you need to do is have your Drive open on one part of your screen and your file or folder location open in another window on your screen and drag and drop your files or folders right into your browser.

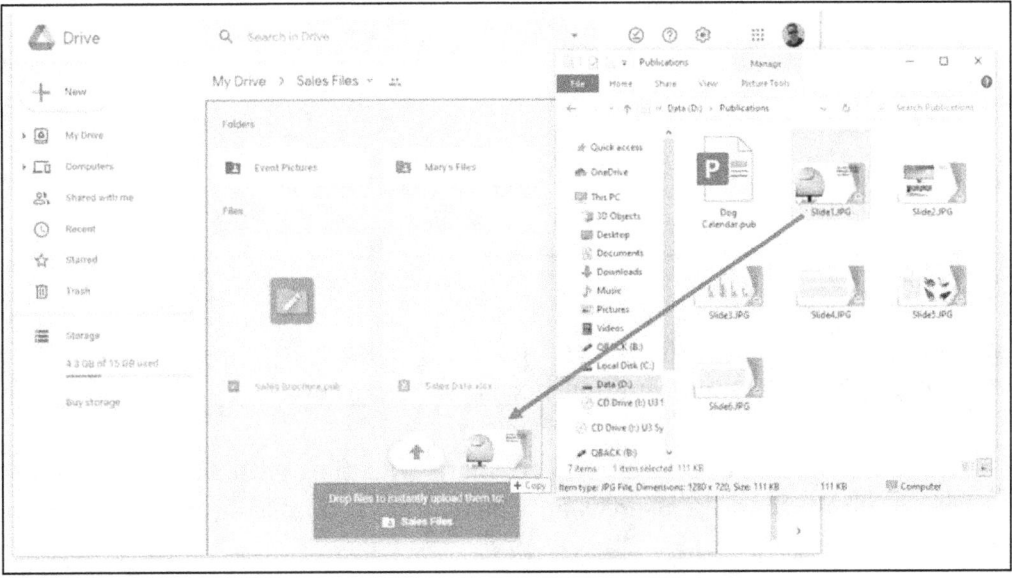

Figure 5.9

Managing Files and Folders

If you end up using Drive to store a lot of files and folders then you will need to know how to manage these files and folders, so things don't get lost and it doesn't take you 20 minutes just to find a file that you need to access.

One of the easiest ways to manage your files and folders is to right click on the one you want to work with and choose the appropriate option from there. Figure 5.10 shows the choices you have when right clicking on each type and as you can see, the options are fairly similar.

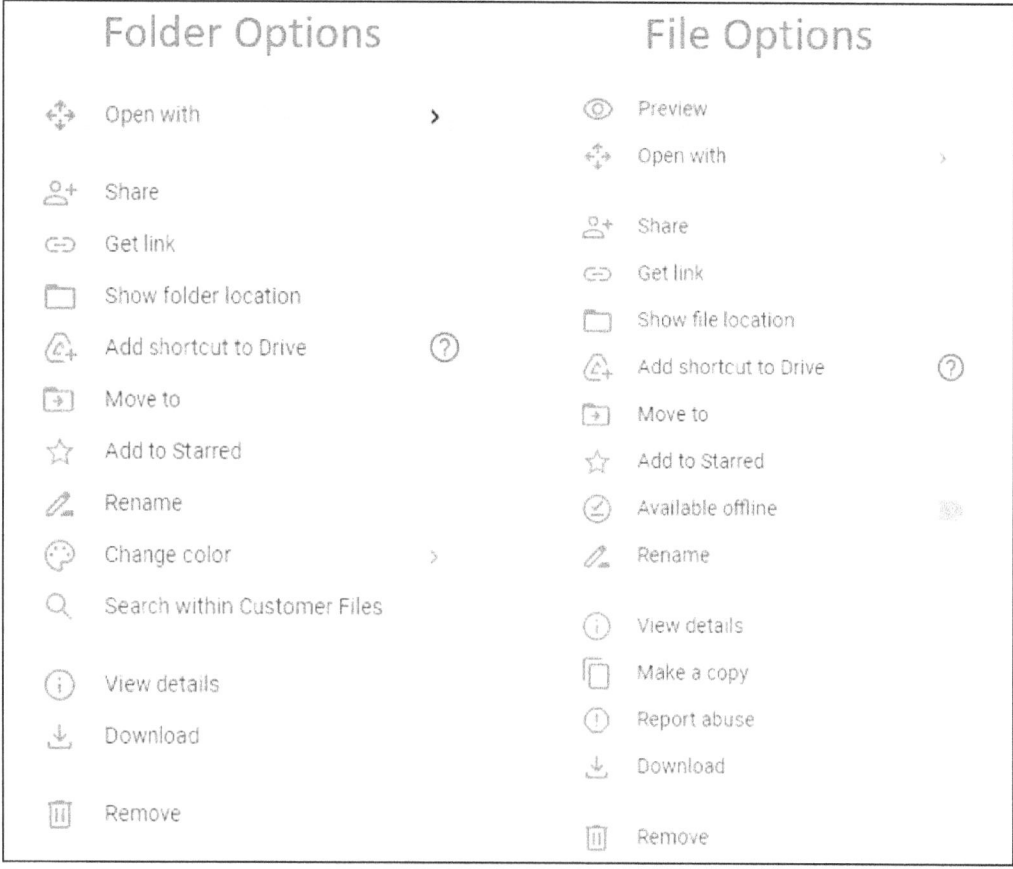

Figure 5.10

I will now go over some of the choices that I feel you should know about since you will probably be using these options more than the others.

- **Share and Get link** – Here you can share your files with certain people or create a link that can be used by anyone to access your file as long as they have that link.

130

- **Move to** – If you need to move a file or folder into a different folder then you can use this option to simply select the folder you wish to move the item into.

- **Rename** – Use this option to rename any files or folders and they will be instantly updated. It should also be updated for anyone who you share the file or folder with.

- **View details** – If you would like to see information about a certain file or folder, you can use this option to see things such as the created date, when the item was last modified and who it is shared with (figure 5.11). The *Activity* tab will show details about things such as when you changed the file or when you shared it etc.

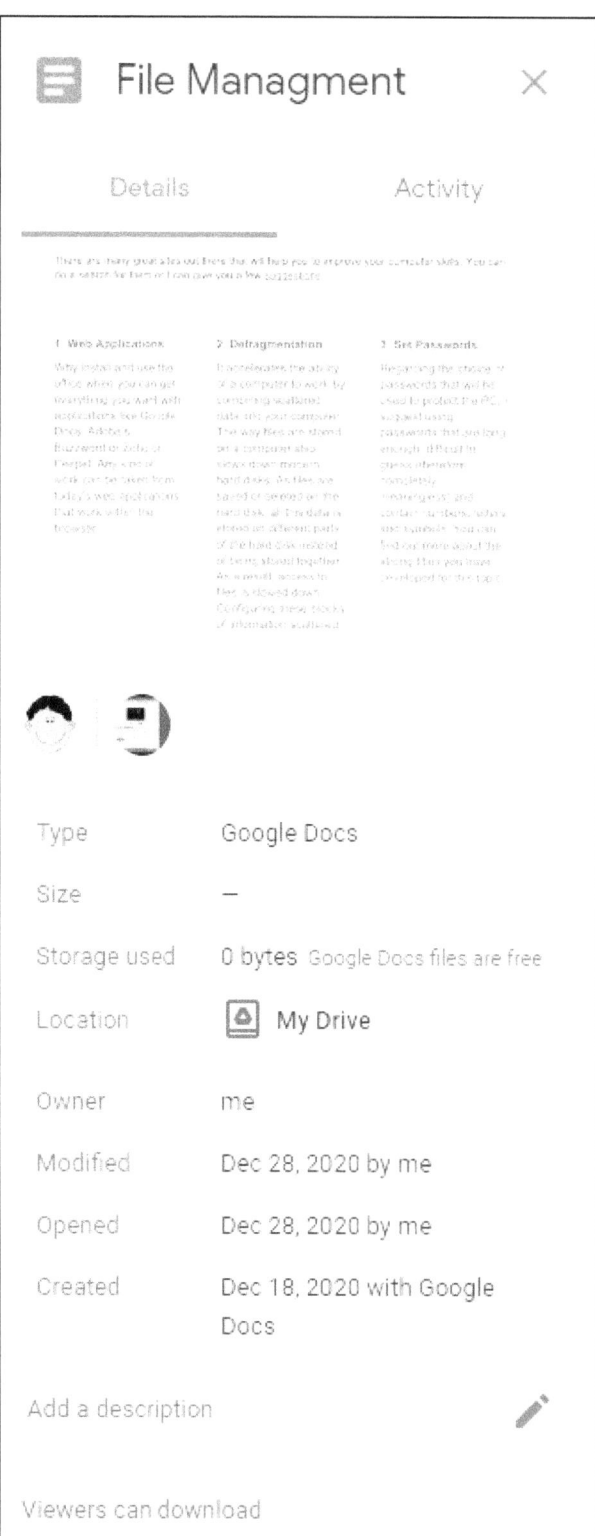

Figure 5.11

If you take a look at figure 5.11 where it says *Storage used*, you will notice that is shows *0 bytes*. This is because files such as Google Docs and Sheets don't count against your total Drive storage space. The area that says *Type* will let you know if your file is a Google Doc file or if it's another type such as a Microsoft Word file.

- **Download** – If you would like to have a copy of a file or folder stored on your local computer then you can download it to your PC using this option.

- **Remove** – This option will send the file or folder to your Trash where it can be restored later if needed.

Google Drive Desktop Client (Backup and Sync)
If you are the type who is used to working with your files and folders on your local PC rather than online then you can use the Google Drive desktop client and have the best of both worlds. The desktop client was designed to let you access your Drive files and folders from your computer like you would any other type of file or folder yet keep them synchronized with the files and folders in your Drive online. You can also use the Drive client to synchronize\backup other files that you have on your computer that are not kept in your Drive.

If you take a look at figure 5.12 you can see that the Computers section is missing under My Drive on the left side of the screen. This is because this user has not installed the desktop client on their computer and logged in with their account.

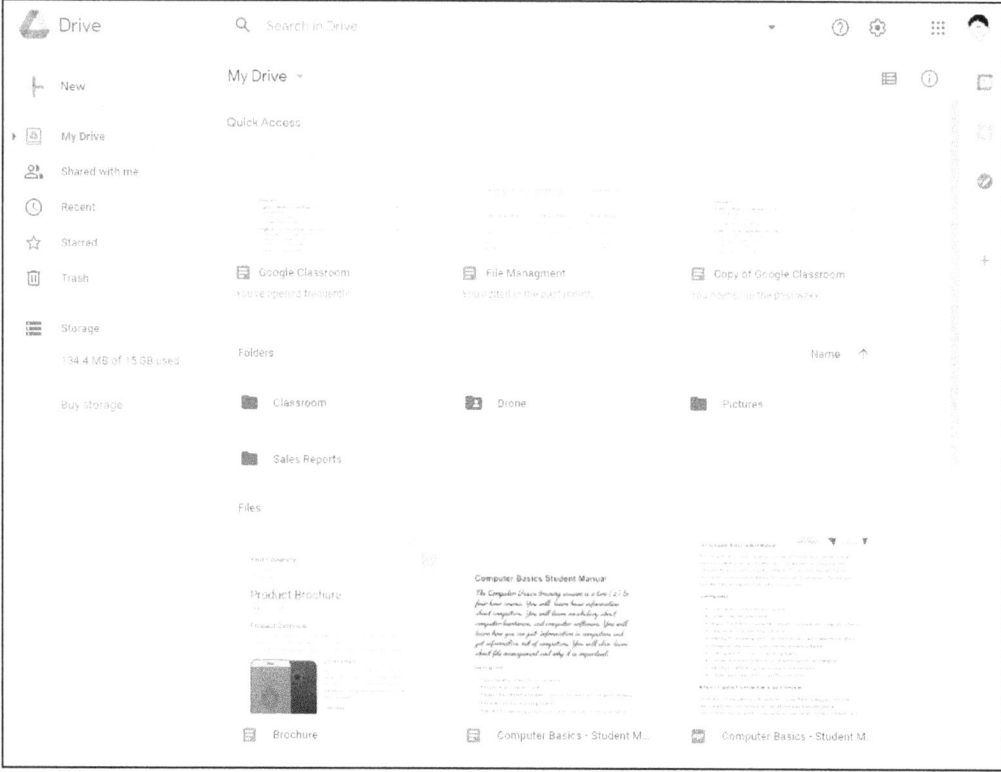

Figure 5.12

Now if I go to the gear icon at the top right of the page I can click on *Get Drive for desktop* to be taken to the client download page.

Figure 5.13

Once I am at the download page I will want to find the section for individuals and look for the download link. Depending on when Google decides to change the way this page is designed, it might look a little different for you.

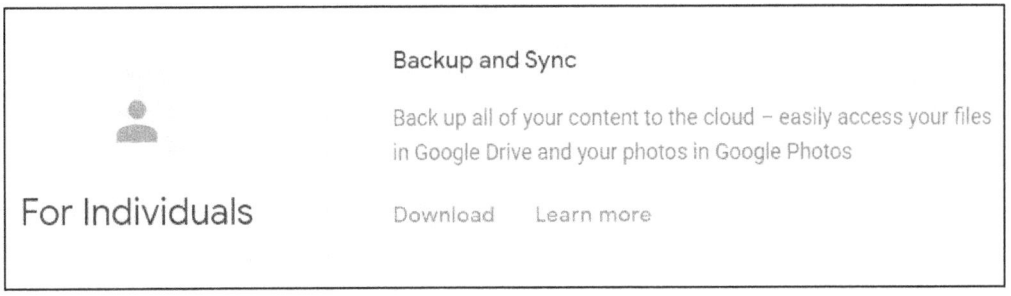

Figure 5.14

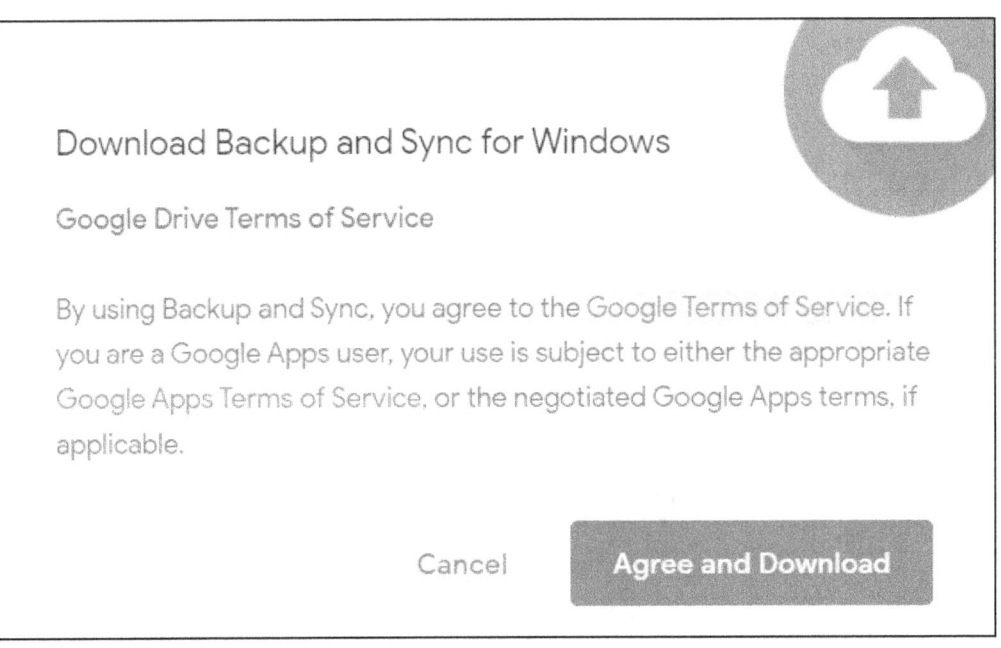

Figure 5.15

The installation process for the Drive client should be automatic and once it's done you will need to log in with your Google account to get started and go through a verification process that usually involves sending a notification to your phone that you need to acknowledge.

Once you are verified you will be asked which folders from your computer you want to have synced\backed up to your Drive.

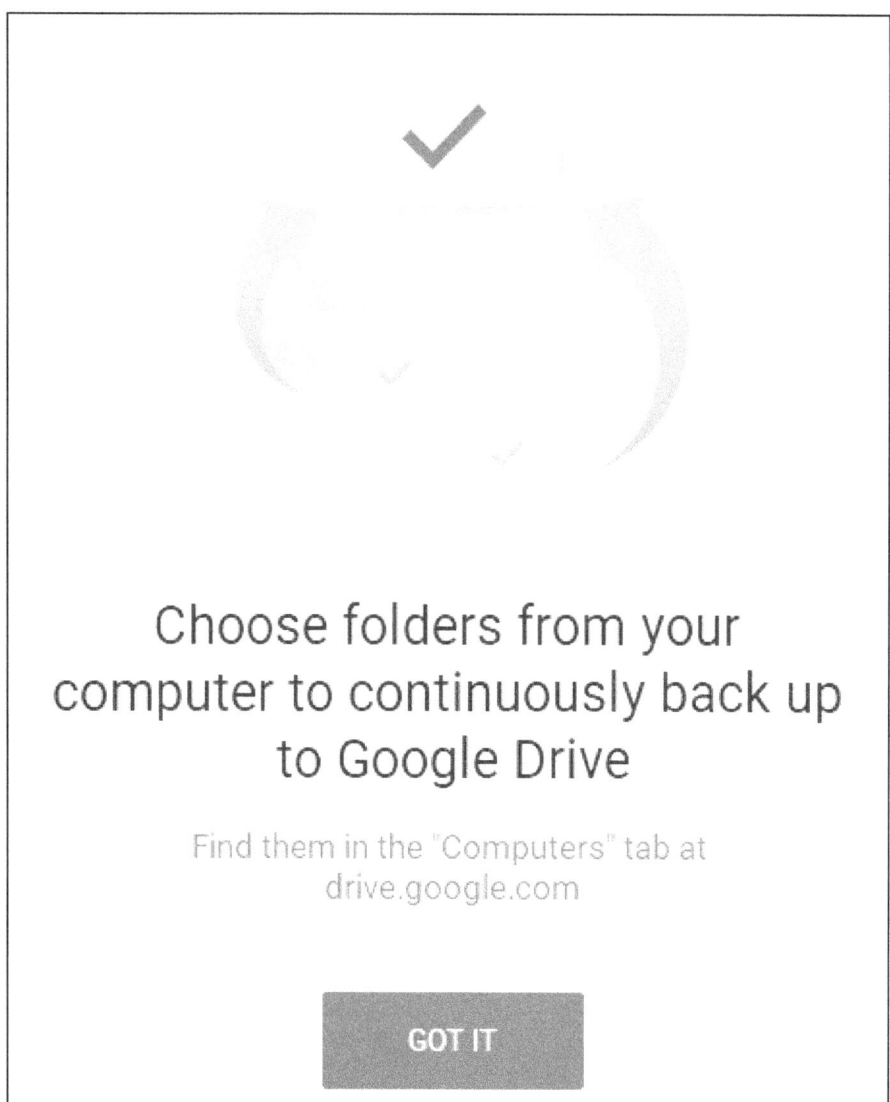

Figure 5.16

By default it will want to backup everything on your desktop, in your documents folder and also your pictures folder. You can check or uncheck the boxes next to these items to configure it however you like. For my example, I just want to backup a certain folder on my computer so I will uncheck all 3 of those boxes and click on the *Choose Folder* link to find my specific folder.

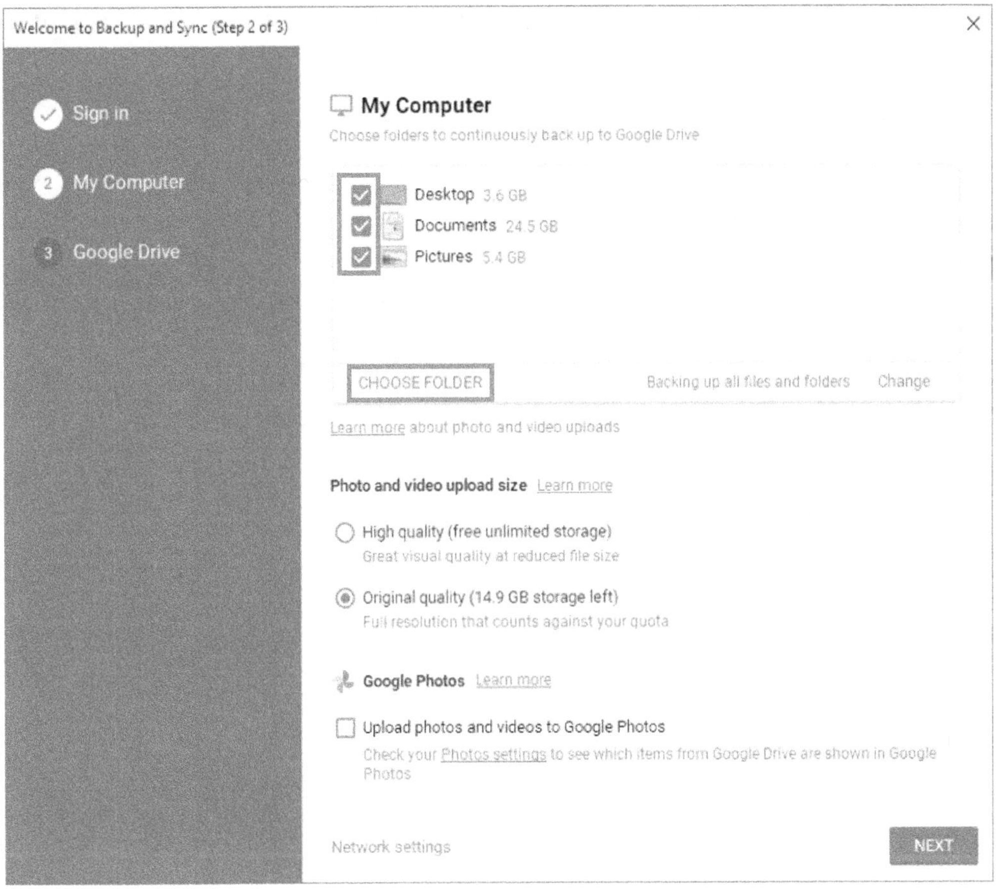

Welcome to Backup and Sync (Step 2 of 3)   ×

- ✓ Sign in

- ② My Computer

- ③ Google Drive

🖥 **My Computer**
Choose folders to continuously back up to Google Drive

- ☑ 🖼 Desktop 3.6 GB
- ☑ 📄 Documents 24.5 GB
- ☑ 🖼 Pictures 5.4 GB

| CHOOSE FOLDER | Backing up all files and folders   Change |

Learn more about photo and video uploads

Photo and video upload size Learn more

- ○ High quality (free unlimited storage)
  Great visual quality at reduced file size

- ⦿ Original quality (14.9 GB storage left)
  Full resolution that counts against your quota

🔗 **Google Photos** Learn more

- ☐ Upload photos and videos to Google Photos
  Check your Photos settings to see which items from Google Drive are shown in Google Photos

Network settings   NEXT

Figure 5.17

Now that I have browsed to my *Client Files* folder and unchecked the other three folders my selection looks like figure 5.18.

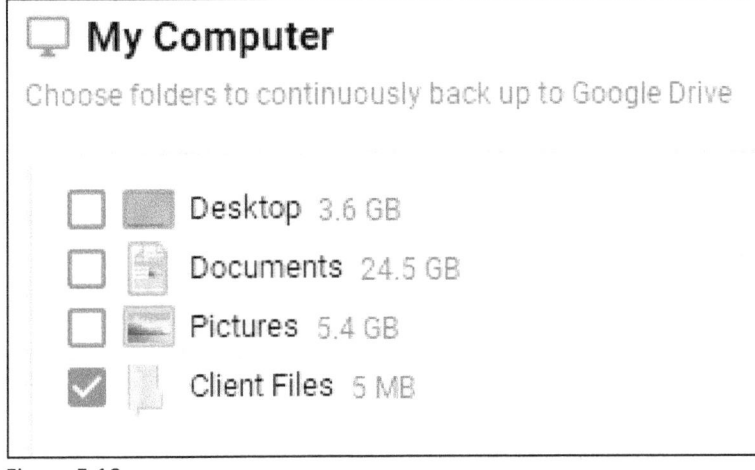

Figure 5.18

Later when I go back to my Drive in my browser I will see that I have the *Computers* section with my Client Files folder shown.

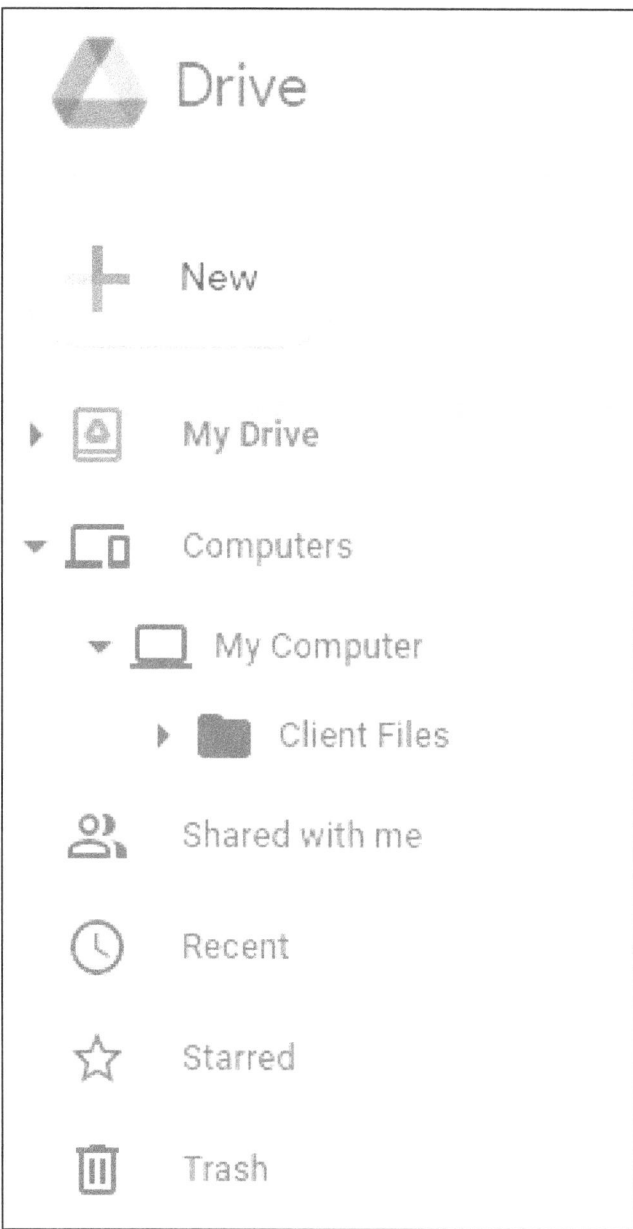

Figure 5.19

You will also be prompted to sync your Drive files and folders with your PC during the Drive client configuration process.

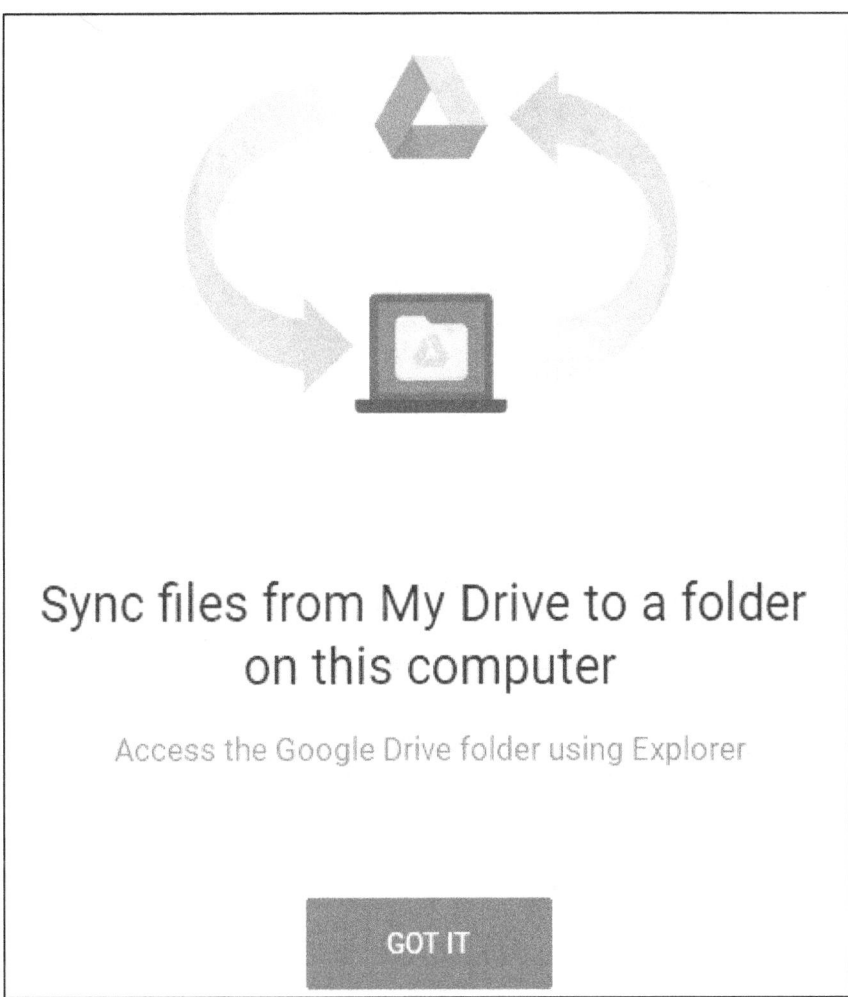

Figure 5.20

You can choose to have all the files and folders from your online Drive be synced to your computer or choose which ones you would like to have synchronized by clicking on *Sync only these folders* and then check the ones you want to use (figure 5.21).

The *Folder location* section is where the Drive client will copy and sync your Drive files on your local computer. By default it will go to your Users folder under your profile name, but you can change that by clicking on the *Change* link.

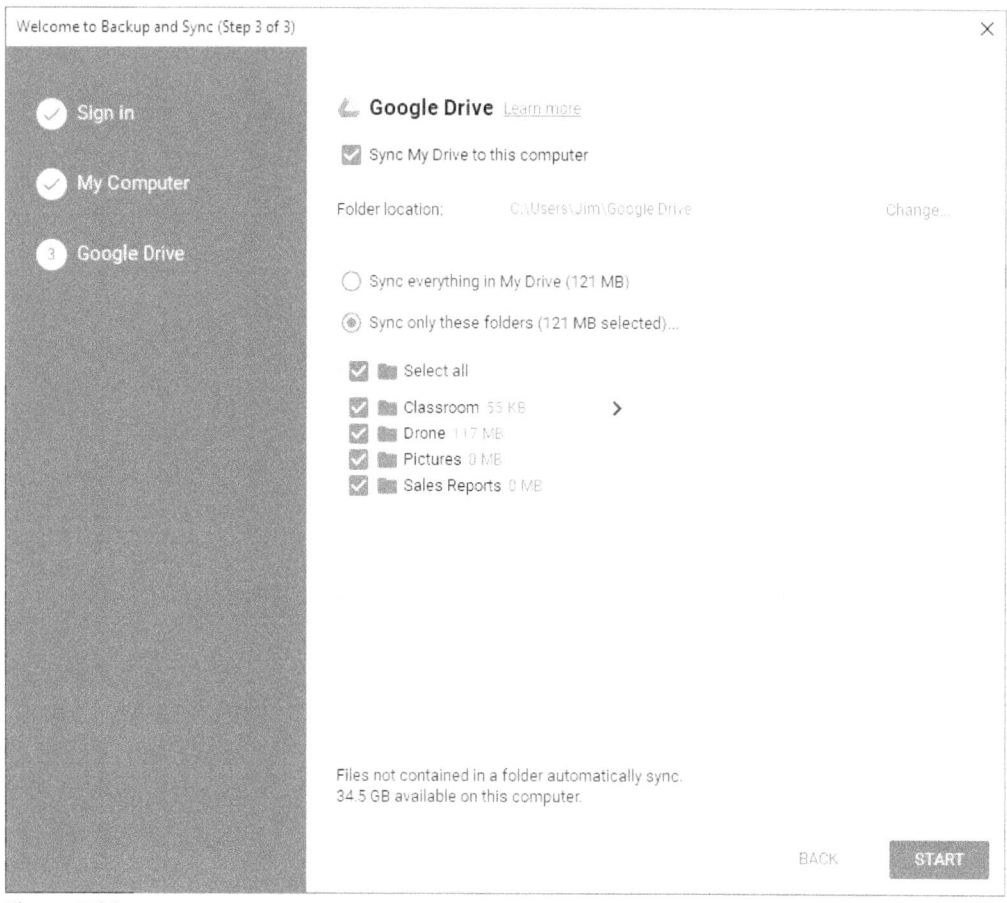

Figure 5.21

If I go to the Drive folder on my local PC located at *C:\Users\Jim\Google Drive* then I will see that now have the same files that were online stored on my local computer.

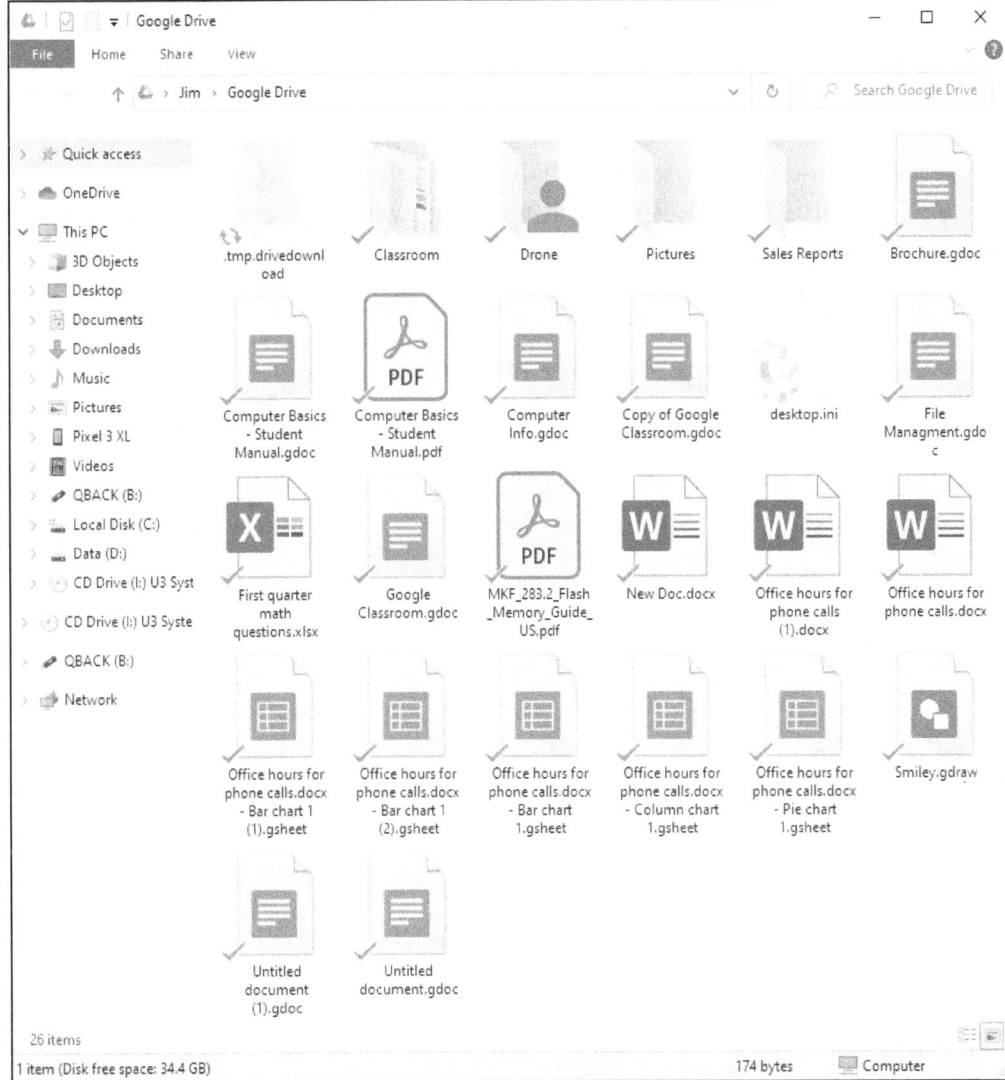

Figure 5.22

Getting used to the Drive client will take a little time since it can be confusing as to what is getting synchronized where so just play around with it a bit and if you don't like what it is doing then you can go to the preferences and modify how your files and folders are being copied. If you are a Windows user then you will find the Drive client in your programs under *Backup and Sync from Google*. You can also find it running in the notification area of your Windows taskbar by the clock.

Inserting a Folder From Drive Into Your Site

If you have a need to share multiple files such as pictures or documents with your website visitors then one way to do this is to simply share a folder on your Drive and then embed that folder into your site. That way, your visitors will be able to see and access the files within that folder right from your site.

The first thing you want to do is to go to your Google Drive, find the folder you want to share and right click on it. Then choose the *Share* option and determine how you want to share the folder. If your site will only be accessed by certain people or you only want certain people to view the folder contents then you can add them in the section that says *Add people or groups.*

If you want the folder to be accessible to all visitors on your site then click on the link that says *Change to anyone with the link.*

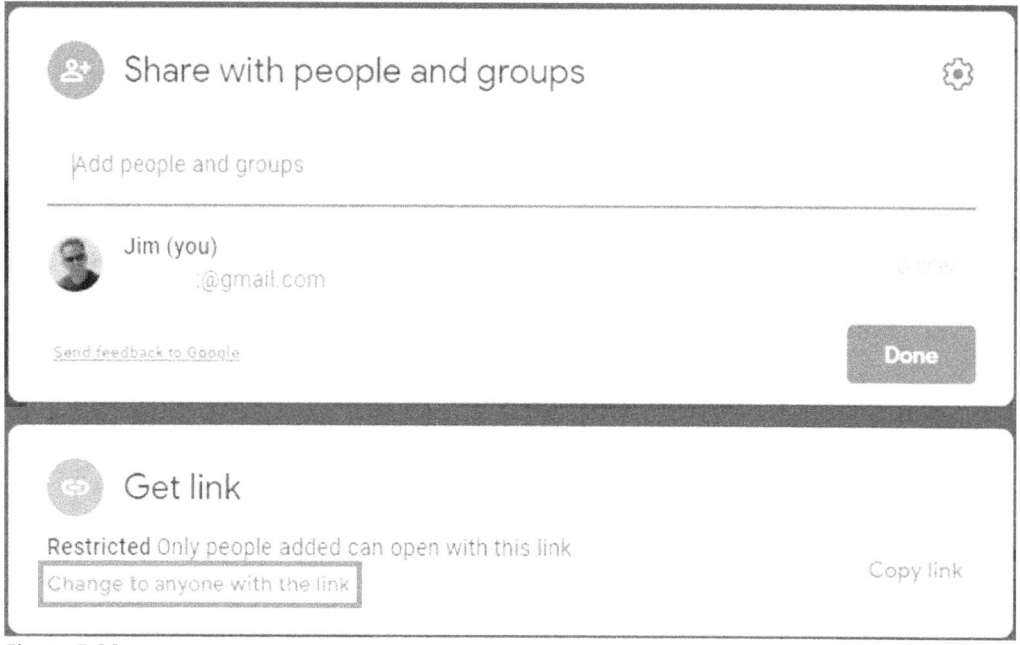

Figure 5.23

From there you should choose the *Viewer* option so your visitors can't edit or delete any files within your shared folder. If it's a non-public site then you can use the Commentor or Editor options if it's safe to do so.

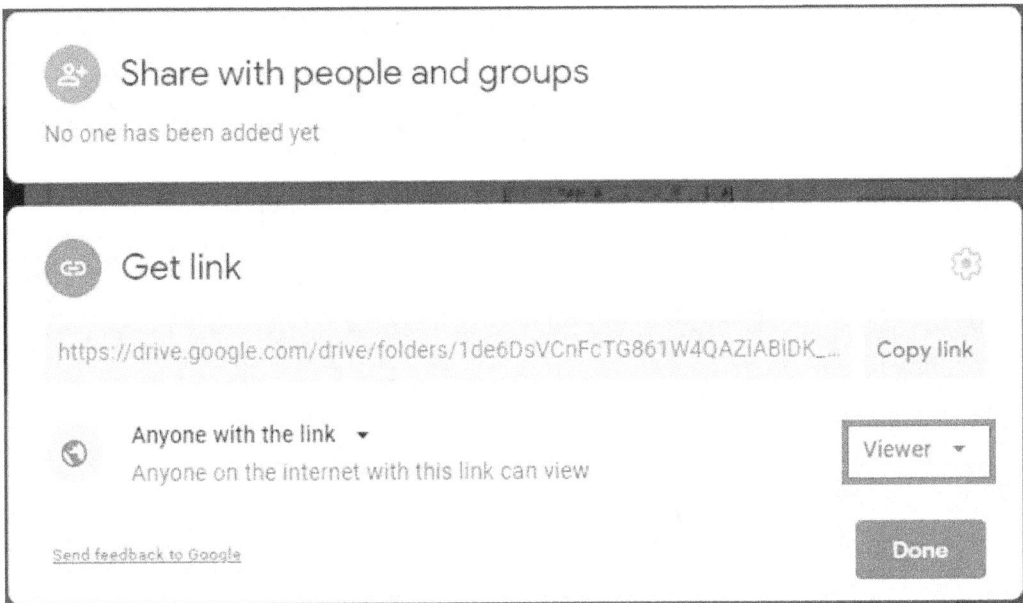

Figure 5.24

Now back in Sites, go to the *Insert* panel and choose the *Drive* option.

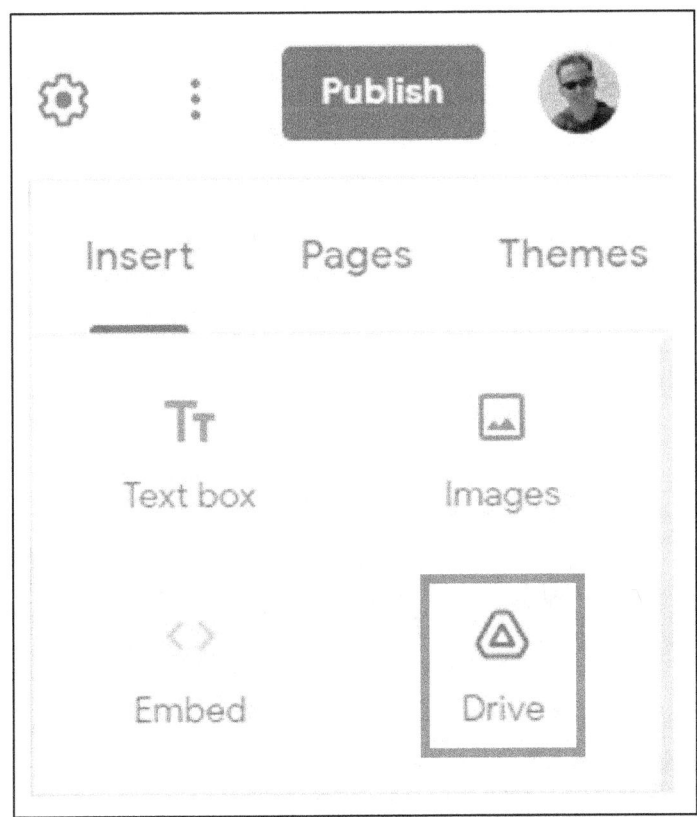

Figure 5.25

Then choose the folder you just shared and click on *Insert*.

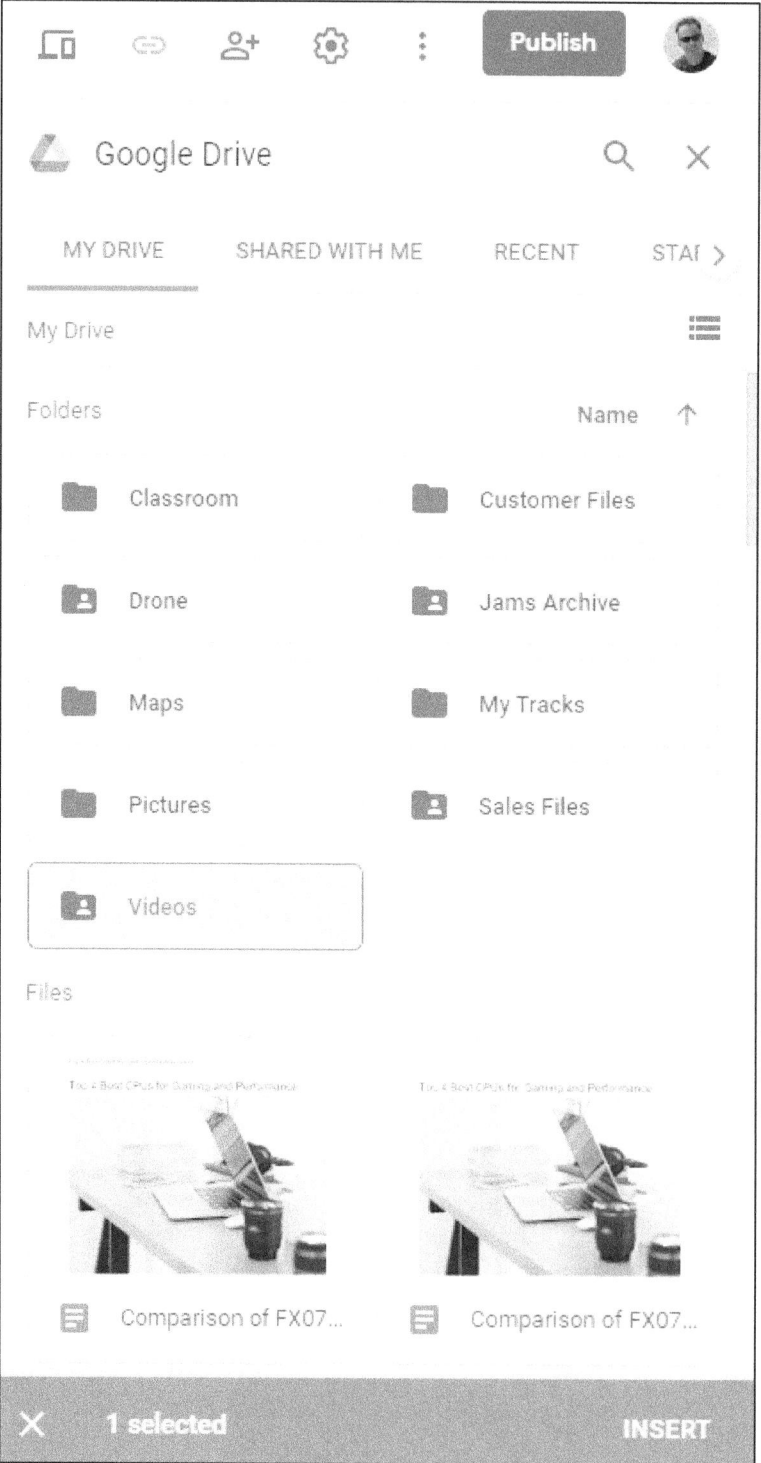

Figure 5.26

Now your shared folder will be inserted onto your page and you can resize or move the section to make it fit the way you like. Then when people go to your site they can view the files that are in that folder and as you update its contents in your Drive, the shared files on your site will also be updated.

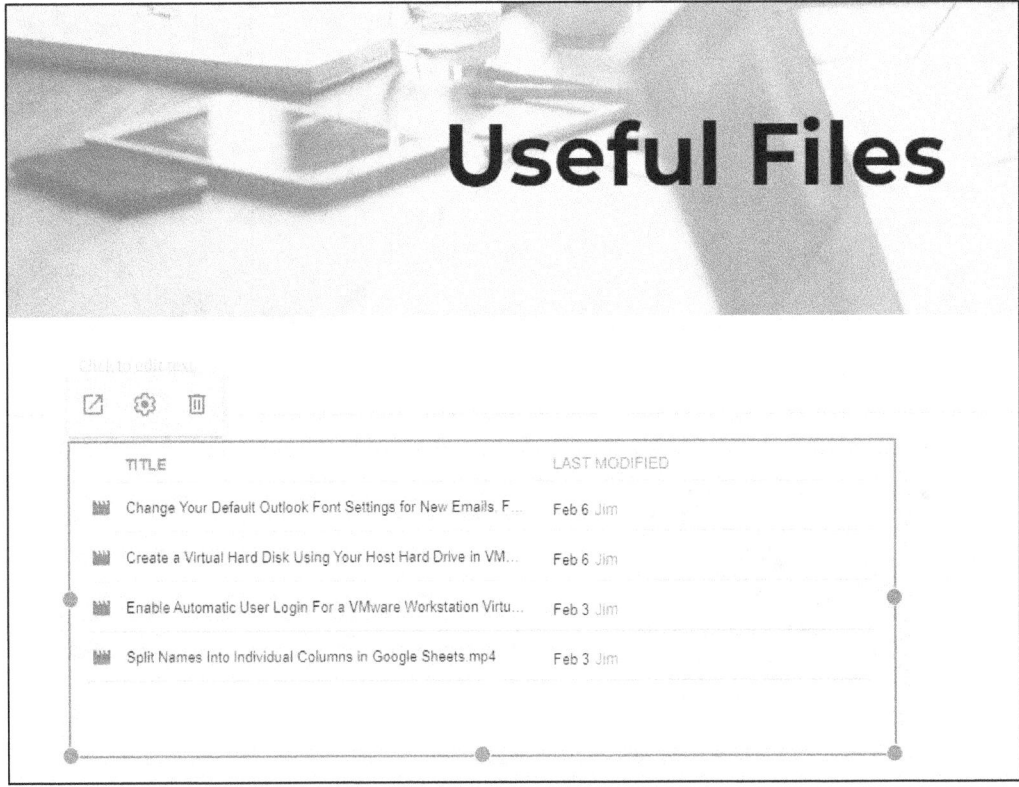

Figure 5.27

Inserting Images From Your Drive

If you would rather just insert individual pictures that you have in your Drive into your site rather than an entire folder, you can do so very easily. Just be sure to set the sharing permissions as we did for the shared folder and then go to the Insert menu and choose Drive once again. Then find the picture you want to use and click on Insert.

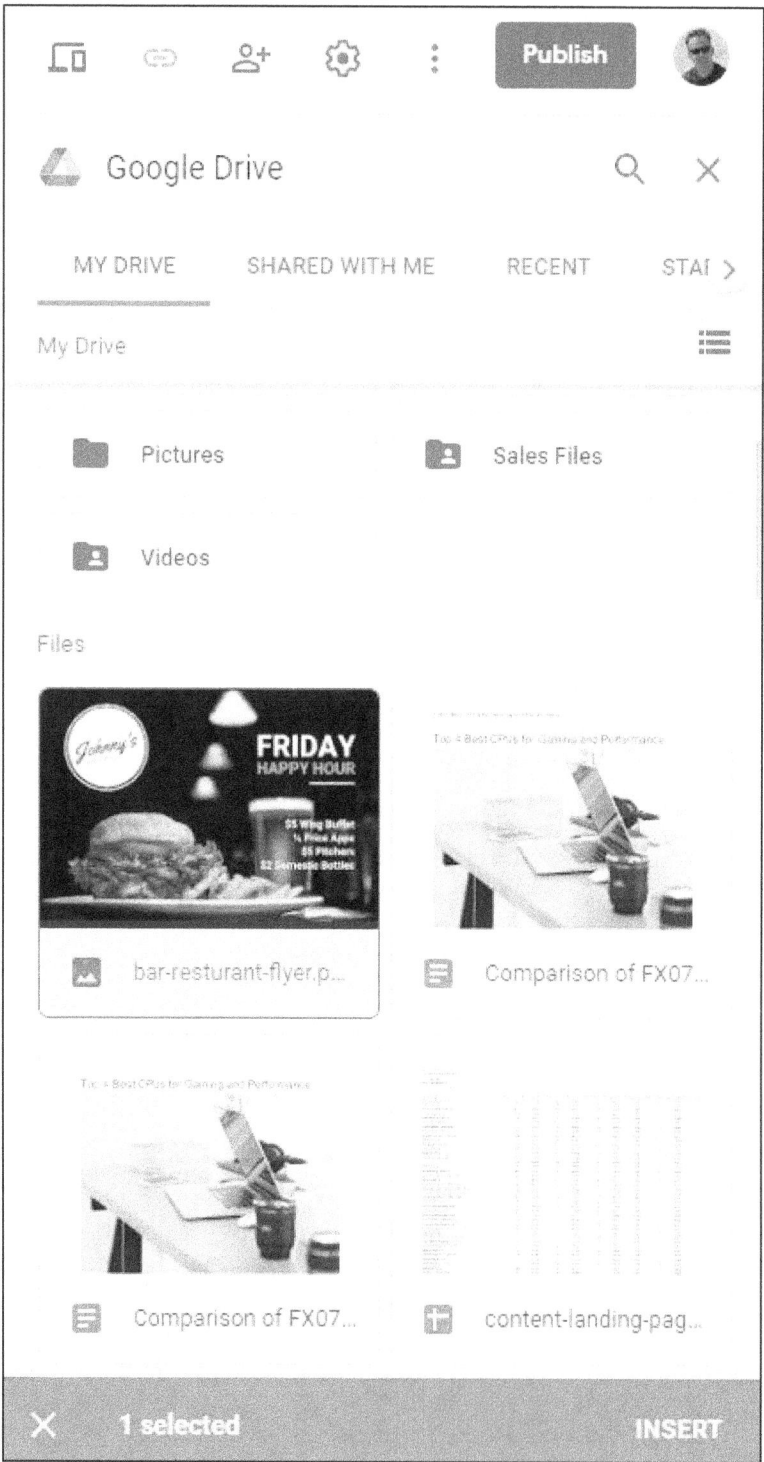

Figure 5.28

Figure 5.29

Chapter 6 – Sharing and Publishing Your Website

Now that you have your website looking the way you like with all of the content in place, it's time to share your creation with the world, or at least with your friends and colleagues! The way you share your website will be entirely up to you. You can just share it with certain people, or you can make it live for the whole world to see.

Sharing Your Site With Others
If your overall intention for who will see your website is only certain people then you can simply share your site and give the people who you choose to share it with access to view it.

You share your website the same way you share other files from your Google Drive by right clicking on it and choosing the *Share* option or if you are in Sites you can use the Share icon from the toolbar at the top of the page.

Figure 6.1

From there you can type in the names\email address of the people you want to share the site with.

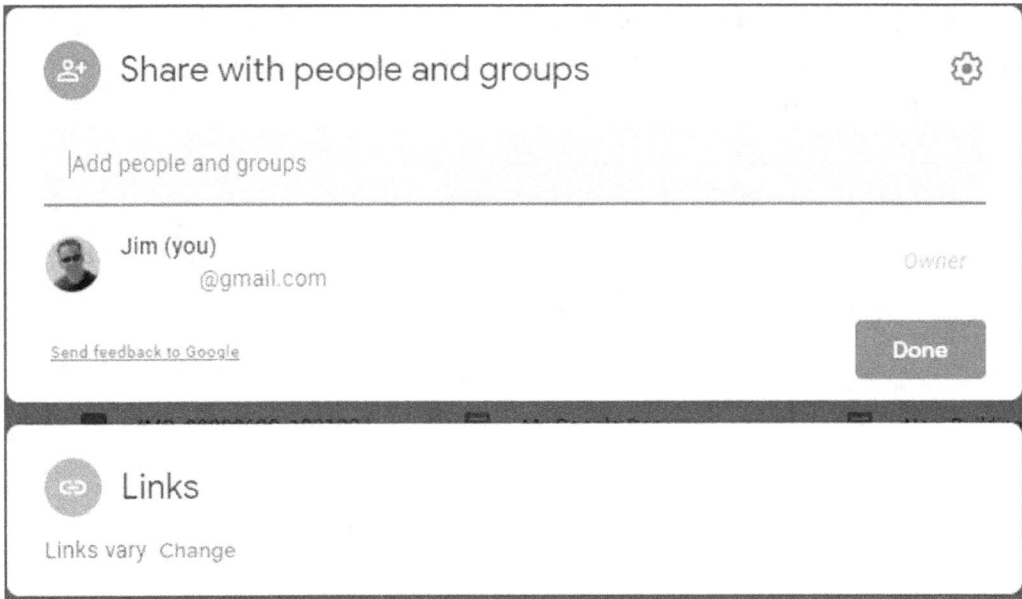

Figure 6.2

You can then determine if you want these people to be editors on your website or just viewers. Once you add the people you want to share the site with you can type in a custom message and click the *Send* button to have them emailed about accessing your new website.

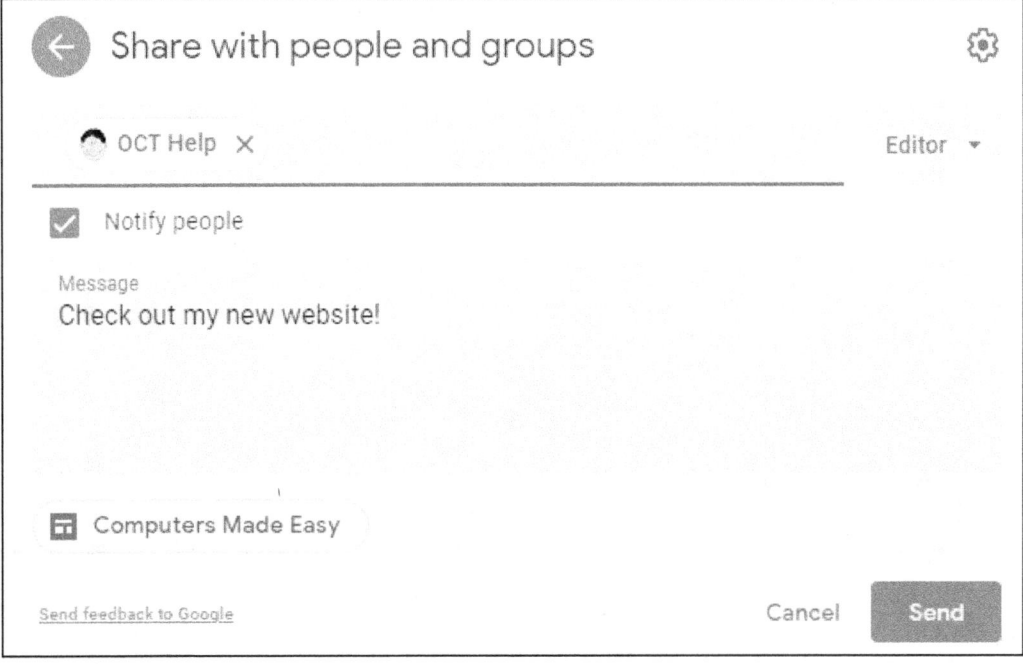

Figure 6.3

They will then get an email with an *Open* button that will take them directly to your website in Google Sites where they can then make changes if you gave them the edit permission.

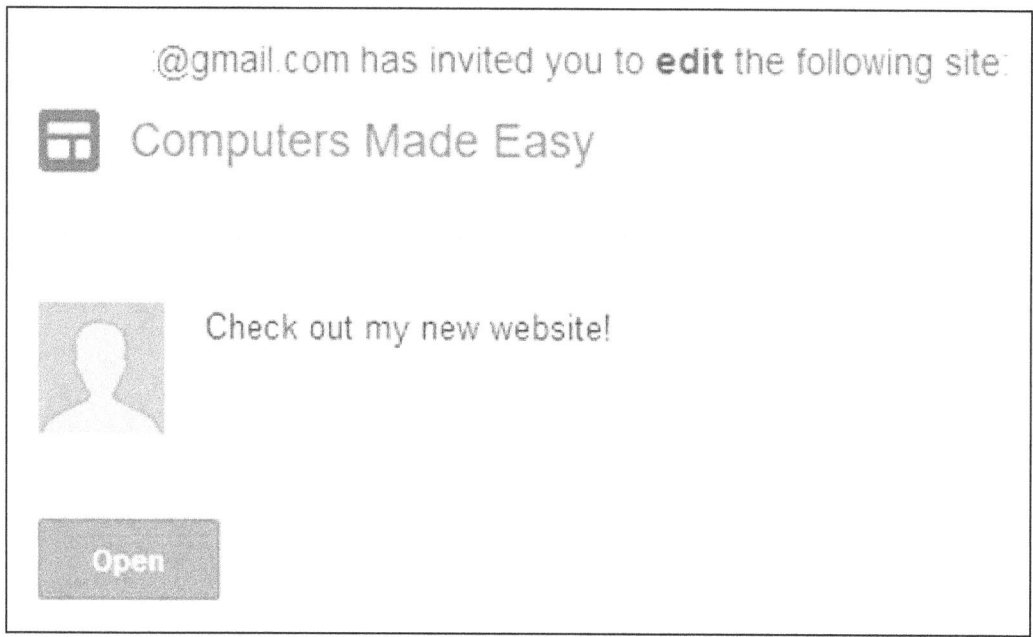

Figure 6.4

If you use the *Published Viewer* option you will notice how you can't check the box that says Notify people (greyed out) if your site is not published and these people won't be able to access your site until it is published. I will be discussing publishing your site later in this chapter.

Figure 6.5

If you click on the *Links* section from figure 6.2 you will have some options as to what people can do with the draft version of your site as well as the published version of your site. So if you want to make your published version restricted you can change it from *Public* to *Restricted*. You can also change your draft from *Restricted* to *Anyone with the link*.

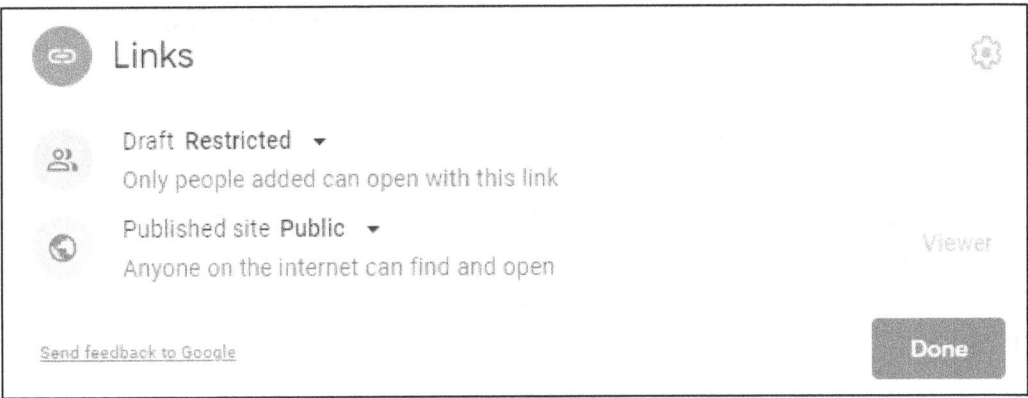

Figure 6.6

Publishing Your Website
If you intend to share your site with the world then you will need to publish your website rather than just share it. Google will host your site and give you a URL (website address) for your site, so you don't need to come up with your own domain name or purchase one of your own unless you want to. You can always use the URL they give you and then switch to your own custom domain name later on. I will be covering this process later in the chapter.

I'm sure you have seen the big *Publish* button every time you work on your website in the Sites interface and that is the button I will be using to publish my website.

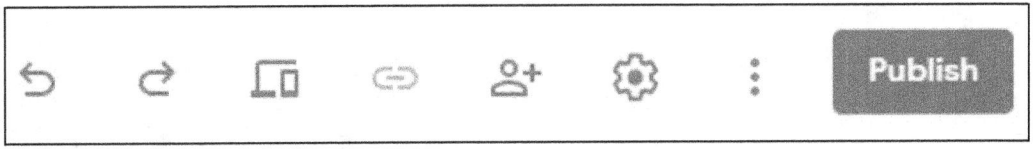

Figure 6.7

When I click the Publish button I will be presented with the *Publish to the web* option box and Sites will most likely add its own name based on information from your site. When I did the for my site it auto-filled the web address section with **computersmadeeasybooks** (figure 6.8) which is not the name I would like to use for my site. The first part of the address (**https://sites.google.com/view/)** is required and can't be changed.

The *Custom URL* section is used for when you obtain your own domain name and wish to use it with Google Sites. I will be going over this process later in the chapter.

The *Manage* option can be used to adjust your sharing settings like I previously discussed.

If you don't want your public site to show up in searches that are performed with search engines such as Google or Bing then you can check the box that says *Request public search engines to not display my site*. There is no guarantee that this will work 100% though.

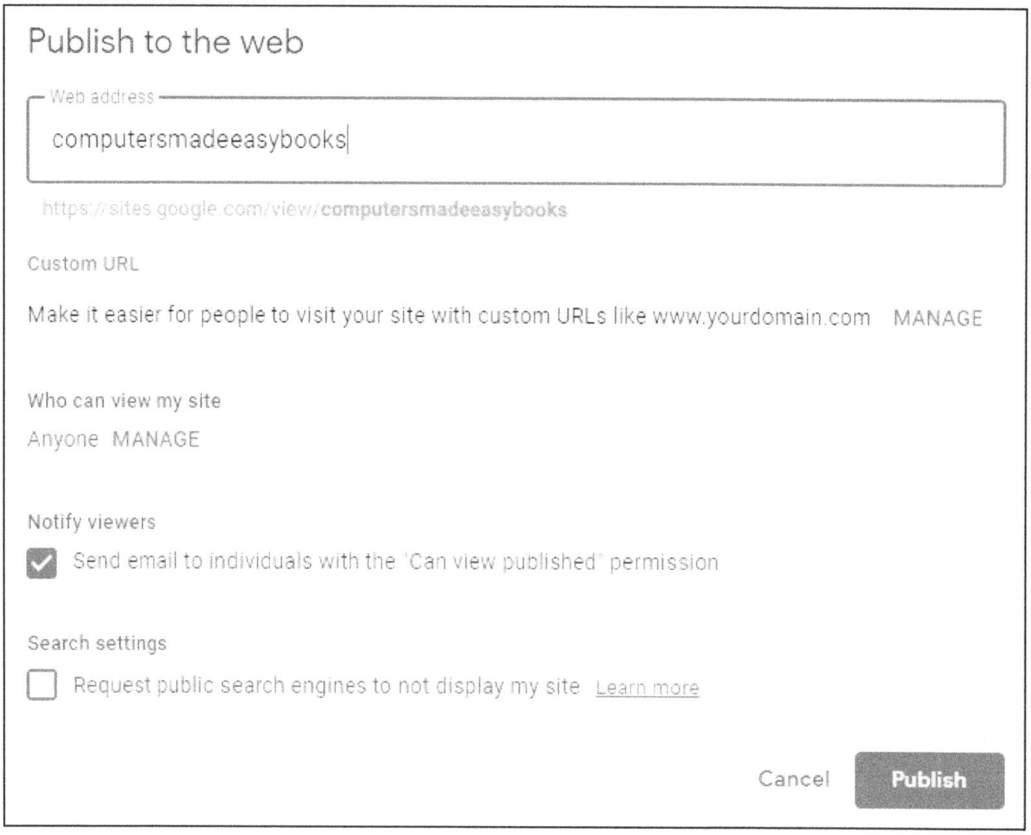

Publish to the web

Web address

computersmadeeasybooks

https://sites.google.com/view/computersmadeeasybooks

Custom URL

Make it easier for people to visit your site with custom URLs like www.yourdomain.com   MANAGE

Who can view my site

Anyone MANAGE

Notify viewers

☑ Send email to individuals with the 'Can view published' permission

Search settings

☐ Request public search engines to not display my site Learn more

Cancel   **Publish**

Figure 6.8

Changing Your Site URL

Since I don't like the web address that was assigned to my site, I will type in something a little easier to read (and remember). As long as the address is not in use by someone else or contains characters that can't be used in the name, I can change it to whatever name I like. So I will use **computers-made-easy** for my URL. Just remember that the beginning of the URL will still be *sites.google.com/view*.

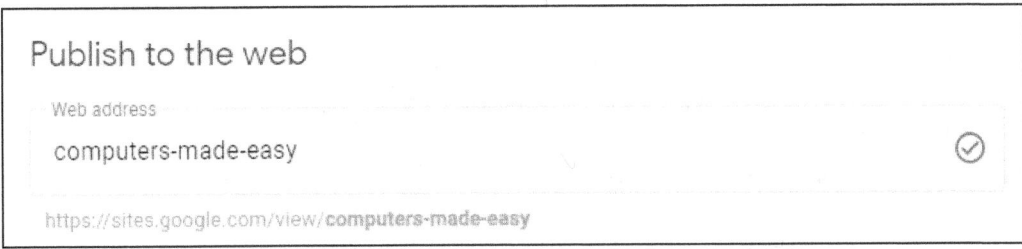

Figure 6.9

When I click on Publish I will get a message at the bottom of the screen that says my site has been published successfully with a link to view the page.

Figure 6.10

I can also view my page from the Publish drop down menu by clicking on *View published site*.

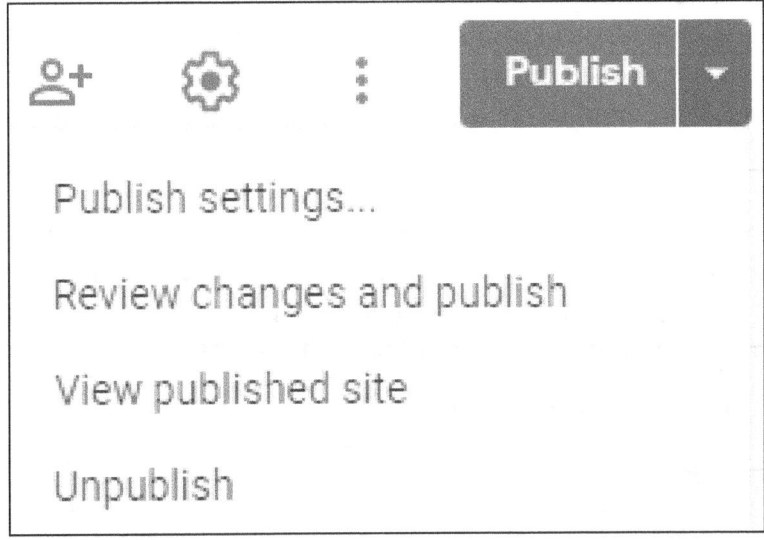

Figure 6.11

If I want to change the address later on, I can click on *Publish settings* and then type in a new address for my site and save the changes. Just keep in mind that you will need to change your site address on any documentation that you might have added it to as well as notify any people that access your site.

When I view my live site in my web browser the address now shows as:

https://sites.google.com/view/computers-made-easy/home

Notice how it says **/home** at the end. That is the address for the home page. If I were to click on the Networking navigation item to go to my Networking book page the URL changes to:

https://sites.google.com/view/computers-made-easy/networking?authuser=0

Another thing that will happen when you publish your site is that people who you gave the Published Viewer permission to (figure 6.5) will get notified that you have published your website.

Figure 6.12

Reviewing and Publishing Changes

Now that my site is live for the world to see, when I make changes in the Sites app, they won't automatically be applied to my live site. What I will need to do is to review the changes and then republish the site again to have those changes go into effect.

So I want to remove my announcement banner and move my image carousel from the image banner into the welcome text section below. When I do that and click on Publish I will get a side-by-side view of the changes I made with the draft (or current changes) on the left and then the currently live site on the right.

Figure 6.13

I will also be shown a summary of the changes on the left side of the screen so I can make sure the proper changes will be applied.

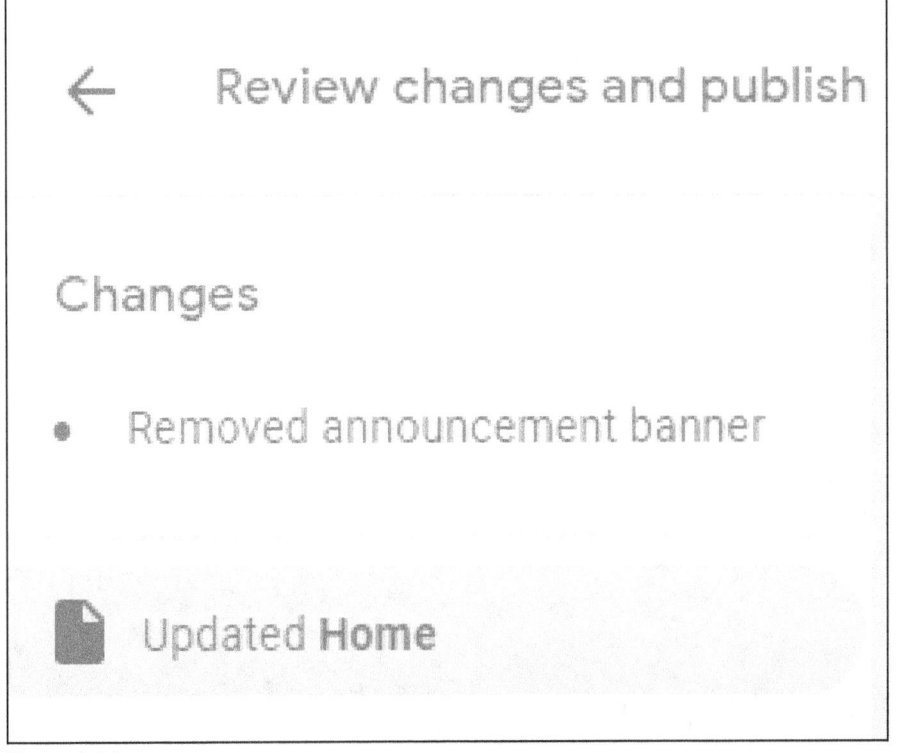

Figure 6.14

If everything looks good, all I need to do is click on the *Publish* button once again and my changes will be applied and then become live on my website.

Unpublishing Your Website

If for some reason you don't want your website to be visible to the world anymore then it's very easy to unpublish your site without worrying about removing it altogether.

When you unpublish your site, it stays within your Google account in your Drive so you can still work on it and also republish it if you want to later on. To unpublish your site, click on the down arrow next to the Publish button and then choose *Unpublish*.

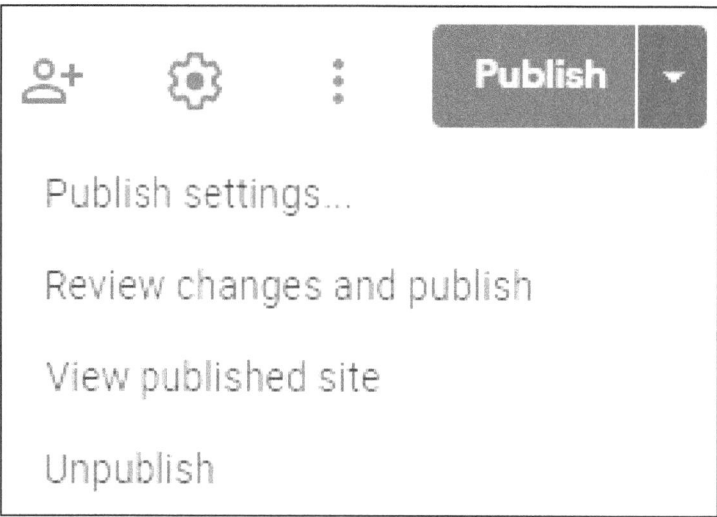

Figure 6.15

You will get a warning saying your site will no longer be live and you will need to click on *Got it* to finish the process.

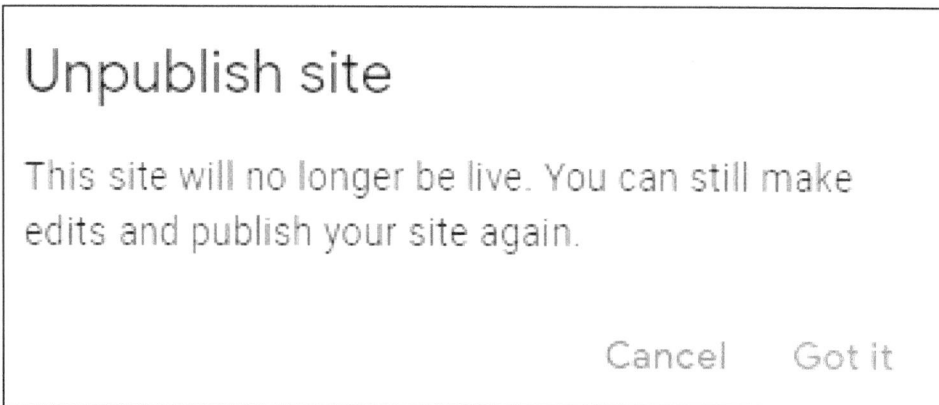

Figure 6.16

When the time comes to republish your site all you need to do is follow the same process you did the first time. Your published URL and settings should stay intact making it easier to republish the second time etc.

Configuring Your Own Domain Name for Your Site
If you would like your website to appear a little more professional then you might want to consider purchasing your own domain name so you can use it with your site. Domains are very cheap to buy and you can get your own for around $10 a year.

The hard part about getting your own domain is finding something that is not already taken by someone else. There are many sites you can use to search for and purchase your domain name from such as GoDaddy and Wix but just make sure you go with a trusted site. You can even use Google for your domain search and purchase one through them. One good thing about using Google for this process is that it makes it easier to apply it to your website if you are creating it using Google Sites.

I am going to use Google Domains to buy the domain name for my book website and then apply my new domain name to my site, so I don't have to use **https://sites.google.com/view/computers-made-easy/** anymore. When I apply my own domain name it will get rid of the Google Sites reference in the URL and will only be **http://computers-made-easy.com** for example assuming that domain was available.

To begin, I will go to Google Domains and start typing in domain names that I want to use to see if something I like is available.

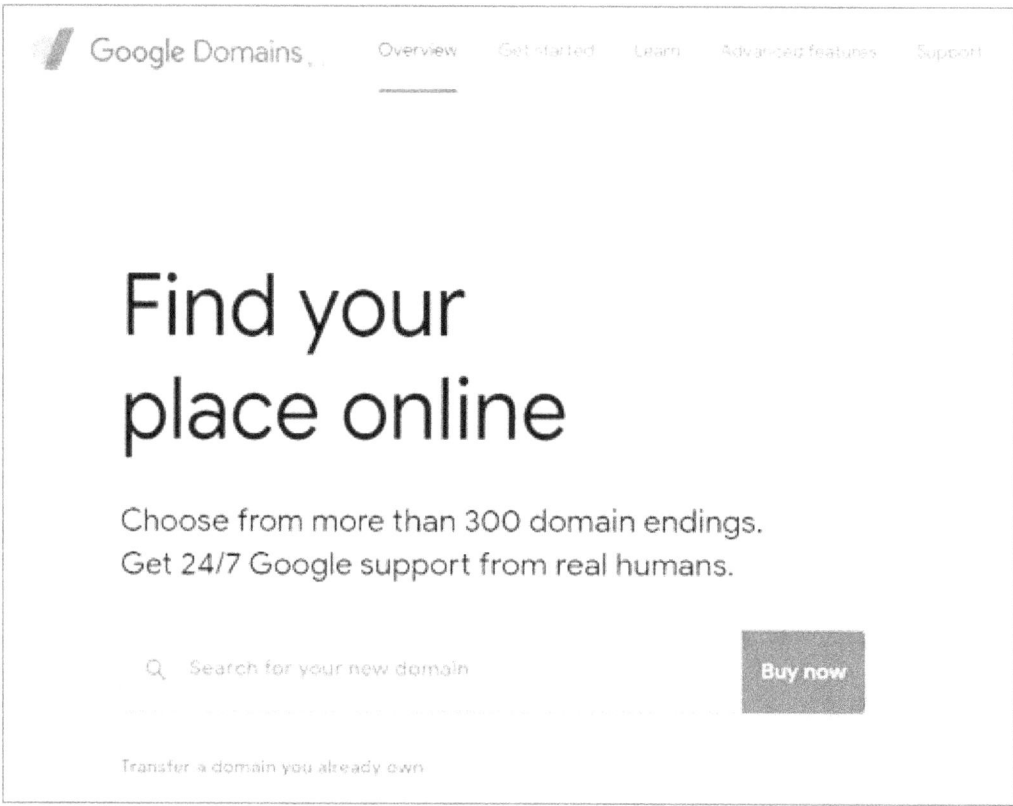

Figure 6.17

If I search for **computersmadeeasy** I am told that the .com, .net and .org endings are not available, and it shows me what endings are available and also gives me some other suggestions that are available.

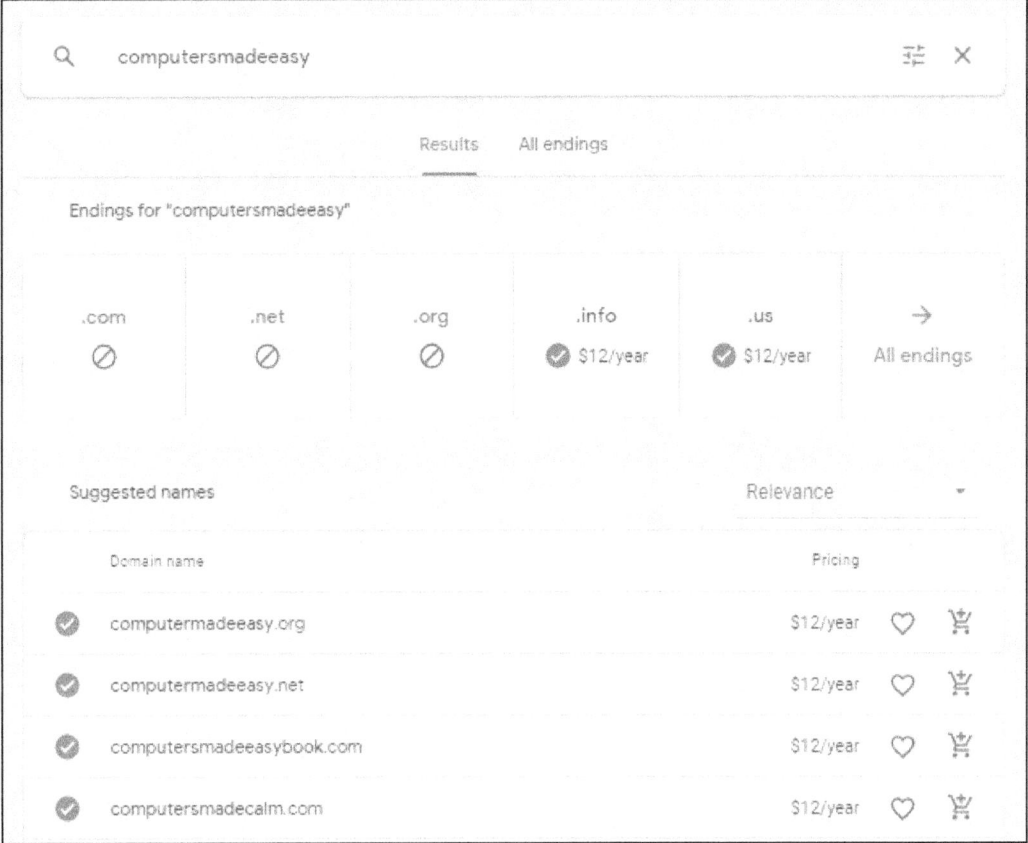

Figure 6.18

It looks as though **madeeasybookseries.com** is as close as I can get to the name of my book series without making it too long of a domain name so that is the one I am going to go with.

Figure 6.19

Then I will choose which ending I want to buy, and I will go with **.com** since it's the most popular and that is what people are most used to seeing.

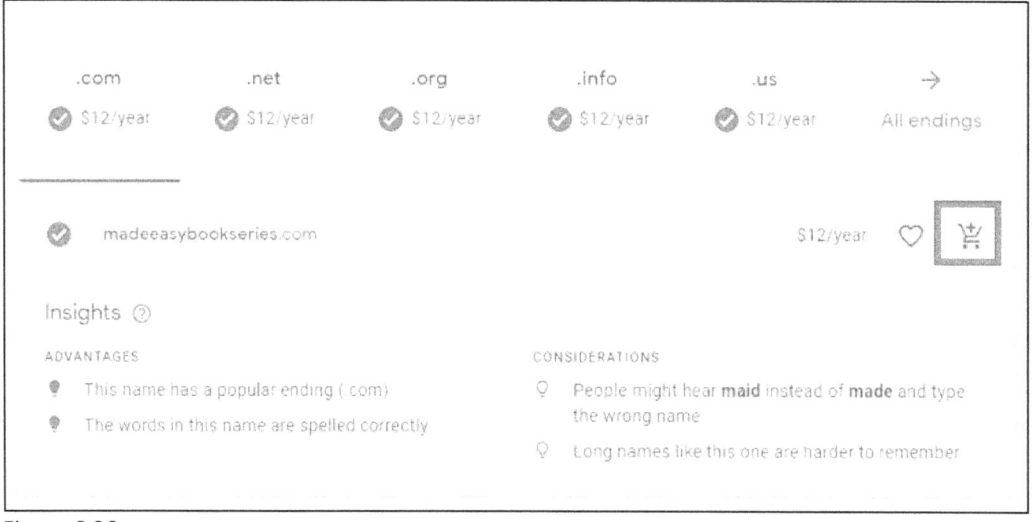

Figure 6.20

Next, I will go to my cart and select any additional options such as having my domain auto-renew each year, so it doesn't expire if I forget. I can also add an email account to my domain such as **info@madeeasybookseries.com** if I want to use that for contact information. Once everything looks good I will click on the *Check out* button to complete my purchase and enter in my billing information.

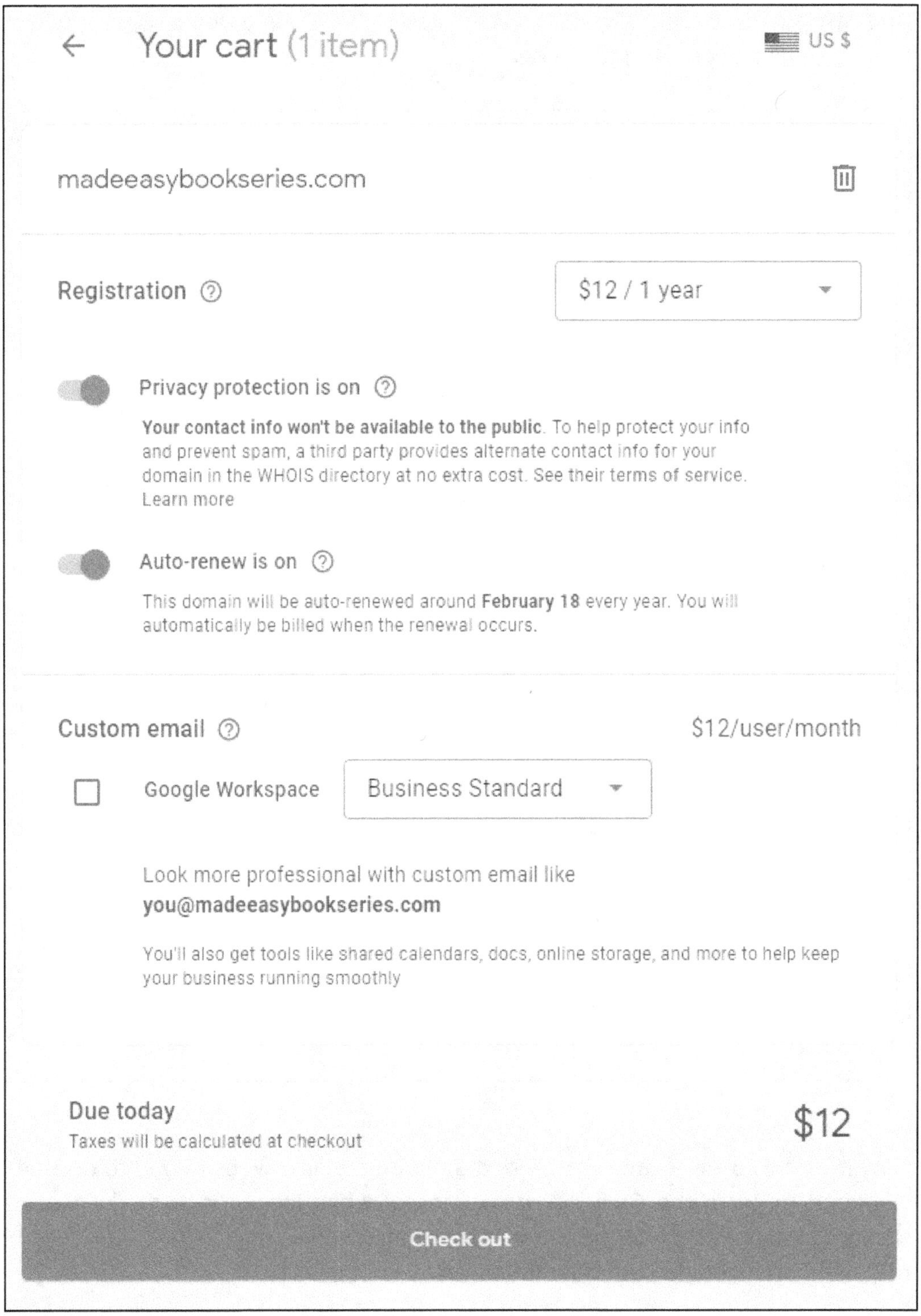

← **Your cart** (1 item)   ▥ US $

madeeasybookseries.com   🗑

Registration ⑦ $12 / 1 year   ▾

🔘 Privacy protection is on ⑦

Your contact info won't be available to the public. To help protect your info
and prevent spam, a third party provides alternate contact info for your
domain in the WHOIS directory at no extra cost. See their terms of service.
Learn more

🔘 Auto-renew is on ⑦

This domain will be auto-renewed around **February 18** every year. You will
automatically be billed when the renewal occurs.

Custom email ⑦ $12/user/month

☐ Google Workspace   Business Standard   ▾

Look more professional with custom email like
you@madeeasybookseries.com

You'll also get tools like shared calendars, docs, online storage, and more to help keep
your business running smoothly

Due today $12
Taxes will be calculated at checkout

Check out

Figure 6.21

After my purchase is complete, I will be taken to the Google Domains page where I can then manage my domain if needed.

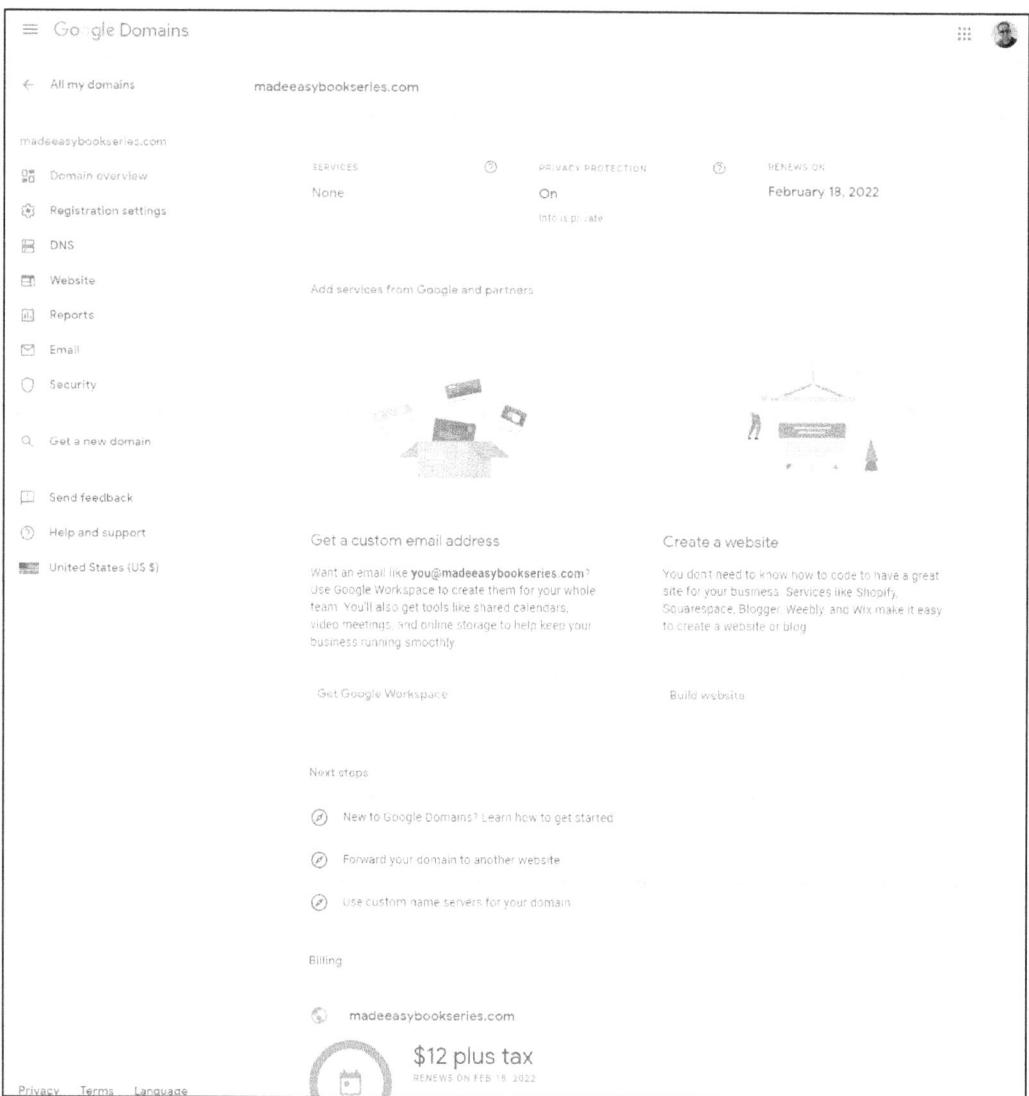

Figure 6.22

Now it's time to associate my new domain with my new website and to do that I will need to go to the *Google Search Console* while logged in with the Google account I have my domain and my site associated with.
https://search.google.com/search-console

If you have any other domains associated with your Google account they will be listed here, and I will now need to add a new property by clicking the down arrow next to my existing site and choosing *Add property*.

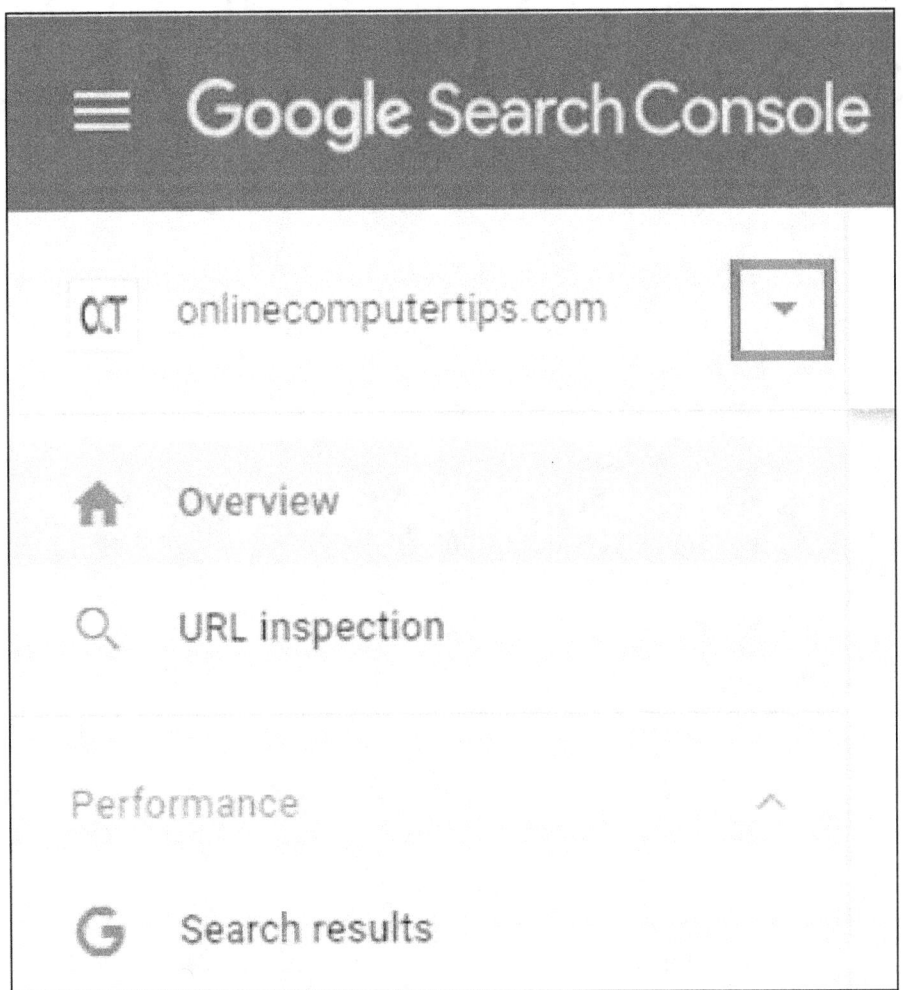

Figure 6.23

Next, I will enter my new domain name in the *Domain* section and click the *Continue* button.

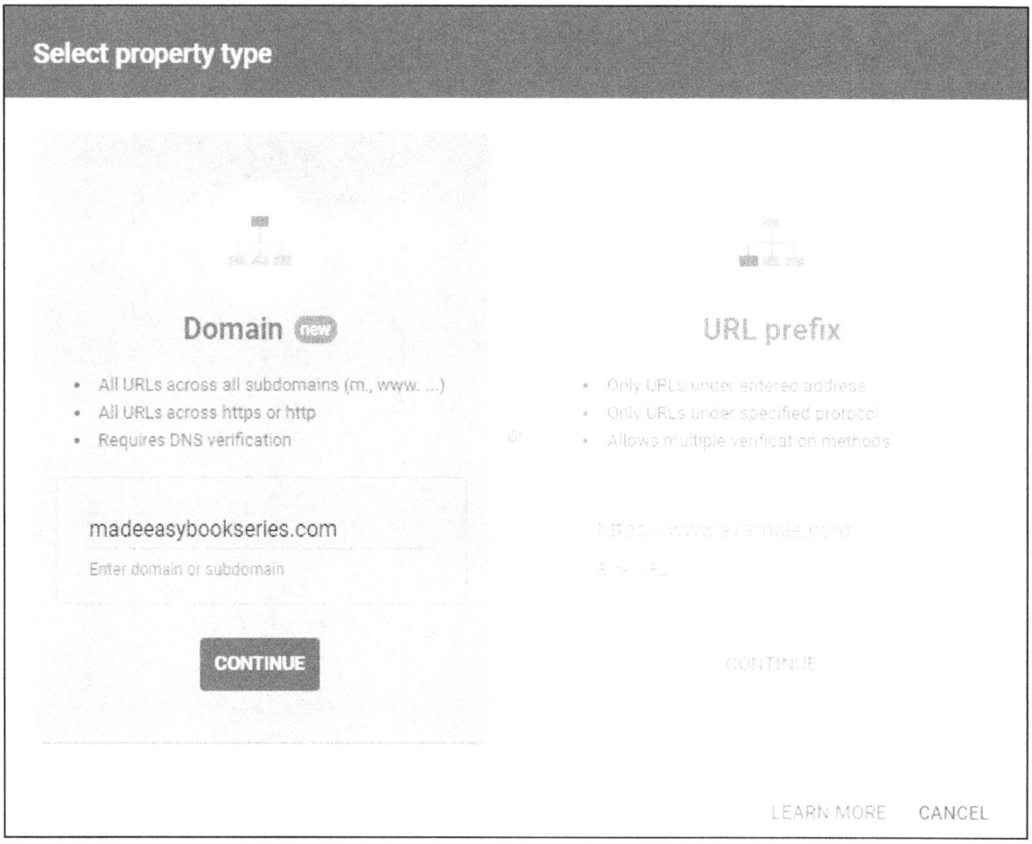

Select property type

Domain (new)

- All URLs across all subdomains (m., www. ...)
- All URLs across https or http
- Requires DNS verification

madeeasybookseries.com

Enter domain or subdomain

CONTINUE

URL prefix

- Only URLs under entered address
- Only URLs under specified protocol
- Allows multiple verification methods

https://www.example.com

Enter URL

CONTINUE

LEARN MORE   CANCEL

Figure 6.24

During this step if you get a message that says **Failed to add domain property "YourNewDomain.com" (Invalid domain)** when adding your property, its most likely because you just created this new domain and Google needs a few hours or so to get things setup so you might want to give it some time and try again.

Once Google checks things on their end I will get a message saying that the ownership of my domain has been verified.

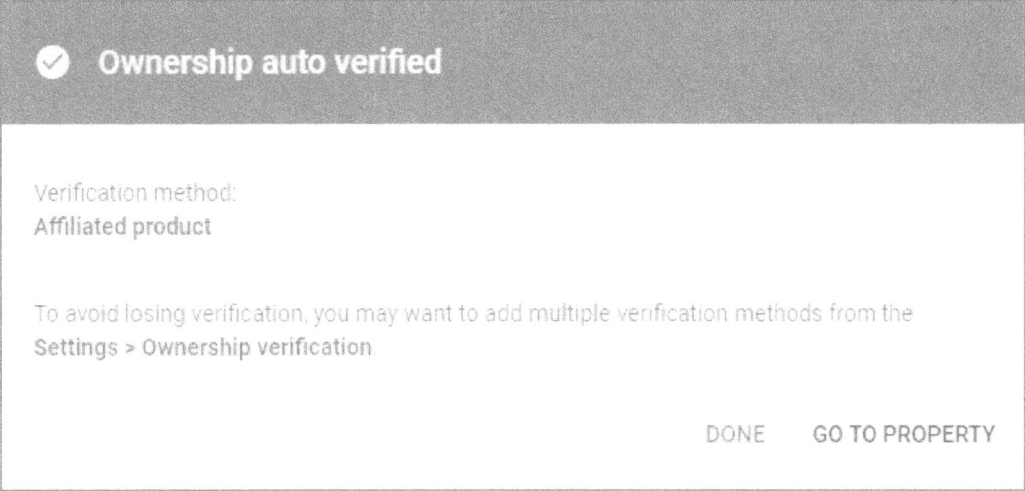

Figure 6.25

Now I can go back into Sites and click on the Settings gear icon and go to the *Custom URLs* section. Next, I will type in **www.madeeasybookseries.com** in the box and click on *Assign*.

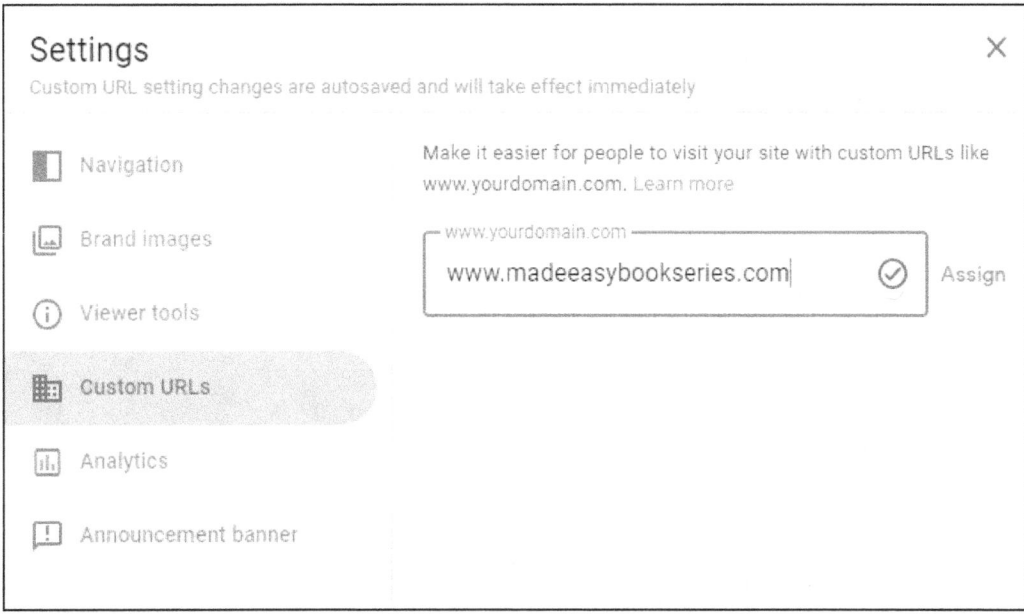

Figure 6.26

If everything checks out then Sites will add it as a custom URL, and it will be shown below.

Figure 6.27

Now I will need to go back to Google Domains and click on the *DNS* section so I can add a custom CNAME record for my site. Keep in mind that I am doing this here because I bought my domain name through Google. If you have another hosting provider your process will be a little different and you might have to contact them to do this for you.

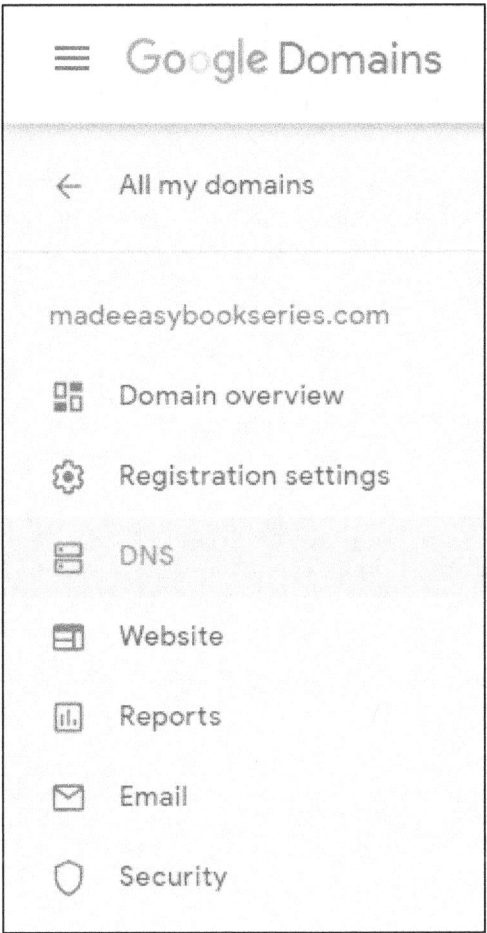

Figure 6.28

Next, I go to the Custom resource record and add **www**, change the type to *CNAME* and then add **ghs.googlehosted.com** since it's hosted by Google and click on the *Add* button.

Custom resource records

Resource records define how your domain behaves. Common uses include pointing your domain at your web server or configuring email delivery for your domain. Learn more

| www | CNAME ▾ | 1H | ghs.googlehosted.com | Add |

| Name ② | Type ② | TTL ② | Data ② | |

No custom resource records set up yet. Learn how to set up resource records

Figure 6.29

You will get a message saying it may take up to 48 hours for the changes to take effect.

Next, I want to add a record which will make it so I don't have to type in the www before the site name. So for the *Synthetic record* I will add **@** in the first box and then type in **https://www.madeeasybookseries.com** in the next box.

I want this to be permanent so I will check the selection for *Permanent redirect* and then I always want to check *Forward path* and *Enable SSL* for security. Finally, I will click on Add and once again be told that it will take some time for the changes to take effect.

Figure 6.30

Figure 6.31

Then after some time has passed I can try accessing my website with its official URL and I should be able to see all of my work.

Figure 6.32

Be sure to check out the finished result of the website that was made during the writing of this book at **https://www.madeeasybookseries.com/.**

What's Next?

Now that you have read through this book and learned how Google Sites works and what you can do with the application, you might be wondering what you should do next. Well, that depends on where you want to go. Are you happy with what you have learned, or do you want to further your knowledge of web design with some more advanced website development software or even learn HTML coding?

If you do want to expand your knowledge and computers in general, then you can look for some more advanced books on web development or focus on a specific technology such as HTML, JavaScript or WordPress if that's the path you choose to follow. Focus on mastering the basics, and then apply what you have learned when going to more advanced material.

There are many great video resources as well, such as Pluralsight or CBT Nuggets, which offer online subscriptions to training videos of every type imaginable. YouTube is also a great source for instructional videos if you know what to search for.

If you are content in being a proficient Sites user that knows more than your coworkers and friends then just keep on practicing what you have learned. Don't be afraid to poke around with some of the settings and tools that you normally don't use and see if you can figure out what they do without having to research it since learning by doing is the most effective method to gain new skills.

Thanks for reading Google Sites Made Easy. If you liked this title, please leave a review. Reviews help authors build exposure. Plus, I love hearing from my readers! You can also check out the other books in the Made Easy series for additional, computer-related information and training.

And don't forget to stay up to date on my Made Easy Book Series website! **www.madeaseybookseries.com**

COMPUTERS MADE EASY	WINDOWS 10 MADE EASY	NETWORKING MADE EASY	CLOUD STORAGE MADE EASY
GOOGLE APPS MADE EASY	OFFICE MADE EASY	android SMARTPHONES MADE EASY	THE INTERNET MADE EASY
WINDOWS HOME NETWORKING MADE EASY	BUILDING YOUR OWN COMPUTER MADE EASY	PHOTOSHOP ELEMENTS MADE EASY	POWERPOINT MADE EASY
PUBLISHER MADE EASY	PREMIERE ELEMENTS MADE EASY	VIRTUALBOX MADE EASY	WINDOWS FILE MANAGEMENT MADE EASY
zoom MADE EASY	GOOGLE MEET MADE EASY	SLACK MADE EASY	GOOGLE CLASSROOM MADE EASY
GOOGLE DOCS MADE EASY	GOOGLE SITES MADE EASY	OFFICE FOR THE WEB MADE EASY	WiX MADE EASY
WINDOWS VIDEO EDITOR MADE EASY	COMPUTERS FOR SENIORS MADE EASY	WINDOWS 11 MADE EASY	SOCIAL MEDIA FOR SENIORS MADE EASY
GMAIL MADE EASY	WINDOWS 11 FILE MANAGEMENT MADE EASY	EMAIL FOR SENIORS MADE EASY	DROPBOX MADE EASY

JAMES BERNSTEIN

You should also check out my computer tips website, as well as follow it on Facebook to find more information on all kinds of computer topics.

www.onlinecomputertips.com
https://www.facebook.com/OnlineComputerTips/

About the Author

James Bernstein has been working with various companies in the IT field for over 20 years, managing technologies such as SAN and NAS storage, VMware, backups, Windows Servers, Active Directory, DNS, DHCP, Networking, Microsoft Office, Photoshop, Premiere, Exchange, and more.

He has obtained certifications from Microsoft, VMware, CompTIA, ShoreTel, and SNIA, and continues to strive to learn new technologies to further his knowledge on a variety of subjects.

He is also the founder of the website onlinecomputertips.com, which offers its readers valuable information on topics such as Windows, networking, hardware, software, and troubleshooting. James writes much of the content himself and adds new content on a regular basis. The site was started in 2005 and is still going strong today.

www.ingramcontent.com/pod-product-compliance
Lightning Source LLC
Chambersburg PA
CBHW082146230526
45467CB00043B/2238